MADE IN ITALY

A Shopper's Guide to Italy's Best Artisanal Traditions, from [cut off] *to Ceramics, Jewelry, Leather Goods, and More*

SECOND EDITION

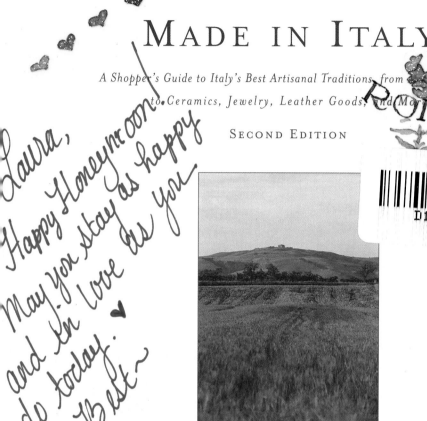

by

Laura Morelli

Laura,
Happy Honeymoon!
May you stay as happy
and in love as you
do today. ♥
All the Best~
Kelly + Bobby
J Kennedy Ct.
West Hartford Ct.

SE

"Pochi, ma buoni . . ." (*"Few, but good . . ."*)

—the Italian craftsman's motto

Photo credits:

Inside cover, pages 15, 26, 30, 39, 45, 46, 51, 67 (right), 64, 84, 96, 97, 102, 104, 105, 107 (left), 108, 110, 111, 112, 114, 115, 116, 121, 125, 127, 128 (right), 137, 142, 147, 153, 155, 156, 159, 169, 180, 181, 185, 188, 197, 199, 202: © Laura Morelli

Pages 4, 12, 32, 37, 49, 51 (left), 55 (right), 74, 79, 100, 157, 176, 192: © Dawn Smith, Shaffer-Smith Photography

Pages 23, 107 (right), 129, 133, 160: © Laura Rainis

Page 55 (left), 95: Courtesy of I.V.A.T., Aosta

Page 58: Courtesy of Acetaia Malpighi, Modena

Pages 65 (left), 66, 68, 69, 71, 87, 90 (left), 103, 119, 122, 128 (left), 139, 161, 163, 165, 211: © istockphoto

Page 66 (right): Yemen, by Ettore Sottsass for Venini, Murano

Page 90 (right): Vases by Tapio Wirkkala for Venini, Murano

Pages 145, 167: Courtesy of Giovanni Apa, Torre del Greco

Pages 189, 194: Courtesy of I.S.O.L.A., Cagliari

Maps: Lorraine Serra, Chiaro Design

Author photo: Jeff Shaffer

First edition published in the United States of America in 2003 by

UNIVERSE PUBLISHING

A Division of Rizzoli International Publications, Inc.

300 Park Avenue South

New York, NY 10010

This edition © 2008 Laura Morelli

Designed by Paul Kepple and Jude Buffum @ Headcase Design

Typesetting for this edition by Tina Henderson

2008 2009 2010 2011 / 10 9 8 7 6 5 4 3 2 1

Second Edition

Library of Congress Catalog Card Number: 2007908485

ISBN 10: 0-7893-1699-4

ISBN 13: 978-0-7893-1699-8

Printed in China

CONTENTS

ABOUT THE SECOND EDITION

Since the initial publication of *Made in Italy* five years ago, my inbox has been flooded with e-mail from readers seeking something meaningful in their travels. They share stories, recommend artisans and shops they've discovered, and ask me how to recognize authentic goods. As our world becomes increasingly homogenized with mega-stores, corporate chains, and mass-production, people are hungry for unique, handmade items, and a chance to make a connection with real people when they travel. In Italy, travelers increasingly seek immersive activities, from stuffing ravioli with pecorino to making leather bookmarks.

But are we willing to wait four months and pay $2,000 for a one-of-a-kind pair of shoes handcrafted by a master shoemaker in Florence? In my experience, the answer is yes. People will wait and pay more for a beautiful object *when they can make a connection with the person whose labor and passion went into crafting it*. It's what draws foreign tourists to the remotest hill towns of Abruzzo and Le Marche, hoping to discover something that brings meaning to their hyper-consumerized lives.

I've been looking forward to updating this guide, which is unique for leading travelers to the most authentic purveyors of Italian tradition, from glassblowers on Murano to ceramics-makers in Deruta. Here's what's new. The listings sections have been completely updated and fact-checked. Many of the artisan enterprises listed in this book are long-standing family businesses that stretch back years, if not centuries. Inevitably, other shops move, change ownership, or close their doors. In addition, I've included new places I've discovered in the last couple of years. Also new to the second edition is a special section on shopping for leather in Florence, probably the most common request I get. Prices are now expressed in euros, to provide greater consistency as exchange rates fluctuate.

I am grateful to Laura Rainis, Zsofi Gera and Giovanna Cucciniello for their diligent research support in revising the listings, and to each artisan who has shared their time and enthusiasm with me, many on more than one occasion.

The original *Made in Italy* marked the beginning of a guidebook series that now includes France, the Southwest, and will feature other destinations around the world. I thank my readers for their feedback and hope these pages enhance your travel experience to Italy, whether via airplane or armchair. *Buona lettura*!

GRAZIE MILLE

One day, after living in Italy just a short time, I realized I had to write this book. It began forming itself in my head the day I landed on Italian soil, and continued to take shape as I strolled through the streets of my adopted hometown and many others, witnessing firsthand the treasures that thousands of people were creating, as if miraculously, in tiny workshops, *botteghe*, and studios across the peninsula.

My second realization was that I couldn't do it alone. Many generous Italians shared their time, their knowledge, and their passion for traditional Italian products. Museum administrators, business people, and aficionados lent a hand. In particular, I thank Vittorio Antonelli, Alberto Bellini, Luigi Bocali, Laura Cardi, Massimo Marchese, Elisabetta Oppo, Fabrizio Raffaelli, Sergio Regis, and Evelino Vagnarelli for sharing their enthusiasm for time-honored craftsmanship. Most of all, I thank every artisan who shared their time and work with me, and patiently endured my questions.

I thank my husband, Mark, and my son, Max, for sharing this great adventure. I thank my parents, who have simultaneously supported and suffered way too many of my open-ended European excursions.

For their support and friendship during the research and writing of this book, I thank Laura Alinovi, Simone Battistini, Mary and Pier Biffi, Tricia Branagan, Veronica Buratti, Rosalia Cantù, Domenico Cosentino, Roberto Invernizzi, Chris and Glenn Landau, Sara Marongiù, Grazia Marchese, Giorgio and Gianna Marchini, Massimo Mondini, Ilwana and Roberto Pucci, Laura Rainis, Chris and Antonella Stainbrook, and Frederick Tschernutter.

I thank my agents, Christy Fletcher and Marly Rusoff of Carlisle & Company, and my editor, Kathleen Jayes, for making this dream a reality. I thank Lorraine Serra and the staff at Rizzoli/Universe Publishing for turning the manuscript into a finished product.

A very special thanks goes to my friend and fellow expatriate writer, the Brazilian poet Solange Menagale. She, more than anyone else, understands why I had to write this book.

THE SPIRIT OF TRADITION

My small village outside Milan has no movie theater and no convenience stores, but it's got an artisan who turns out the most stunning hand-crafted cellos you'll ever see. Tucked into a cobblestone alley off the main street, his humble studio is a mosaic of sawdust, hand tools, strings, and planks of wood waiting to be turned into masterpieces of song.

The poetry of the gestures of manual labor, repeated day after day, year after year, century after century, is the essence of European life and tradition. For international visitors, the image of the Old World artisan laboring on a unique, handmade item remains imprinted on the memory long after the return home. From supple leather bags to blown glass, colorful ceramics, stunning wrought iron furniture, finely crafted wood, and, of course, scrumptious food, Italy means quality goods and time-honored workmanship.

I want to take you on a journey. It's a journey to see an 88-year-old woman in a Sardinian village whose able hands swiftly work a wooden hand loom her grand-mother taught her to use when she was just five. It's a journey to an Umbrian hill town to watch an artisan paint a picture of a rabbit on a terra-cotta pot, while drawing inspiration from a 500-year-old ceramic fragment at his side. It's a jour-ney to the gastronomic mecca of Parma, to watch an inspector poke an aging ham hock with a horse-bone needle, and draw it under his nose to rate its quality com-pared to thousands of similar specimens he has tested over four decades.

Across Italy, handcrafted objects, or *prodotti artigianali*, emerge from humble workshops, artisan studios, and tidy homes of countless Italian towns and villages. Italian craftspeople sustain a passion for traditional occupations that is unrivaled in the Old World. From wrought iron to delicate embroidery, crisp table linens, col-ored glass, and woodcarving, they bring to life the same forms that captivated their ancient ancestors. That pride in workmanship, local tradition, and skill has been passed down through generations, and still shines through the shop windows lining cobblestone streets on this sun-filled peninsula where time seems to stand still.

WHY I WROTE THIS BOOK

The first time I visited Venice as a wide-eyed 16-year-old, I knew I was supposed to buy Murano glass, but I had no idea why. All I knew was that I was whisked to the famous "glass island" on an overcrowded, stinky boat, and whisked into an overcrowded, stinky glass factory, then pressured to buy something by someone speaking English with a really bad accent. I waited behind two dozen American and Japanese tourists to pay an exorbitant price for a little green glass fish, which still sits on the windowsill of my study as a testimony to the bewildering experience.

Still, it was the artistic traditions of Italy that lured me back again and again after that first trip. As I pursued advanced studies in art history, I continued to return not only to Venice but also to Rome, Florence, Milan, and other towns to see the celebrated works of Leonardo da Vinci, Michelangelo, Tintoretto, the Lorenzetti, Modigliani, Balla, and other painters and sculptors. I stood in line for hours at the Uffizi and sought out many smaller art museums and churches around the country. I had to experience the mystery and effect of those masterpieces firsthand, as if standing before a Renaissance painting or a gilded altarpiece could impart some sense of meaning and reality that my own fast-paced, New World culture had lost . . . or maybe never had.

Years later, my family and I accepted a once-in-a-lifetime opportunity to move from the United States to Italy on a company transfer. I was elated. I imagined spending hours exploring the museums, galleries, and church treasuries again, and looked forward to arriving in this art lover's paradise. I relished the thought of experiencing again the pleasure that comes in understanding and appreciating beautiful objects and the best of human creativity.

Upon arrival, my anticipation soon turned to disillusion. We were living in a small town north of Milan that looked nothing like Venice, Rome, or Florence. There were no great museums and there was no great art; only quiet residential streets, cornfields, and nondescript industrial outskirts. There was no Michelangelo. There were no tourists.

With no great paintings or cathedrals to distract me, I found myself wrapped up in the more practical aspects of getting integrated into Italian life and my new home. We moved into a house that needed built-in bookshelves and *armadi*, the ubiquitous armoires that serve as closets in Italian homes. I contracted with a local family of carpenters to do the work. After two months of waiting with no response, I called to complain. The young carpenter explained their slow place by spouting the company philosophy: *"Signora, siamo pochi, ma buoni"* ("Ma'am, we're few, but good").

My aggravation turned to wonder when they finally appeared. At long last, a white van pulled up in front of my house and the carpenters emerged with tool-boxes, sawhorses, and large planks of raw lumber. Over the course of three days, this grandfather, father, and son transformed the courtyard outside our house into an artisan's workshop. With saws, sandpaper, and their hands, they created a set of bookcases and armoires as if by magic, then installed them in the gaping spaces in the walls. As the father and son tamped the wood gently with a mallet, the grandfather observed and critiqued, and made a few tweaks of his own.

The result was stunning: fine strips of different woods created an inlaid effect. Each shelf was solid as a rock, and doors slid silently from side to side with the push of a finger. Drawers glided in and out. It was a masterpiece.

That's when I realized that in Italy, the craft tradition of the past is also a *living tradition*. The medieval craft guilds may be long gone, but their arts, their techniques, and their soul, still thrive on Italian soil. The skills, the forms, the knowledge, and, more importantly, the spirit of the past, is kept alive in the hands of thousands of artisans who take great pride in this tradition of craftsmanship. I was riveted.

Suddenly, I wanted to know everything. Where did they get their materials? How did they learn their craft? What was their inspiration? And my curiosity extended to other objects as well—ceramics, glass, leather, textiles, and more. I wanted to witness it firsthand. I longed to watch people fashioning animals out of papier-mâché, stamping leaf patterns into leather albums, carving wood into musical instruments, weaving patterns into blankets. And what is so great about Murano glass anyway, I wondered.

It was the beginning of a journey that would take me to every corner of the Italian peninsula and become my obsession.

Over the course of my research, I continually asked myself what it was about Italian culture that fosters this profusion of world-class objects. I believe it hinges on several factors. First, Italians place a high cultural value on beauty or *bellezza*. When you learn Italian, you're struck by the prominence, frequency, and above all

THE WORLD'S BENCHMARK

For me, the most impressive thing about Italian workmanship is that—even with today's sophisticated technologies—no one has improved on the hand-wrought designs of these unsung masters. Even in the twenty-first century, their work is still recognized around the world as a benchmark of quality.

the versatility of the word *bello*—and every iteration of it: Che *bello*, che *bella*, *bellino*, *molto bello*, and of course, *bellissimo* or *bellissima*. *Che bello* connotes not only the concept of beauty, but can also be used in the same way that we might say in English, "That's great," or "How wonderful." Of course, *bellezza* is omnipresent in Italian society. It is valued and cultivated not only in the world of artisanal production and in architecture and the fine arts, but also in fashion, industrial and automotive design, and even the preparation and presentation of food.

Another cultural phenomenon that informs craft production is the regionalism that pervades Italian culture. There is something unique and special about every town, every region. Perhaps more than any European country, Italy is still profoundly one where *campanalismo*—pride in one's own town or city—reigns supreme, and the history of producing things for local use is still strong. In talking with countless craftspeople, one thing I heard over and over was pride in carrying on an important local tradition to the next generations, and the expectation that their children would do the same. Still today, young people feel obliged to follow in the footsteps of their parents, and the historical importance of clan, so inherent in Italian culture, lives on today.

The work of today's Italian craftspeople is a testament to the past, an honor to tradition. If these traditional craftspeople disappeared, think how soulless Italian towns would be. Their works would be shut away in museums and the cobblestone streets would be reduced to chain fashion stores. Thankfully, today in artisan studios across Italy, production is limited, quality is high, and a sense of carrying the torch of tradition is stronger than ever.

As an art historian, one of the most interesting things I find about studying today's traditional craftspeople is that their work opens a window onto the past. By looking closely at the ways in which the torch of tradition is passed, from mother to daughter, from father to son, from master to apprentice, we can learn something about the technical aspects of each trade, and how they have been practiced over time; and the oral traditions that play a vital role in the transmission of knowledge.

Of course, there are important differences between workshops of the past and those of the present. In Gubbio, I found the teenaged son of Giorgio Rampini not painting swirls on pots. Rather, his father tasked him with packing wares and shipping ceramic plates DHL to Cinncinati and beyond, as well as responding to e-mail and updating the company web site.

THE QUEST FOR QUALITY

If you've traveled to Europe, you can probably tell a story similar to my Murano glass-buying fiasco. In fact, if you're like me, collecting souvenirs of your European experience is one of your favorite pastimes. As visitors to Italy, we are bombarded continually with beautiful, wonderful objects. We browse museums, souvenir shops, local markets, and street stalls, and gorgeous treasures in gold, glass, paper, leather, ceramic, and iron lure us. But it's not always clear what to buy, how to find it, and, more importantly, how to differentiate between treasures and trash. Never mind figuring out if you're getting a good value.

The goal of *Made in Italy* is to enhance your appreciation of, and, in some cases, introduce you to, the most typical, handcrafted products from each of Italy's 18 regions. This is not a simple shopper's guide. Rather, I want to lead you beyond the tourist traps and souvenir shops to discover the traditions and the people behind extraordinary regional traditions like Tuscan terra-cotta, Venetian marble paper, Neopolitan papier-mâché angels, Volterra alabasters, Sicilian marionettes, and Alpine copper cookware. I want to share what makes the regions and their world-class products special, and to help you bring home great values in your suitcase.

This book is about why you're supposed to buy Murano glass . . . and more.

PREPARING TO SHOP

There are thousands of excellent books, magazines, and electronic resources to help you plan your trip to Italy—where to stay, where to eat, and what to see. This is not one of them. *Made in Italy* is a specialty guide, a supplement to the more traditional travel guides. I hope you take it with you.

Made in Italy won't tell you where to stay or how to navigate a museum, but you'll still find practical information of all sorts: what to buy when you visit a particular place, where to find it, how to know if you're buying something authentic, and what you should pay for it. Let's start with a few general tips.

NAVIGATING ITALY

I find city maps with street indices indispensable, especially in the larger towns. You may be able to find maps of Rome, Florence, and Venice with street listings in your local bookstore before you leave, but you can always pick them up in train stations, bookstores, tourist offices, or the corner newsstand—the ubiquitous *edicole*—once you arrive in Italy. The artisan studios and shops listed in this book are scattered and toting a good map will save you a lot of time.

SHOPPING IN ITALY

When you shop in Italy, it doesn't take long to figure out you're on Mediterranean time. Most stores and businesses open around 9-10 A.M., then close about 12:30 P.M. (a little earlier in the north, a little later in the south). They reopen around 3:30 in the afternoon (again, adjusting a bit for north or south). Most shops stay open until 7:30 or 8 at night, a little later in the summer resort towns.

For North Americans, the prolonged midday siesta often seems an aggravating inconvenience when there is so much to see and so little time. If you are still browsing at 12:30, prepare to be escorted politely to the door. The midday meal is sacred to Italians, and a few foreign travelers with money to spend aren't going to change that, so just relax and enjoy. Do as the Romans: go get yourself a nice plate of tortellini, sit at a sidewalk table, soak up the sun, and people-watch until the stores reopen in the afternoon.

European shopping etiquette dictates that you should always ask a salesperson before touching anything, especially if it is visible in the shop window. Italians take great pride in their window displays, as window-shopping is the country's second-favorite pastime (after eating). You just might get your hand slapped or, at best, curt service, if you dare touch without asking first.

PACKING TO SHOP FOR CRAFTS

I learned how to pack the hard way: by dragging heavy bags through the streets of Europe and living to regret it. I have even popped off suitcase wheels in the crevices of cobblestone streets. I have made many trips to Europe and returned with a lot of handcrafted goods, so please take my advice.

After you've laid out what you want to pack, be ruthless. Put at least 50 percent of it back in your closet; trust me, you don't need it. The quickest way to spot Americans in European airports is by the size of their suitcases.

I usually pack one small, wheeled suitcase with clothes and necessities. Then I throw in an empty, soft duffel bag and a dozen gallon-sized Ziploc bags. These are for packing my purchases, which I pad with clothes. Breakables go in my carry-on, preferably packed in bubble wrap, which I've either brought with me or purchased locally a stationery store (*cartolaio*). My carry-on bag has a zippered side pocket, where I store receipts for everything I purchased overseas; that way they're handy in case a customs official flags my bulging suitcase for inspection (read more about customs in "Getting it Home").

MONEY MATTERS

Life is expensive in Italy. Recent exchange rates and the power of the euro have made finding a bargain more challenging than ever. The combination of a relatively strong economy, government regulations, and a high cost of living keep prices high, even when exchange rates are favorable to foreign travelers. Besides, certain Italian goods like clothes, sports cars—and crafts—are highly valued in the international marketplace for their quality and uniqueness, and are priced accordingly.

And don't forget the 20 percent value-added tax, or IVA, that keeps prices high. Larger retail stores are usually set up to offer tax-free rebates to non-Europeans who make a minimum purchase, so take advantage of those whenever possible. Retailers offering this service usually post a tax-free sticker in their store window; if not, ask for it (luckily, the Italian word for tax-free is tax-free!). You must show the retailer a passport that proves you are not a citizen of one of the European Economic Community countries, and fill out a form with your name, address, passport information, and details of the transaction. Then, you must pay the full price, and wait for the 20 percent tax to be rebated to you, either as a credit to your charge card or by check. Keep these forms and receipts in your wallet or carry-on luggage, as you will need to have these documents stamped by customs officials before you board an international flight. You must also remember to mail in the forms to a central office in Switzerland, using the pre-addressed envelope that is part of the paperwork. The process sounds cumbersome but after you've done it once or twice, it becomes easy.

AVOIDING SCAMS

Generally, you don't have to worry about falling victim to scams when it comes to purchasing Italian crafts. The biggest danger is tourist traps selling cheap wares—some not authentic, some not even made in Italy—to gullible travelers. One of the goals of this book is to help you distinguish between authentic wares and cheap knockoffs, and to lead you to the best artisans.

Italy is relatively safe. Assaults are uncommon, but pickpocketing and purse snatching rank among the country's most frequent crimes. If you're a tourist, you're a target. On a crowded sidewalk in Florence, a thief speeding by on a moped even snatched my friend's purse right off her shoulder. Keep your cash on your body and pay attention to your surroundings, especially in larger cities.

No matter how expensive life may be in Italy, certain items are still a bargain. You may consider $120 a lot to pay for a medium-sized ceramic plate from one of Deruta's most esteemed artisans, but you'd pay twice that amount for the same item at a retail gift shop or department store in the United States. The same goes for Parmigiano-Reggiano cheese, any Italian wine, and many other goods listed in this book.

Cash is still king in Italy and some merchants do not accept credit cards. Italy is one of the last European countries to widely adopt credit card payment; fees charged to the merchant, as well as a history of scams, has stigmatized the practice. Rest assured that paying with a credit card in Italy is absolutely safe; by all means take advantage of it whenever possible, as it offers favorable exchange rates. The majority of businesses in larger cities honor credit cards, but you may not be able to whip out your credit card so easily in small towns or when paying in smaller, family-run artisan shops and studios. Be prepared to pay in cash.

You already know that it's not a great idea to walk around a foreign country (much less your own) with a wad of cash in your back pocket, especially since pick-pocketing ranks among the most common crimes in Italy. Luckily, automatic teller machines are easy to find—even in small towns—so you should be able to withdraw cash from your home bank as long as it participates in one of the major international banking networks. The machine will dispense cash in local currency, and you'll usually get a better exchange rate than you would by converting cash or travelers' checks at a local currency exchange booth.

About Knock-offs

Avoid buying luxury brand knock-offs on the street. In recent years European authorities have cracked down on these copyright-infringers. I have personally seen American tourists pay a hefty price for "brand-name" bags from an illegal street vendor, only to turn around and have the *caribinieri* ply the goods from their hands. Even if you make it back to your home airport, a U.S. Customs official may confiscate them. It's not worth it!

GETTING IT HOME

Figuring out how to get it home is one of the great challenges of European shopping.

As a general rule, the more you can cram into your carry-on bag, the better. I once stuffed so much Parmigiano-Reggiano cheese into my carry-on luggage that I had to carry my passport between my teeth all the way to the boarding gate. Schlepping goods home in your carry-on is preferable for a number of reasons. First, you reduce the chance of breakage or loss. Second, you spare shipping charges, which can add up to significant savings. Third, when a customs agent flags your bag for inspection, you'll have everything handy.

Yes, just when you get it all packed, it's time to meet Mr. Customs Official—I mean, Mr. Customs Official, Sir. When you return home, you must claim everything you bought on the forms the flight attendants pass out on the plane. If you're an American citizen, you're granted an $800 personal exemption, which means that you don't owe any customs duties on the first $800 worth of goods you purchased overseas for personal use or for gifts. Be prepared to document your purchases with receipts, and remember to carry receipts in your handheld luggage.

Before you travel, brush up on the latest U.S. Customs regulations at www. customs.ustreas.gov. At the time of this printing, you are allowed to bring into the United States unlimited amounts of crafts (keeping in mind that you'll owe duty if it totals more than $800 for one person). But there are restrictions on certain items, such as food. For example, you are allowed one liter of alcoholic beverages duty-free; anything above that is subject to duty. You can bring back hard cheeses like Parmigiano-Reggiano but not soft, fresh ones like ricotta. Baked goods like Panettone bread or cookies are allowed, but fruits, vegetables, and meats (including cured ham) are not, so enjoy these while still on Italian soil.

Oddly enough, handicrafts are dutiable, but fine art is not, a regulation I've

YELLOW LIGHT ON CERAMICS

In theory, you can bring as many ceramic wares into the United States as you like. However, the U.S. Customs Service has red-flagged pottery from Italy and other countries because of high lead content. The concern is over lead seeping into food and beverages that might be served in wares such as pitchers, cups, plates, and casserole dishes. Most Italian ceramics producers no longer use lead-based glazes. However, if there's any question in your mind, use the wares for decorative purposes only.

never understood. If you can convince the customs official that what you've got is fine art and not craft, you've saved yourself some money.

One last thing: don't forget that you still have to pay duty on items purchased in the duty-free shop. Duty-free means that you do not owe duty on the items in the country in which you purchased them, not the one you're entering.

The other way to get things home is to ship them. Many of my friends have related horror stories about mailing items between the United States and Italy, and I can tell a few of my own. Let's face it: the Italian postal service does not have the best reputation when it comes to reliable deliveries. (When I lived in Lombardy, my local postal carrier delivered mail strapped to the back of his moped with a frayed bungee cord. As he sped away, he left a trail of exhaust and fluttering envelopes. No telling what got lost over the years!)

However, there are many good reasons to ship, such as the ability to track a particularly valuable delivery, and file a claim if it's lost or damaged. I've also chosen to ship when traveling with small children, because I simply didn't have enough hands. Shipping is generally better than sending something home in your suitcase, for the simple reason that airlines have lower insurance limitations to cover lost or damaged luggage, and cannot be tracked like a FedEx package.

If you stick to the major international shippers like FedEx, UPS, and DHL, you'll generally enjoy reliable service and be able to file a claim if something is lost or damaged. Before you travel, check the web sites of these carriers for rates, local phone numbers, and drop-off locations. Shipping via express service from overseas is not cheap, but may be worth it if you've purchased something particularly valuable or unique.

It's paramount to pack your goods properly. I often carry bubble wrap in my suitcase since it's difficult to locate overseas. It's also important to insure your package, keeping in mind that some shippers include a certain amount of insurance in the shipping cost. If your item is worth more than that, a little more for insurance can go a long way in peace of mind. I would not dream of shipping a unique, handcrafted item uninsured.

The other option is to ask the merchant to ship your item for you. Many Italian businesses are experienced in shipping abroad, others are not. Remember that there are many variables from the time you leave the shop to the time your items arrive at your doorstep. When you have your merchant ship for you, you're entrusting them to send the correct piece, pack your item well, ship it as you agreed, and respond to you if the item is lost or damaged.

As a general rule, it's a good idea to have the merchant ship for you only if they are clearly set up to provide this service. Do they advertise the fact that they ship in their store? Will they let you watch to make sure they pack the right item and pack it properly? What shipping service will they use? Do they have special containers to protect fragile items like ceramics or glass? Make sure that you get a copy of the air-bill with a tracking number you can track from home. Finally, exchange full contact information, including telephone and e-mail, with the merchant so that you can follow up if necessary.

You may think that shipping large items is out of the question, but I have had great experiences shipping furniture from Europe. Many antiques and furniture companies have special contracts with freight brokers and can negotiate rates that are sometimes surprisingly reasonable, especially if the merchant is shipping multiple items to the same country. It doesn't hurt to ask!

How to Use This Guide

This book divides the Italian peninsula into five geographical zones, north to south. Each chapter opens with a brief narrative portrait of the area, highlighting the history and uniqueness of its regional handcrafted items, plus an explanation for what makes them among Italy's finest.

Literally every town in Italy boasts scads of local traditions and craftspeople, many excellent. To include them all would turn this book into a multivolume, Yellow Pages–style directory, and would require several lifetimes of research. My goal is to make this book useful; therefore, I have focused on the major destinations of international travelers. However, I also include lesser-known places and people that merit a detour from the well-beaten tourist path. My aim is to present a well-balanced view of Italian craft production and highlight the major centers.

In selecting the artisans represented here, I used several criteria. First, their production must be done primarily by hand; in fact, most of the artisans in this book rely exclusively on handmade techniques. Many trades that used to be primarily done by hand (the majority of textile production, for example) are now industrialized, and so do not appear here. Many of these are dying arts, or were dying until recently, and are now enjoying a renaissance.

Secondly, I focus on artisans who continue a major, well-defined historical tradition, such as Murano glass, Deruta ceramics, and Parmigiano-Reggiano cheese. These artisans are important purveyors of Italy's cultural patrimony, and many items are protected by law or given special denominations to indicate their high quality.

Artisanal foods of Italy—handmade items that represent the best of Italian tradition—are the subject of numerous books, and wine is a subject unto itself. Although tempted to include many of the regional culinary specialties, I have

A Word about the Web

Many of the artisans listed in this book have Websites, and I have listed them whenever possible. Some of them sell products online; some do not. Nearly all of these Websites are in Italian. Some offer an English translation, but the quality varies from site to site. You may find it useful to browse these sites in planning your trip, purchasing goods, checking on the status of your order, or communicating with artisans and shop owners after you return home. At a minimum, it's a great way to explore fabulous images of these crafts from the comfort of your living room.

included only those whose status transcends Italy's borders—Parmigiano-Reggiano cheese, *prosciutto di Parma*, traditional balsamic vinegar of Modena, and a few others. There are thousands of excellent books on Italian food, and this is not one of them. But a few culinary items fit the criteria for a book on the best of Italian artisanship. These are foods that have a long and historic tradition; that involve some skill to produce, much like finely blown glass or wrought iron; and that truly stand out from the crowd as world-class.

Lastly, I focus on artisans who sell their works directly to consumers, either from their workshops or from retail spaces they operate. Because I want you to experience the techniques and spirit of craftsmanship firsthand, I have only listed resellers when it's the only source for buying the works of a particular artisan. For example, some of the artisans in Deruta distribute their wares through shops in Italy and abroad; you can even find them at high-end department stores in the United States. But I have provided the addresses of the artisan studios so you can see them work firsthand.

Today in Italy, there is a greater appreciation than ever before for these important historical arts, and much more support for the craftsperson. In fact, some of the craft traditions covered in this book had all but died out until the last few decades. Venetian gondolas, lace of Burano, the coralworking of Trapani, and many others, were in danger of disappearing.

Many of these industries had simply faded away or were automated during the Industrial Revolution (after all, the blacksmith played a vital role in town life for many centuries, but how many blacksmiths do you know today?). The silk workers of Como now churn out fabrics for Versace, Ferragamo, and other stars of the Milan catwalks. Vigevano, southwest of Milan, and Ponte a Egola, near Pisa, produce thousands of leather uppers that end up in shoes all over the globe. The jewelers of Vicenza and Valenza host the world's largest jewelry trade fairs and export their wares from Japan to the Middle East to here in America, where we see them on television shopping channels.

But quietly, alongside the small and medium-sized industrial firms that form the backbone of the Italian economy, a handful of dedicated artisans have planted a flag in the soil to preserve the legacy of the artisanal and the handmade. Even in Valenza, Piemonte's gold capital with nearly one thousand jewelry manufacturers in a town that measures little more than one square mile, a couple of craftspeople insist on entirely handmade production.

In the past two decades, scads of local organizations have sprung up to help sustain and promote artisans who choose these careers. Regional craft organizations such as Sardinia's ISOLA and the Valle d'Aosta's IVAT have even established trademarks that serve as a recognized mark of quality akin to the "DOC" moniker assigned to certain classes of fine Italian wines. These grassroots efforts have fueled new enthusiasm into these arts.

The Confartigiano, a chamber-of-commerce-style national organization, promotes the craft industry and even recruits apprentices among Italy's youth. Individual trade organizations dedicated to wrought iron, glass, ceramics, and other crafts are well organized and in some cases, well funded.

In the listings, I have provided the current addresses, phone numbers, and Websites, if applicable, to the best of my ability as of the date this book goes to press. Obviously, these are always subject to change. As a final disclaimer, I am not affiliated with any of the artisans and retailers listed in this guide, and do not endorse any one of them in particular, though I have highlighted my favorites in the sections entitled *Bellissima!*. I have done my best to offer an unbiased, even-handed approach that I hope will enhance your enjoyment of Italy and its enchanting traditions.

Throughout the book, I offer suggestions for finding the highest quality, most authentic examples of traditional Italian crafts. If you find something that's not in this book and you love it, by all means buy it. Shopping in Italy is all about discovering things that are meaningful and pleasurable to you personally, and I hope you find wonderful objects that bring you years of satisfaction and happy memories of golden sunshine, cobblestone streets, church bells, and pasta.

I would love to hear about your experience using this guide, and about the people, places, and treasures you discover in Europe. Drop me a line at laura@lauramorelli.com, or through my Website at www.lauramorelli.com, where you can also subscribe to my newsletter, Laura Morelli's The Real Deal. Until then, happy reading, happy browsing, and *buon viaggio*!

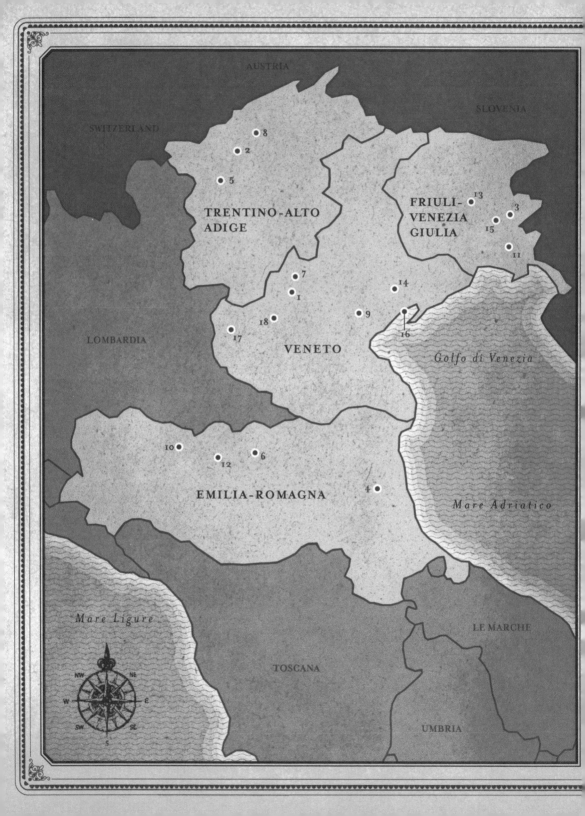

Chapter 1

NORTHEAST ITALY

EMILIA-ROMAGNA · FRIULI-VENEZIA GIULIA
TRENTINO-ALTO ADIGE · VENETO

SOUTHERN ITALIANS MAY CALL THEIR NORTHERN countrymen "Germans," but you'd never mistake Milan for Munich. Still, in many ways, northern Italy's traditions are closer to that of Germany and Austria than they are to Rome or Sicily. North of Parma, the Mediterranean diet of the south gives way to hearty mountain food. Instead of pasta or a light fish course, locals dine on stick-to-your-ribs risotto and veal cutlet pan-fried in butter, not olive oil. In artisans' shops across the northernmost reaches of Italy, you'll find wooden clogs, copper cookware, wooden sculpture, cuckoo clocks, and fur coats.

Northeastern Italy comprises four of the country's most diverse regions: Emilia-Romagna, Italy's breadbasket and home to some of the world's finest cuisine; Trentino-Alto Adige, a unique Italo-Germanic culture in the heart of the Alps; the Veneto, which boasts the prestigious cities of Venice, Padua, and Verona; and Friuli-Venezia Giulia, a mountainous region whose people are as colorful as the scenery.

In terms of crafts, Venice plays a unique and critical role. Perhaps in no other Italian town are the local handicraft traditions—carnival masks, blown glass, and gondolas, for example—as virtually synonymous with the city. Venice is a feast for the eyes, with colorful, exotic *palazzi*, mosaic-encrusted churches, and candy-striped gondola moors making wavy reflections in the dark waters of the canals. With some 100 islands linked by 400 bridges and 150 canals, Venice appears like a surreal Gothic vision against the Italian landscape.

But Venice's role reaches far beyond the water-logged city. Historically, Venice was a major point of entry for luxury goods from the Byzantine and Arab worlds, and the city's traditional products bear witness to its historical position as a crossroads between East and West. In the Middle Ages, the powerful Republic of Venice alternately pummeled and traded with some of the most illustrious cities of the East, especially Constantinople (now Istanbul). As Venetian Crusaders plundered Eastern cities and brought home their booty, local artisans were influenced by the modes of the Byzantine and Islamic world. In turn, many of the goods produced in the Republic of Venice were exported or copied elsewhere on the Italian peninsula.

Venetian wares are fancy: handmade wooden furniture with delicate scrolls, painted flowers, and curved legs; Murano glass with delicate gilding and rich color;

lace collars with intertwined vegetal motifs and animals; mosaic work on vases, tables, lamps, buildings, and anything else imaginable. The city's famous annual carnival gives birth to outlandish, fantastic masks and costumes. If you're looking for whimsy and opulence, look no further.

West of Venice, the Dolomite mountain range rises in craggy peaks, and you couldn't feel farther away from the exotic, ultra-civilized atmosphere of Venice. I consider Italian and Austrian culture at opposite extremes in many respects, but in this region of Trentino-Alto Adige, they coexist in a disconcerting and wonderful way. Against dramatic mountain scenery, onion domes stand alongside Roman ruins. Artisans produce both cuckoo clocks and terra-cotta pots. Only in Trentino-Alto Adige can you enjoy a plate of authentic fettucine alfredo while taking a break from some of Europe's best skiing.

The famous Brenner Pass has linked Austria and Italy in trade, tourism, and warfare for centuries. The northern part of the region, Alto-Adige, also known as Südtirol, is more Germanic in culture. A strong Teutonic accent in the local language reflects its geography. Trentino refers to the southernmost part of the region, one that shares more in common with Italian culture. Trentino-Alto Adige is home to the stunning Dolomite mountain range, including some of Europe's tallest peaks and most popular ski resorts, such as Cortina d'Ampezzo and Madonna di Campiglio.

The handmade crafts of Trentino-Alto Adige share one thing in common: they represent trades that can be carried out throughout the winter months, when snow blankets the highest elevations and isolates many small villages for several months. There is a strong regional tradition of handicrafts such as ceramic stoves, woodcarving, straw weaving, lace, copper crafts, and knickknacks carved from horn and bone.

East of Trentino-Alto Adige lies another region with a conglomerate name: Friuli-Venezia Giulia. My cousins from Udine sum up the character of this region best: "We're warm people living in a cold region." What accounts for the gregarious, jovial quality of these rustic mountain lovers? I suspect that it has something to do with their local specialty—grappa. Or maybe grappa is the natural outcome of the fun-loving, hardworking local residents who sought an effective way to stay warm throughout the snowy months.

Whatever the reason for its friendly people, Friuli-Venezia Giulia has been unjustly overlooked by international tourism. This mountainous area is tucked into the northeastern corner of Italy, bordering Slovenia, Austria, and the Veneto. Like the Veneto, Friuli-Venezia Giulia is marked by its historical role as a meeting point of East and West. Its main port city, Trieste, lies almost in Slovenia on the

Adriatic Sea. Its most important inland city is Udine, famous for grappa and white wine production. In addition to wine and spirits, the region produces the world-famous San Daniele ham, a leaner, milder version of *prosciutto di Parma*. The region also turns out stunning mosaic tiles and wooden clogs you'll see on the feet of country landowners all over the region.

Emilia-Romagna occupies the southernmost rim of northeast Italy, forming a link, both geographically and culturally, with central Italy. This is truly the breadbasket of Italy, as Emilia-Romagna is home to some of Italy's finest and most distinctive cuisine. Tortelli stuffed with pumpkin, grainy shavings of Parmigiano-Reggiano the size of postage stamps, wafer-thin slices of pink cured ham, and roasted veal so tender it falls off the shank count among the region's specialties. All are paired with local wines—unique, rich, bubbly, effervescent reds. The region's principal cities—Parma, Modena, Bologna, Reggio nell'Emilia—boast a dizzying number of excellent restaurants and food shops.

Traditional farm estates, or *cascine*, characterize the flat, often monotonous countryside of Emilia-Romagna. These grand brick or stucco conglomerates surround a central courtyard usually filled with rabbits, quail, and other animals that also figure prominently on local menus. It's also here that pigs are fattened on the whey left over from the production of Parmigiano-Reggiano cheese, and later turned into *prosciutto crudo*. Outside the farms, wildlife flourishes in the Po river delta, a broad expanse of fertile wetlands.

There is a saying in Emilia-Romagna that I have always considered the world's greatest understatement: *"A Parma, si mangia bene"* ("In Parma, one eats well"). Three foods of Emilia-Romagna—traditional balsamic vinegar of Modena, Parmigiano-Reggiano cheese, and prosciutto ham—form a holy trinity of culinary delights in Emilia-Romagna. In the last century, these local products have risen above the confines of their region to conquer the taste buds of the whole world. Best of all, the three taste great together.

While its cuisine stands out as the region's preeminent art form, Emilia-Romagna also boasts impressive ceramics, with important centers of production in Imola and Faenza. Wrought iron and textile production is also based on traditional craft methods. And who could forget design? Emilia-Romagna is also home to Ferrari and its glorious design and automotive legacy.

THE TRADITIONS

BALSAMIC VINEGAR OF MODENA

Aceto Balsamico Tradizionale di Modena

I once spent four hours driving in the rain just to taste three drops of balsamic vinegar, dribbled onto my spoon by a vinegar producer on the outskirts of Modena. But then, this is not just any vinegar. This is traditional balsamic vinegar of Modena, the king of vinegars and one of Italy's most prized culinary legacies. Over the past three decades, balsamic vinegar of Modena has come to be treated in the same way as fine wines—with highly controlled production and labeling methods. The local consortium monitors every producer, from grape harvest to end product, assigning a designation much like the D.O.C. moniker for fine wines that serves as a quality symbol recognized around the world. Today, some 90 producers are authorized to carry the consortium's distinctive label, all in an 80-square-kilometer zone around Modena. Most are family-run operations started by ancestors generations ago.

No one knows how long Italians have been making this aromatic vinegar, but documents attest that aristocrats exchanged it on important occasions as far back as the eleventh century. Traditionally, the best balsamic vinegars were made at home instead of commercially, and were a prized gift. Some folks willed the precious juice to their heirs, and it was even included in women's dowries!

Balsamic vinegar begins on the vine with ripe, white Trebbiano grapes. The vinegar is made by boiling grape juice (not wine, as in other vinegars), and moving the juice year after year into increasingly smaller casks made of different kinds of wood, including oak, cherry, and chestnut. Often the barrels are stored in attic-level storage rooms, where they are exposed to summer heat and winter cold. As it ages, anywhere from ten to 25 years, it becomes more concentrated, richer in flavor, and more expensive. Rich, syrupy, fragrant, and almost black, its distinctive taste is immediately recognizable.

You'll find plenty of inexpensive bottles with labels reading *aceto balsamico di Modena* in your local supermarket, but this vinegar bears no relation to the real stuff. It may be produced from wine made near Modena, with flavors and colors added, but it is not aged in casks, and could never be enjoyed straight from the bottle. The artisanal product carries a label that includes the word *tradizionale* and comes wrapped in a smartly designed box with the consortium logo.

I save the real stuff for drizzling over shavings of Parmigiano-Reggiano cheese, or as a dressing for steamed vegetables, pan-fried *frittate*, and meats for special dinner parties. One of the most surprising uses for balsamic vinegar is in desserts and sweets. In Italy, you can find it used as a filling for chocolates, and incorporated into pastries and pastry cream. You can even serve it over strawberries and vanilla ice cream. Occasionally I even put a drop on my spoon and sample it straight from the bottle.

PRICE POINTS

I picked up an eight-ounce bottle of 25-year-old vinegar directly from a top producer in Modena for about 50 euros; the same bottle sells for $175 in a popular American culinary catalog. In contrast, the mass-produced bottles go for around $6 in American grocery stores.

THE REAL DEAL

Only about 20,000 bottles of the artisanal product are produced a year, compared with a huge production of 30 million bottles of the commercial product exported to supermarkets from Japan to the United States. Look for the consortium logo and the words *aceto balsamico tradizionale di Modena* to assure you're getting the real thing. It's the word *tradizionale* that's missing from the mass-produced vinegars—a small distinction, but a big difference!

BELLISSIMA!

The taste of traditional balsamic vinegar varies from producer to producer, and even from batch to batch. My favorite is the 25-year-old *extra vecchio* produced by the Malpighi family (page 57).

CARNIVAL MASKS

Maschere di Carnevale

C arnival in Venice hearkens back to the Middle Ages; the city held its first in the eleventh century. In early times, carnival was the one time of year when social divisions were blurred; behind the mask it was impossible to tell aristocracy from the lower classes. By the glory days of the Venetian Republic in the sixteenth century, masks had become as elaborate as the costumes and jewelry for which Venetians were world-renowned.

Today's fancy carnival masks are outdone only by the stunning costumes, complete with feathers, velvet, scarves, ruffles, pearls, jewels, gold, and other adornments. Traditionally, this free-for-all celebration preceding Lent includes parades, balls, practical jokes, and ten days of general revelry. Outlawed at the end of the eighteenth century and revived again in 1979, carnival draws ever increasing crowds to Venice each February.

Over time, many archetypal masks developed, all immediately recognizable to Venetians. Many of these characters came from the popular theater troupe, the *Commedia dell'Arte*, whose stock characters included a pair of lovers, two elders, a Capuchin monk, a captain, and a host of servants, the most famous of which was *Arlecchino* or Harlequin. Other typical characters became popular, including the

Plague Doctor, whose sinister-looking, beaked-nose mask is historically accurate. In times of plague, doctors wore these masks as they were thought to help ward off the harmful effects of the bubonic plague by preventing the disease from coming near the doctor's nose.

Venetian mask craftsmen first model their masks from clay, so that they have a form that can be used again and again. Papier-mâché paste is pressed over the clay form, then left to dry. Once dry, the craftsman buffs the mask, cuts eyeholes and other facial features, then paints and decorates the mask by hand.

Carnival masks abound all over Venice, from craft stores to street vendors. There are a few traditional mask types, including the plague doctor and the joker, though after hours of strolling Venice's streets, you may find they all begin to look the same. A few shops offer unique creations, so keep your eye out for one-of-a-kind masks.

PRICE POINTS

Venetian masks are a relative bargain considering their uniqueness. You can pay as little as $10 for an acceptable handmade mask, or over $100 for one crafted by one of the city's most famous artisans.

Considering the relatively low cost of handmade Venetian masks, you may decide to splurge on a custom design, which should set you back no more than about two hundred euros. Steer clear of the metal masks you see in trinket shops and street vendor stalls; they are not traditional, and most are not even made in Venice.

BELLISSIMA!

Since carnival was revived in the 1970s, the Max Art Shop (page 63) has distinguished itself as one of Venice's most innovative mask producers.

CURED HAM

Prosciutto di Parma e Prosciutto di San Daniele

L *a nebbia.* In Italian, it means fog, and throughout the countryside of Emilia-Romagna, *la nebbia* enshrouds the flat landscape, so that silhouettes of medieval castles and ancient farm estates loom like dark giants in the white soup. This is not London fog, or the wet, cold mist that hangs along the coast of Maine. This fog is dry and billowy, and imparts an inexplicable aroma that is at the same time salty, sweet, and clean.

It may be a bane for drivers, but this peculiar air is a boon for local ham producers in the Langhirano region just south of Parma. All year round, eastward breezes waft salt air off the Mediterranean and over the hills and plains of north-central Italy. It blows through vents pierced in the walls of seasoning rooms, where hundreds of ham hocks hang quietly for up to two years. According to the experts, this air accounts for the unmistakable flavor and aroma of this region's premier product: *prosciutto di Parma*.

In the first century B.C., the Roman scholar Varro described the distinctive flavor of cured hams in this region. And what flavor it is: sweet, mild, and less salty than other cured hams, with a lean, pink flesh streaked with thin lines of fat. The zone of production for *prosciutto di Parma* extends from the province of Parma southward between the Stirone and Enza rivers. This production area is protected by Italian law.

Production begins with pigs raised in Italy and fed on a diet of grains and the whey left over from the production of local Parmigiano-Reggiano cheese (see page 48). They must reach an age of ten months and weigh 140 kilograms before slaughtering. Only the rear haunches and legs of the pigs become *prosciutto di Parma*, trimmed into a distinctive rounded shape with the leg attached. The hams are branded with the month and year of slaughtering, then are sold to individual producers, where the seasoning process begins.

First, the raw hams rest on ventilated racks inside a refrigerated meat locker, where they are rubbed with salt multiple times over several weeks to extract as much moisture as possible. Then, they're showered with lukewarm water to rinse the salt, and are hung to dry in another refrigerated chamber. Finally, producers transfer the hams from the refrigerators to special curing rooms located partly below ground, with windows on opposite walls to allow the curious air of Parma to circulate. Producers cover any meat not covered with skin with a protective layer of a fat, salt, and pepper mixture called *sugna*. Then, the hams are hung with twine on large steel or wooden frames, and left to cure for a minimum of 12 months.

But the hams aren't left alone at that point. Specially trained inspectors from the *prosciutto di Parma* official consortium circulate among the some 200 producers to inspect the hams at every stage of production. The consortium, established in 1963, controls the production of *prosciutto di Parma* and promotes it worldwide. In a process called *spillatura*, inspectors use a needle crafted from the bone of a horse leg to pierce the skin of the ham in five places, then smell. Special characteristics of the bone allow for optimum testing of the aroma. If any part of the ham has gone bad, they must throw out the entire hock. After the hams are aged, inspectors grant the quality seal—the five-point ducal crown burnished into the skin of the hock— to only the best ones.

Today, the specially denominated region around Parma produces some 9.5 million hams annually, sold to markets as far afield as North America and Asia. But Italians keep the majority of the stuff to themselves. In local markets, groceries, and specialty food stores across Italy, a special deli counter is reserved for ham. Ham hocks hang from twine behind shiny, steel electric slicers that carve them into wafer-thin slices. You can buy real *prosciutto di Parma* virtually anywhere in Italy, from grocery stores to village markets.

Hams are sold boneless or with the bone in. The bone-in hams can be stored up to a year at 62–68 degrees Fahrenheit. They must be sliced from the side first, until the bone is exposed, then the large bone must be extracted by hand. Boneless versions are more easily sliced, but last only up to three months refrigerated. Slices will keep for a couple of weeks in the refrigerator.

You can buy prepackaged *prosciutto*, already sliced and ready to serve from sealed packages. However, the best *prosciutto* is eaten immediately after it's sliced. I like to serve it as an antipasto with ripe figs or cantaloupe, but most Italians like to eat it by itself or on crusty bread. All over Italy, you can amble up to the bar and order a sandwich or panino with *prosciutto di Parma*. Locals like to serve *prosciutto di Parma* with a light, fruity white wine, but the complex flavor of the ham also stands up to bolder reds like Barolo.

Prosciutto di Parma is the most famous of Italy's cured hams but by no means the only good one. A cousin to *prosciutto di Parma*, San Daniele ham is produced in the hills of San Daniele, in the northern mountainous region of Friuli. Compared with *prosciutto di Parma*, San Daniele ham is sweeter, less salty, and leaner. It's a matter of personal taste, but many hold that San Daniele is the best cured ham in Italy. It's my favorite.

Like *prosciutto di Parma*, San Daniele is produced in a small geographical area that boasts the ideal microclimate for curing hams. The hams sit in seasoning rooms for about a year, and then are stamped with the special San Daniele logo. But there are a few important differences. San Daniele is cured with the hoof on, so you'll recognize this eye-catching ham hock right away in the markets and food shops. (If the sight of the ham hock repulses you, buy a package of the ham pre-sliced.)

PRICE POINTS
You can buy an entire hock of *prosciutto di Parma* in Italy for around 200 euros. In the U.S., authentic *prosciutto di Parma* stamped with the ducal crown runs around $20 per pound.

THE REAL DEAL
Look for the five-point ducal crown that's been fire-branded into the skin of the *prosciutto di Parma*. This is the brand of the consortium of *prosciutto di Parma*, the organization that regulates the raising of the pigs and the production of the ham. It's the only guarantee that you're buying the real thing. A decade ago, the consortium also began fire-branding the initials of the producer below the ducal crown, so that every ham can be traced back to its origins. Call the consortium at 0521/243987 to set up a visit to one of the region's producers.

BELLISSIMA!
An entire hock of *prosciutto* is considered a traditional holiday gift in Italy, one very much appreciated by Italians.

GLASS
Vetro

I love the charming island of Murano, which has all the allure of Venice but boasts friendlier people and fewer crowds. And that's even before we start talking about glass. Lower prices and a more pleasant shopping experience mean that I always board the boat at the end of the day with an armful of shopping bags.

Venice has been a glass-making hub at least since the ninth century. The great number of glass-firing ovens—that reached as much as 2,700 degrees Fahrenheit—caused so many fires in the mostly wooden city, that in the 1290s, city officials transferred all glass workshops from the center of Venice to the outlying cluster of islands called Murano. The glass blowers became renowned throughout Europe for their stunning and colorful creations, and Murano glassmakers held a virtual monopoly on European glass making until the sixteenth century.

Archeological finds show that Venetian glassblowing techniques have changed little since ancient times, and some centuries-old museum pieces look amazingly contemporary, with colorful stripes and swirls. The glassblowing process begins when a specialized glass artisan called a gaffer lifts a molten blob of sand mixed with a variety of materials with the end of the blow pipe. Next, he blows, twists, pulls, and cuts the shape over a hot flame. Special glassmaking tools forged by a blacksmith are then used to form specific shapes such as handles, spouts, stems, and other shapes. To create color, cobalt, manganese, and other materials may be added to the mix. The gaffer continues to shape the piece until it results in its final form—a vase, a goblet, a plate. In addition to this basic process, Venetian glassmakers have developed and refined many specialized—and purely Venetian—glass techniques over the years, some with amazing results, like the popular flower-like patterns known as *millefiori* (see A Murano Glass Primer, below, for some of these techniques).

In addition to the glass museum, a tour of one or more glass factories is the main attraction on Murano. Even if you don't buy, it's worth the trip just to see the impressive glass-blowing demonstrations. Molten glass on the end of a rod miraculously transforms into gorgeous vases, glasses, and candlesticks before your eyes. The range of quality is staggering. You'll see everything from silly figurines of Donald Duck to drop-dead gorgeous tableware with so many zeros on the price tag it will make your head spin.

You can catch a factory tour just by showing up during hours of operation (most remain open during the traditional Italian lunch break), or by taking an

A MURANO GLASS PRIMER

Here are a few glass terms you'll see when you start looking at Murano glass:
• **Murrina:** The *murrina* technique involves slicing canes of glass to expose transverse patterns, and it can be used to create repeating decorative elements.
• **Millefiori:** Literally "thousand flowers," it refers to the technique of slicing rods of layered glass to expose a flowerlike design on a disk of glass. You see these disks used a lot as pendants and earrings. *Millefiori* is a particular type of *murrina*.
• **Vetro battutto:** The glass is "hammered," giving it a rich, textured finish.
• **Vetro pezzato:** Large bits of different colored glass are pieced together like a patchwork quilt.
• **Vetro tessuto:** Lined or ribboned effect resembling fabric (*tessuto*).

organized excursion from Venice. If you opt to accept the offer of one of the many persistent hawkers hanging around San Marco, be ready for high-pressure sales tactics, but don't feel obliged to buy.

The more reputable houses are set up to pack and ship your treasures home, and can usually ship anywhere in the world. Still, my advice for getting your glass home is to carry it with you. This may seem impractical, but shipping these delicate pieces home is both costly and hazardous. One of my friends shipped a carton of goblets home to Connecticut. Finally, after six weeks, they arrived shattered. Luckily, she had insured the package, but so much for her one-of-a-kind souvenir of Venice! If you decide to ship anyway, use one of the top express carriers (FedEx, UPS, or DHL), and insure, insure, insure.

Today, the island of Murano is synonymous with glass. Everything imaginable is made from Murano glass, including jaw-dropping goblets, vases, candlestick holders, miniature animals, paperweights, chandeliers, lampshades, dinner services, tiny pieces of glass candy, beads, and every kind of jewelry you can dream of. There is tremendous variety in quality, price, and style. When it's cheap and tacky, it's hideous; when it's well done, it takes your breath away.

PRICE POINTS

Prices for Murano glass vary according to the techniques used to execute the piece. You'll pay more for more intricate designs and more threads (the colored bands of glass swirled into a finished piece). Also, some glass houses—especially Venini, Pauly, Barovier & Toso, and Seguso—command higher prices than others because of the quality of their work and the tradition behind it.

Big-name designers like Versace and Valentino have produced pieces for some glass houses, and of course you'll pay a premium for signed pieces. I lusted after a collection of vases signed by Franco Raggi and Daniela Puppa in the shop window at Barovier & Toso on Murano, each of which ran in the 500 to 600 euro range. The prices can go much higher than that, but still much less than you will find anywhere else in the world. The most valuable Murano glass pieces fetch six figures at auction.

BELLISSIMA!

Don't miss the outrageous glass chandeliers at the Pauly showroom in St. Mark's Square (page 65).

GONDOLAS

Gondole

Well, you may not take one of these home unless you're willing to row it across the Atlantic yourself, but don't let that stop you from appreciating the fascinating craft of boat building while you're here.

Gondolas are the sport utility vehicles of Venice . . . and cost about as much. They carry everything—luggage, commercial goods, camera-toting tourists, lovers, pets, and more—through the snaking canals of this island city. So central are boats to Venetian life, that it would be almost unfathomable to live here without one.

In its golden age, the entire city was filled with gondolas. In the seventeenth century, some 10,000 gondolas glided through the narrow canals, transporting goods and people all over the city. Today, about 400 *gondole* glide through the waters of Venice. Most of today's gondola makers live and work in Dorsoduro, a quiet and wonderful section of town south of the Grand Canal.

Originally, gondolas were the primary mode of transportation for Venetians.

Organized into guilds, boatmen adhered to an elaborate bureaucratic system similar to the one taxi cab drivers follow in today's largest cities. They awaited passengers at specified *traghetti*, or boat stops, and charged standard fares. Venetian gondoliers had a reputation for cursing, fighting, and extorting their passengers, and historical Venetian chronicles are filled with legal charges against them for these offenses.

Wealthy Venetians employed their own boatmen to maintain their boats, dock them in private boatyards, and remain at their masters' disposal to ferry them around the city. By the sixteenth century, some of these boats were so outlandishly ornamented that city authorities banned gondola ornamentation in 1562, including hefty fines for those who broke the rule. For some nobles, however, the fine was a small price to pay to uphold their social status, and they gladly paid the price to keep up appearances with red velvet curtains on the *felze*, or passenger compartment, as well as elaborately gilded and carved details.

The *ferro*, or F-shaped decoration on the prow, had evolved as a standard gondola accessory by the seventeenth century. The *forcola*, or oarlock, whose purpose is to help the gondolier maneuver the craft in narrow canals, has become a work of high art over the last two hundred years. Several specialized forcola makers in Venice are true sculptors.

The craft of the Venetian gondola maker—the *squerariolo*—begins with nine different kinds of wood—beech, cherry, elm, fir, larch, lime, mahogany, oak, and walnut. The oak is the most critical, for the planks run the entire length of the boat, up to about 30 feet. The left side of the boat is wider than the right, giving the correct counterbalance to the force created by the gondolier, who rows only from the right side.

Every year, the Venetian Regatta parades the most beautiful gondolas through the canals of the city, and it's a great chance to see these historic boats in action (see the Calendar of Events on page 214).

PRICE POINTS

The basic shell of a gondola—without the seats, upholstery, and decoration—will set you back about 20,000 euros. Fully outfitted, it can go for up to 30,000 euros or more and will take about three months to complete.

THE REAL DEAL

Once a thriving industry, today only a dozen or so new gondolas are produced in Venice each year by a handful of artisans.

BELLISSIMA!

For a unique Venetian experience, visit one of the last gondola makers still in operation (page 66).

GRAPPA

Grappa

Throughout Italy, grappa always seems to command tones of respect and awe for its potency. Grappa is made by extracting alcohol from the skins, stems, and seeds of grapes left over after fermentation for wine (known as pomace, or *vinacce* in Italian). These are distilled into a strong, alcoholic concoction known all over the world. Though grappa is produced in Piemonte, Tuscany, and other regions of Italy, the northeastern region of Friuli is Italy's largest grappa producer. It's not surprising, given the cold clime of this region, and, at 50–60 percent alcohol, the warming effects of grappa on a chilly fall night.

The grape skins are steamed in baskets encased within giant copper cauldrons that are works of art in themselves. The resulting liquid streams into copper distillation columns, where the impurities are separated from the liquid. Then the grappa is transferred to wooden casks to age.

Grappa comes in different grades, some of the more potent of which are capable of singeing your eyebrows. The Italian government prohibits home distillation, in part because of the ethanol and methanol contained in the skins and seeds.

Grappa is traditionally served after a meal as a *digestivo*, usually along with or after coffee. However, people drink it at all hours in bars throughout Italy. Some prefer it chilled, while others prefer it at room temperature. It is best served in a small flute, and top glass designers have created glasses resembling small champagne flutes to maximize the flavor and bouquet.

Throughout northern Italy, grappa is incorporated into recipes served from appetizers to desserts. In Piemonte, a drizzle of grappa is added to a sauce of oil, vinegar, and anchovies, which is served over cooked meats and vegetables. During the Venice carnival, pastry chefs make chocolate cakes filled with pastry cream mixed with grappa. In Friuli, people traditionally drink a glass of grappa on New Year's Day morning to chase away evil spirits in the new year.

Today, producers go out of their way to package the potent after-dinner drink in beautiful handblown bottles of every shape and size, with artistic labels and decorative corks. Stock up at a local wine shop and you'll have finished half of your holiday shopping. One of the most treasured gifts I've ever received is a bottle of homemade blueberry grappa my neighbor made from berries she handpicked in the mountains north of Bergamo. The slender bottle is chock full of the gorgeous berries, which surrender their color to the liquid over time.

Grappa is produced in the fall, just after the wine harvest, so plan your trip accordingly if you want to see it being made. Several distillers offer tours. Always call in advance to arrange a visit.

PRICE POINTS

Grappa used to be considered a poor man's drink, as it is concocted from the skins and seeds left over from the production of "great" wines. However, the drink has enjoyed a recent vogue, and the quality has improved. Today there is a huge range of prices, depending on the grape used, how long it ages, and the brand.

THE REAL DEAL

Some of Italy's most well-known grape varieties—Moscato, Lambrusco, Gavi, and Brunello—turn into rich grappa. More recently, distillers have turned to other fruits—strawberries, raspberries, and pears, for example—to make unique and innovative *grappe*.

BELLISSIMA!

The distiller Nonino, located outside of Udine (page 60), is credited with raising the humble *digestivo* known as grappa to a stylish drink.

JEWELRY

Gioielli

I taly is the largest gold jewelry exporter in the world. Vicenza, a prosperous city west of Venice, hosts a mega–trade show for the gold industry twice a year. At Vicenza Oro, jewelry traders meet to deal and keep track of the latest jewelry fashions. Thousands of jewelry fans and professionals convene here to talk shop, buy, and gawk at the season's best.

A document from 1399 attests that goldsmiths were already operating in Vicenza at that time, and by the Renaissance, the city's artisans gained a reputation throughout Europe for their skill at crafting gold and gems into beautiful creations. Over the centuries, many new jewelry enterprises were drawn to the city.

Today, with so much money to be made in the international export markets, the smaller, artisanal jewelry producers are few and far between. But a handful of high–quality artisans have put a stake in the ground and decided to specialize in artisanal jewelry. The results are dazzling.

BELLISSIMA!
Davide Penso's studio in Murano (page 69) contains some of the Veneto's most creative jewelry designs.

LACE

Merletti

T he image of the elderly woman working lace is one of Italy's most timeless. From the Alps to the islands, women gather at the thresholds of their homes, spinning tales as they spin lace, and repeating gestures they have used thousands of times over the course of their lives.

Although artisans create lace all over Italy, Venetian lace boasts the most prestigious pedigree. The earliest Venetian laces were produced inside convents and were reserved for church vestments, altar cloths, and other delicate church finery. Trade guilds took over the craft in the fifteenth and sixteenth centuries. Portraits of nobles wearing outlandishly fancy lace collars—the kind you see in the seventeenth-century paintings of Rembrandt and van Dyck—helped make Venetian lace

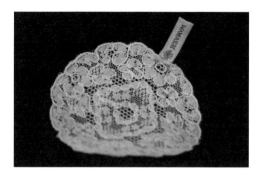

a status symbol among aristocracy from Ghent to Paris. Artisans all over Europe copied Venetian designs from actual examples and pattern books.

By the end of the seventeenth century, rival French and Dutch producers caused the Venetian lace industry to decline. It enjoyed a revival toward the end of the 1800s and now continues, in part, thanks to today's lively Venetian tourist trade.

There are two main types of handmade lace: needle or point lace, and bobbin or pillow lace. In the Veneto, needle lace prevails, made with a single needle and thread. The pattern is traced or drawn onto parchment, then tacked to a piece of linen for support. Artisans fasten a few threads to the design, then work the pattern. Once finished, the linen is cut free from the completed piece. (Bobbin lace, by contrast, is made by weaving threads wound around tiny wooden spools.) Lace is crafted using geometric patterns such as circles, stars, rosettes, and triangles. Animals, flowers, scrolls, and other naturalistic elements also play a part in fancier designs.

The island of Burano, a 45-minute boat ride from Venice, is the undisputed capital of Italian lace production. The tradition began in the fourteenth century, when Duchess Morosina Morosini, wife of the Venetian doge, established a lace workshop employing 130 workers on the island of Burano. Over the next few centuries, Burano lace became highly coveted throughout the European royal courts; for his coronation, Louis XIV of France wore a fine lace collar that took Burano lacemakers two years to produce. Typical Buranese needle lace became known as *punto in aria*, or "points in the air," because of its delicate effects.

Burano is a quiet island filled with brightly painted houses, picturesque boats, and endless *botteghe* selling lace tablecloths, doilies, jewelry, knickknacks, and breathtaking babies' dressing gowns.

PRICE POINTS

Today, much of the lace in Burano is machine-made. Genuine, handmade Burano lace is rare, taking weeks of labor. For a machine-made lace doily, you'll pay 5 to 10 euros, versus more than 100 euros for a handmade version.

THE REAL DEAL

Today's lace-making machines weave cotton thread many times faster than the hand. The machine-made versions are sterile, stiffer, and perfect, while the handmade laces are delicate and contain imperfections only the human hand can craft. However, some machine-made lace is so fine that it is difficult even for experts to tell the difference. Venice is a city full of tourist traps, so always buy from a reputable dealer and be careful that you're not paying handmade prices for machine-made lace.

BELLISSIMA!

To feast your eyes on some of the world's most exquisite lace, head to Burano's impressive lace school and museum, the Scuola di Merletti (page 68).

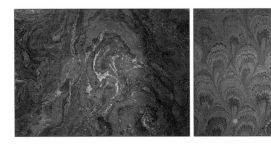

PAPER AND STATIONERY

Carta

I f it's your first trip to Venice, you'll be struck by the number of shops selling gorgeous marbleized paper, blocks of elegant stationery, Old World leather-bound books and albums, and a host of related items from fountain pens and wax seals to unique calendars, agendas, and diaries.

Why this penchant for paper? Venice claims an important place in the history of bookmaking and paper production. The art of paper making traveled from Asia to Europe during the Middle Ages. Venice, with its strong ties to Constantinople and the East, was the natural place for this art to gain a European foothold. From Venice, the tradition of marbleized paper trickled south to Florence and then to the rest of Europe.

Bookmakers held special status in medieval and Renaissance Venice, and the art of the Venetian bookbinding studio, or *legatoria*, goes back to the 1450s, with the advent of the first books printed with moveable type. One of the most influential publishers of the era was Aldus Manutius, whose Venice-based *legatoria* typeset many scholarly books in Greek and Latin destined for cities all over Europe.

The tradition of facing the inside covers of leather-bound books with marbleized paper began not because of a desire for decoration, but rather for a practical reason. Early bookmakers found that the end papers that came into direct contact with the leather bindings became damaged and discolored, so they faced the inside book covers with hand-colored papers. Later, in order to cut the high cost of leather bindings, bookmakers began using leather only for the spine, disguising the cover boards with decorative papers. These papers became a prime place for creativity in decoration.

PRICE POINTS

You'll see Venetian paper covering books, desk accessories, bookmarks, and hundreds of other accessories, but the cheapest way to buy it is by the sheet. It makes lovely giftwrap. Wax stamps with initials, agendas, bookmarks, and other knickknacks make great personalized gifts.

THE REAL DEAL

Though many of the marbleized papers (*carta marmorizzata*) you find in Venice today are machine-printed, there are still a few *legatorie* making paper the old-fashioned way. Traditionally, marbleized paper is created by swirling oil-based paints into a large pan of water, then laying the paper gently and briefly on the surface of the water to transfer the pattern. Traditional patterns include peacock feathers (*pavoni*), snail shells (*chiocciole*), and streaked or "combed" marble (*marmo pettinato*).

BELLISSIMA!

Venice's most exquisite paper can be found at Legatoria Piazzesi (page 67).

PARMESAN CHEESE

Parmigiano-Reggiano

I honestly don't know what I ate before I discovered real *Parmigiano-Reggiano*. When I fly home to the United States, I pack my carry-on luggage full of the big, golden triangles. My family and friends are waiting with out-stretched hands when I disembark, but I always reserve a chunk or two to savor, making it last till I return again to Italy. It is no wonder that *Parmigiano-Reggiano* is known as the king of cheeses. One taste of the real thing and you'll laugh at the imitations in the jars that line American grocery store shelves.

Parmigiano-Reggiano is produced in a *zona tipica*, with Parma and Reggio nell'Emilia at its heart and fanning out across north-central Italy from Bologna to Mantova. The area is protected by the government. *Parmigiano-Reggiano* starts with cows fed on a diet of grass, hay, and special grains. Their milk is collected immediately after milking and mixed in a giant cauldron, with naturally fermenting whey (the left-overs of which are fed to local pigs raised for *prosciutto di Parma*). Calf rennet is added to initiate curdling, then the milk is drained, cooked, and decanted. The cheese is then left to rest inside a wooden mold that forms its distinctive wheel-like shape. The milk cools and dries for several days before being salted in a brine solution. The rind forms naturally with the hardening of the outside of the cheese, matur-ing into a hard, golden-colored casing. Finally, it is left to age, usually for a min-imum of two years. The giant golden wheels, some the size of automobile tires, rest on shelves inside specially constructed aging rooms.

No one knows for sure how long *Parmigiano-Reggiano* has been made in Italy, but it's been celebrated for more than 800 years in European literature and folk-lore. The French playwright Molière is said to have dined solely on *Parmigiano-Reggiano* in his old age. In his *Decameron*, the fourteenth-century author Boccaccio describes a paradise consisting of a giant mountain made of grated *Parmigiano-Reggiano*, with people rolling pieces of macaroni and ravioli in it. Sure sounds like heaven to me!

You'll find plenty of expensive wedges of industrially produced "Parmesan" cheese in gourmet shops and supermarkets across the United States, and of course you'll find endless varieties of grated cheese in jars, but only the rind will tell you if you've found the real thing. The words *Parmigiano-Reggiano* are stamped in pin-dot writing around the circumference of the rind (horizontal lines running through those words mean that the wheel of cheese was rejected by the consortium because it

failed quality control). If you can see the entire rind, you'll also find the fire-branded logo of the consortium, a number indicating the identity of the producer, and the year of production. It must be aged for a minimum of 12 months, but it is better if left to age from 18 to 24 months. The longer the cheese ages, the darker the color, the richer the flavor and aroma, and the higher the price. Real *Parmigiano-Reggiano* has a wonderful, grainy texture, strawlike color, and distinctive scent.

Italians portion *Parmigiano-Reggiano* with a special knife consisting of a short handle and a teardrop-shaped blade that allows you to break apart the cheese into crumbly, irregularly shaped triangles or wedges. You can pick up these inexpensive tools in *casalinga* ("housewife") shops and grocers all over Italy; they make unique gifts for Italophiles back home.

You can buy good *Parmigiano-Reggiano* all over Italy, in supermarkets, outdoor produce markets, and specialty shops. My secret: load up on it in one of the country's many hypermarkets, the gigantic supermarket and discount department stores that sell everything under the sun. You certainly don't have to go to Emilia-Romagna to buy *Parmigiano-Reggiano*, but isn't it more fun and authentic that way?

PRICE POINTS

A wedge of *Parmigiano-Reggiano* in Italy costs about half of what it does in the United States, yet still ranks among the more expensive cheeses in Italy.

THE REAL DEAL

Parmigiano-Reggiano is regulated by a consortium of producers with a board of directors and entourage of inspectors who judge the quality of the cheese from udder to table. Before the giant golden wheels of cheese are released to the market, a consortium inspector taps the rind with a special metal hammer, telling him as much about what's happening inside the cheese as a stethoscope tells a doctor what's going on inside a patient's body.

PORCELAIN AND CERAMICS

Porcellane e Ceramiche

T he ceramics of northeastern Italy may surprise you. If you came here looking for Italian *maiolica*—white pots and jars decorated with bright, Mediterranean splashes of color—you won't find it in the two major ceramics capitals of the Veneto: Nove and Bassano del Grappa. You'll have to head to the southernmost reaches of the region—specifically to Faenza in Emilia-Romagna—where *maiolica* is the reason for the very existence of the town.

The success of two towns in the Veneto—Nove and Bassano del Grappa—stems from good old capitalism. In the 1720s, European nobles went mad for Chinese export porcelain, with their transparent white glazes and fancy, frilly forms. The Dutch and English produced good enough imitations to enjoy wild success. Not to be outdone, the Republic of Venice decided to start creating its own ceramics, imitating the delicate, rococo forms that were sweeping the royal courts. The Venetian Senate granted artisans in Nove, a sleepy town to its west, the exclusive right to produce these luxury wares. Today, artisans in the two towns continue the tradition, and there's an excellent selection of fancy porcelain to suit every taste.

When most people think of Italian pottery, they think of *maiolica*, the brightly colored wares for which the town of Faenza is known. Considering the importance of Faenza as a world ceramics capital (after all, the term *faïence* is just a Frenchified version of the town's name), it is surprisingly quiet. Located in the heart of Emilia-Romagna halfway between Bologna and the Adriatic Sea, today Faenza is home to about 60 working ceramics firms whose artisans quietly turn out small masterpieces.

Maiolica refers to the technique of painting with ceramic pigments against a white glaze background over terra-cotta or earthenware. It is often confused with majolica, a variation of the word that appeared only in the nineteenth century to describe English pieces. Traditional Italian *maiolica* was fired in the kiln at relatively low temperatures (about 1,820 degrees Farenheit) to achieve a glossy finish and colorful, painterly effects.

This colorful ware was popular with the noble classes for decorating villas and country estates throughout Italy during the Renaissance and baroque periods. Fine pieces of *maiolica* were exchanged between acquaintances, and special pieces were commissioned for engagements, important political deals between families, and other special occasions.

All summer long, Faenza hosts the annual Ceramic Summer (*Estate Ceramica*), with special exhibitions, competitions, and other fanfare surrounding the famous local product (see Calendar of Events, page 214). But this event is not a new phenomenon. Already in the 1500s, Faenza was famous for its annual weeklong *fiera* which drew crowds from across Europe to see local ceramics exhibited in all their glory.

A Faenza Ceramics Primer

There's no single style of Faenza ceramics, but today artisans who follow historical tradition take their inspiration from one or more of the main ceramic periods of Faenza:

• **stile arcaico (archaic style)**: This is the monochromatic style of the Middle Ages, with dark blue geometric patterns against a white ground.

• **stile severo (severe style)**: My personal favorite. This is the quintessential Renaissance spirit, with noblewomen shown in profile and symmetrical decorative motifs in the form of leaves and peacock feathers. Blue, gold, and ochre predominate.

• **stile bello (beautiful style)**: Storytelling or historiated pottery became all the rage in the 1500s, with religious and mythological scenes covering an entire plate or vessel.

• **stile compendiario (abbreviated style)**: Not much painted decoration here, it's true, but the artisans more than make up for it with elaborate basket patterns and pierced effects through the white glaze.

• **stile Berettino (Berettino style)**: This refers to a rich decoration of white scrollwork against a dark blue ground.

• **stile a garofano (carnation style)**: Carnations and other flowers characterize this type of decoration, and blues, greens, and ochres predominate. The style was influenced by French and Asian pottery popular in the eighteenth and nineteenth centuries.

PRICE POINTS

Quality and price vary tremendously in Faenza, but generally, you can find good deals on ceramics. You might pay 60 euros for a small, hand-painted vase in Faenza, compared to 100 euros for a comparable item in one of the central Italian *maiolica* meccas like Deruta. I picked up a large, nineteenth-century platter at an antique market for 450 euros. The most valuable pieces on the market today—those produced in Faenza between 1500 and 1530—command up to seven figures at auction.

THE REAL DEAL

In recent years, the Italian Association of Ceramic Cities (the Associazione Italiana Città Ceramiche, or AICC) has invented a handshake emblem to designate ceramics that adhere to certain historical standards, much as the term D.O.C. is given to wines that follow particular guidelines and authentic standards for a particular region. In Faenza, this "ceramic D.O.C." is a trademark with an image of a handshake, one of the traditional decorative motifs of Faenza ceramics. Look for it prominently displayed at the entrance to the town's ceramic merchants that have earned this designation. Of the 60 or so ceramic shops active in Faenza, about 20 are denominated with the D.O.C. All of those in the listings are D.O.C. producers (see page 56).

BELLISSIMA!

Mirta Morigi (page 57) is one of Faenza's most interesting artisans. By incorporating historical ceramic motifs into entirely modern forms, she takes Faenza tradition to a new level.

STOVES

Stufe

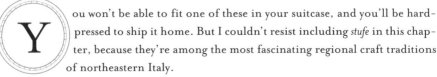

ou won't be able to fit one of these in your suitcase, and you'll be hard-pressed to ship it home. But I couldn't resist including *stufe* in this chapter, because they're among the most fascinating regional craft traditions of northeastern Italy.

Stufa is Italian for stove, but the word doesn't begin to do justice to these handsome, giant ceramic space heaters that are not quite architecture and not quite sculpture. They were produced in Trentino Alto-Adige beginning in the Middle Ages, and local artisans have continued to create and improve these stunning pieces. During the age of grand villas and *palazzi* in the seventeenth and eighteenth centuries, fancy ceramic *stufe* warmed the formal salons and receiving areas of these luxurious residences. Stoves from this era often reach eight or ten feet high, a testament to the enormous, fancy living areas they once heated.

Stufe are pieced together using clay formed in molds and fired in very hot ovens. Artisans then hand-paint designs on these ceramic panels, ranging from formal and ornate floral patterns, scrolls, vegetal motifs, and animals, to rustic folk-art designs. If you browse the local antique markets and shops, you'll find lovely old pieces that can be converted to use as space heaters in modern homes, or simply transported to your living room as a decorative accent. A few artisans still produce these masterpieces according to traditional methods, and they can give you advice about how to best install and use them in your house. They come in round, octagonal, and square forms, and they make a unique conversation piece and collector's item.

PRICE POINTS

An antique or reproduction stove costs several thousand euros, but you'll be hard-pressed to find a more unique conversation piece for your home!

THE REAL DEAL

Some of the more authentic regional *stufe* incorporate local folk-art motifs such as rosettes and scrolls in repetitive patterns.

BELLISSIMA!

The owners of the antique shop *Casa Cozzio* in Madonna di Campiglio (page 61), have arranged one of the region's most impressive collections of antique *stufe*.

WOODCRAFTS

Legno

Woodcarving craft guilds sprang up in the Dolomite Mountains at the end of the Middle Ages, and by the sixteenth century, the craft constituted a booming industry in this isolated mountain region. Woodcrafts are easy to produce indoors when the snow isolates many mountain villages in the Val Gardena, near the Gardena Pass linking the Italian peninsula with Austria. Ortisei, northeast of Bolzano, is one of the north's major centers for woodcarving.

The earliest wood artisans crafted religious sculptures destined for town churches and lone chapels on mountain peaks. Rustic Madonnas and vivid saints enlivened the otherwise sparsely decorated chapel interiors. Artisans painstakingly crafted delicate, lacelike gothic altarpieces of wood, then gilded and painted them with religious scenes for a rich effect. You can still see these stunning works of art in the many churches and mountain chapels in the region.

In the 1870s as many as 300 wood craftspeople operated in Ortisei. Today, a handful of artisans in the Val Gardena continue the centuries-old craft of creating wooden sculpture totally by hand. From whimsical, gnomelike figures to stunning painted nativity scenes, these pieces make great gifts and collector's items.

BELLISSIMA!
Conrad Moroder (page 61) is Ortisei's leading woodcarving studio.

THE LISTINGS

EMILIA-ROMAGNA

FAENZA

If you want to see Faenza like the locals, bring your bicycle; it's the way most people get around this small, flat town.

CERAMICS
Ceramiche

Ceramics Museum
Museo Internazionale della Ceramica
Viale Baccarini
0546/697311
www.micfaenza.org

Before heading to the shops, tour the impressive ceramics museum, with its airy, bright modern spaces. In addition to classic *maiolica* of Faenza, there are examples of ceramics from other periods and places from South America to France and Holland, from the Renaissance to the modern era. The museum also hosts an annual international ceramics competition, inspiring creative entrants from Canada to Australia (see Calendar of Events, page 214). A limited number of pieces are for sale in the museum shop.

Carla Lega
Via Fratelli Rosselli, 6/A
0546/30274

Born and bred in Faenza, Carla Lega spent many childhood days in her father's ceramic studio. But instead of slavishly copying historical models, Carla Lega struck out to craft new, innovative plates and vessels with a contemporary spirit. Her work features metallic glazes and sophisticated, sleek forms, often decorated with floral motifs. If you wish to commission a custom piece from this friendly studio, call in advance.

Laura Silvagni
Corso Garibaldi, 12/A
0546/663077

If you're lucky, you might catch Laura Silvagni painting a piece in the back of her small, tightly packed shop on the Corso Garibaldi. Her specialty is crafting reproductions of Renaissance wares. The well-lit space displays thousands of tiny treasures—bells shaped like ladies with long dresses, small plates, pharmacy jars, eggs, Christmas ornaments, oil and vinegar jars, and many other beautiful trinkets. Signora Silvagni's expanded workshop on the Via Sant'Ippolito provides another opportunity to appreciate her fine work (see below).

Ceramiche l'Odissea
Via Scaletta, 6
0546/660461
www.ceramicheodissea.it

In a rustic, crumbling stucco building on a picturesque street, Odissea puts on no airs. Real artisans with real pots stacked up next to the kiln work diligently here crafting the "beautiful lady" plates for which Faenza is famous. "Beautiful lady" plates were popular in the Renaissance as gifts for the beautiful lady in your life. Alongside a profile of a lovely female, the words *Bella Giulia* or my personal favorite, *Bella Laura*, would be painted on a scroll. Daniele Del Faggio and Morena Moretti produce works in all of the historical styles of Faenza, but occasionally turn out something truly innovative.

Cooperativa Artigiani Ceramisti Faentini (Immagine Faentina)
Via San Silvestro, 1
0546/672151
www.immagine-faentina.net

This artists' cooperative produces *maiolica* according to old-fashioned traditions, and this studio is a great place to take in the spectrum of historical Faenza designs produced today.

Gatti
Via Pompignoli, 4
Piazza della Liberta
0546/634301
www.ceramicagatti.it

Dante Servadei crafts some of the most stunning reproductions of historical Faenza ceramics. He also produces contemporary, copperlike reflective ceramics, a technique invented by Servadei's uncle, Riccardo Gatti, in 1928. Look for the cat logo (gatti is "cats" in Italian).

La Vecchia Faenza
Via S. Ippolito, 23A
0546/26357

The excellent ceramicist Laura Silvagni (see above) has expanded her workshop at a new location on the via San Ippolito, a quiet street in the eastern part of town. Taking over a space once occupied by the venerable artisan Gino Suzzi, Signora Silvagni kept the name La Vecchia Faenza, which is perfect for this enterprise, as it sums up the accurate and well-executed historical reproductions made here.

Mirta Morigi
Via Barbavara, 19/4 (workshop)
Corso Mazzini, 64 (showroom)
0546/29940
www.mirtamorigiceramista.it

Mirta Morigi began playing with ceramics as a hobby, but it quickly became her passion. For the last 20 years, she has operated a large studio in a courtyard building off a quiet side street, full of green, soothing plants and old terra-cotta pots. Morigi and her assistants funnel most of their creativity into excellent modern wares that make references to the past. For example, they'll craft a square terra-cotta plate that incorporates haphazardly placed shards of traditional Faenza ceramics. They also make cool, whimsical animals crafted of ceramic, like polka-dotted lizards and funny frogs that perch on the edge of pots.

Vittoria Monti
Via Cavina, 22
0546/25264

A huge range of wares are stacked neatly on the metal shelves of this unassuming workshop. From plain terra-cotta tiles to plates with vegetal decoration, religious themes, napkin rings, and more, this shop has it all. Enter through narrow doors from the vicolo Carina, or through the courtyard facing Corso Matteotti 4.

MODENA

BALSAMIC VINEGAR
Aceto Balsamico Tradizionale di Modena

Most producers of *aceto balsamico tradizionale di Modena* are family enterprises without marked storefronts or signs, so reservations are always recommended if you want to see how it's done first-hand. However, most producers are happy to have visitors. It's one of Italy's best experiences!

Consorzio Produttori Aceto Balsamico Tradizionale di Modena
Strada Vaciglio Sud, 1085/1
059/395633
www.balsamico.it

If you want to see how it's made, arrange a tour of one of the region's producers through the consortium. The consortium establishes minimum standards for balsamic vinegar production, and its inspectors put the stamp of approval on every bottle that comes to be called *aceto balsamico tradizionale di Modena*. Visit their website to request a tour.

Acetaia Malpighi
Via Pica, 310
059/367763
www.acetaiamalpighi.it

The Malpighi family began growing their own grapes and producing balsamic vinegar as a hobby in 1850, sharing prized bottles with family and friends. Today, young Massimo Malpighi (below) is the heir to this legacy and a gracious host. The small estate comprises a neat-as-a-pin brick villa and a series of outbuildings housing rows of vinegar casks. Nearby, vines hang heavy with grapes, colorful pheasants forage beneath a grove of acorn trees, and white swans glide across a still pond. There's no sign at the gate, no advertising, and no hint that behind this peaceful, unassuming facade lies one of Modena's leading balsamic vinegar producers. Reservations are essential. The Malpighis recently opened an appealing inn and restaurant. Make reservations for both on their web site.

Azienda Agricola Galli
Via Albareto, 452
059/251094

Signora Galli is one of the grand matriarchs of balsamic vinegar of Modena. This elderly woman continues a tradition of homemade production of *aceto balsamico* in her exceptionally lovely estate on the outskirts of Modena.

The day I visited, Signora Galli's gregarious daughter-in-law showed me approximately 80 barrels made of different woods that lay silently in the attic-level room of one of their tidy outbuildings, and even treated me to homemade pie and chunks of *Parmigiano-Reggiano* drizzled with the family's 25-year-old balsamic vinegar as we gazed out onto endless rows of vines heavy with Trebbiano grapes. Again, reservations are necessary.

Monari Federzoni
Via Carrate, 24
059/801711
www.monarifederzoni.com

Traditional balsamic vinegar of Modena is excellent, but you can't cook with it, as the product breaks down when heated. For good-quality industrially produced vinegar for cooking and everyday use, go to Monari Federzoni. The Monari Federzoni family had already been producing balsamic vinegar in their Modena home for centuries when, in 1912, Elena Monari Federzoni began selling her family's vinegar to the public. Today, Elena's grandchildren and great-grandchildren run the family business. Call ahead to make an appointment to see their facility, a rather industrial-looking complex in the Modenese countryside.

Pasticceria San Biagio
Via Emilia, 77
059/217284

If you thought balsamic vinegar was only for salad, think again. This pastry shop—a feast for the senses—will stretch the limits of your imagination with its many uses for balsamic vinegar: it's incorporated into pastry cream and piped into flaky crusts; it's used as a filling for dark chocolate; it's even served by the spoonful straight from the bottle if you visit at festival time (see page 213).

PARMA

CURED HAM
Prosciutto di Parma

Consorzio del Prosciutto di Parma
Via Marco dell'Arpa 8/b
0521/246211
www.prosciuttodiparma.com

This is the home of the official consortium of producers of *prosciutto di Parma*. You can buy the cured meat in stores and markets all over Italy, but if you're interested in coming to Parma to see firsthand how it's made, contact the consortium to arrange an appointment with one of the region's producers. You should make arrangements in advance of your trip.

Trattoria Corrieri
Via Conservatorio, 1
0521/234426
www.trattoriacorrieri.it

Check out the "salami room" in this unpretentious, local restaurant located in the historical center, one block back from the river. The waitstaff slices wafer-thin slices of *prosciutto di Parma* and other local sausages and cured meats on vintage slicing machines. They also serve well-prepared local specialties like *tortelli di zucca*, *risotto alla parmigiana*, and *osso buco*.

Market
Piazza della Ghiaia

Every morning except Sunday, you can sample the best prosciutto right where it's made. This is one of the best markets in Italy.

PARMESAN CHEESE
Parmigiano-Reggiano

Ristorante Parizzi
Via Repubblica, 71
0521/285952
www.ristoranteparizzi.it

Yes, that big cart the waiter just wheeled right under your nose is full of lovely golden hunks of *Parmigiano-Reggiano*. And this is just the appetizer. At Parizzi, Chef Marco Parizzi zips off traditional dishes of Emilia-Romagna with impeccable quality

and finesse. Behind an unassuming façade on a busy street, the well-appointed dining room, complete with stone walls and white tablecloths, welcomes guests. The menu changes according to season. Dine like a king, then waddle over to the lovely medieval cathedral and baptistery of Parma, just a few blocks away. Reservations, please.

REGGIO NELL'EMILIA

PARMESAN CHEESE
Parmigiano-Reggiano

Consorzio del Formaggio Parmigiano-Reggiano
Via Kennedy, 18
0522/307741
www.parmigiano-reggiano.it

This is the official consortium that controls the quality of *Parmigiano-Reggiano* cheese. Contact them at least two weeks in advance to arrange a visit to a local producer.

FRIULI-VENEZIA GIULIA

CIVIDALE DEL FRIULI

GRAPPA

Domenis
Via Darnazzacco, 30
0432/731023
www.domenis.com

Now in its fourth generation of family ownership, Domenis is one of the region's most well-respected makers of grappa. The family makes the potent spirit using traditional copper alambics in its no-frills distillery on the outskirts of Cividale di Friuli. Call in advance to arrange a visit and a tasting.

PERCOTO

GRAPPA

Nonino
Via Aquileia 104
0432/676331
www.nonino.it

Nonino is one of Italy's top grappa producers, and the family has been instrumental in elevating the image of grappa from a poor man's drink to that of an elegant *digestivo*. The Noninos are also at the vanguard of grappa bottle design. Some of their bottles, designed by Murano glass artists, have become collector's items. Their distillery is located in Percoto, south of Udine. Call two weeks in advance to arrange a visit of the distillery.

SAN DANIELE DEL FRIULI

CURED HAM
Prosciutto di San Daniele

Consorzio del Prosciutto di San Daniele
Via Umberto I, 26
0432/957515
www.prosciuttosandaniele.it

This is the San Daniele counterpart to the group in Parma. They sponsor a festival during the last week of August that attracts *prosciutto* fans from around the world (see Calendar of Events, page 215). Contact them in advance of your trip to arrange a visit with one of the some two dozen producers of prosciutto di San Daniele.

UDINE

GRAPPA

Banear
Via Cocul 2, Treppo Grande
0432/968811
www.banear.it

Against a backdrop of vines producing plump chardonnay and sauvignon blanc grapes, grappa producers at Banear quietly labor away, making up to 260,000 gallons of grappa every year, in addition to sweet dessert wines and a red cabernet sauvignon. Treppo Grande is located on the eastern outskirts of Udine.

TRENTINO-ALTO ADIGE

BOLZANO

STOVES
Stufe

Thun
Via Castel Flavon, 24
0471/285214
www.stufethun.com

Oscar Thun runs the leading workshop
for artisans creating *stufe* using traditional
methods. Thun's artisans create models based
on historical prototypes, as well as beautiful
modern interpretations. The workshop is
located in a picturesque, historic farm building, or *cascina*, on the outskirts of Bolzano.

MADONNA DI CAMPIGLIO

STOVES
Stufe

Casa Cozzio
Via Cima Tosa, 3
0465/441337

After a day on the slopes of the craggy
Dolomites, head into the Piazza Righi in
the center of town. This fascinating antique
shop has amassed an impressive collection
of local *stufe*—the giant ceramic room heaters
so typical of northern Italy—from different
historical periods. Also check out local
handmade furniture, from fabulously ornate
chairs and mantelpieces fit for a palazzo
to rustic dressing tables and beds for the
simplest abode.

ORTISEI

WOODCRAFTS
Legno

Artiginato Gardenese
Via Rezia, 9
0471/796634

Just down the street from Conrad Moroder's
shop (see below), this artisan's workshop
produces wood dolls and statuettes, along
with religious figurines, animals, and other
collector's items.

Conrad Moroder
Via Rezia, 204
0471/796187
www.moroder.com

One side of Conrad Moroder's workshop and
showroom fronts the village of Ortisei, while
the other side opens to vast gardens, creating
the impression of a palatial estate for this five-
generation wood-carving family. The workshop creates heirloom-quality wooden toys like
Pinocchios, trains, wagons, clowns, dolls, pull
toys, marionettes, and other accessories, but
also a vast array of religious sculptures.

Craft Museum
Museo della Val Gardena
Via Rezia, 83
0471/797554

Before you head out for the shops, visit the
local museum to see impressive examples of
local woodcarving from the Middle Ages to
the present.

VENETO

BASSANO DEL GRAPPA

GRAPPA

Grappa Museum
Poli Museo della Grappa
Ponte Vecchio
0424/524426

The Poli family of grappa distillers operates this small museum dedicated to the history and techniques of grappa production. Here you can understand how the pomace turns into the potent spirit known as grappa. Stick around for a *degustazione*, or better yet, visit the family distillery in Schiavon, outside of Bassano del Grappa, where Jacopo Poli now heads the fourth generation of this artisan grappa enterprise (call ahead at 0444/665637 to arrange a distillery visit).

PORCELAIN AND CERAMICS
Porcellane e Ceramiche

Ceramiche La Gardenia
Via Rivarotta
0424/828033
www.ceramichelagardenia.it

The Stocchero brothers specialize in porcelain lighting; their chandeliers resemble wedding cakes. They also craft table lamps, gifts, religious objects, and mirror frames wrought with delicate frills and flowers.

NOVE

PORCELAIN AND CERAMICS
Porcellane e Ceramiche

Barettoni
Via Molini, 3
0424/590013
www.barettoni.com

The Barettoni family operates the porcelain works of the old Antonibon family, who once held a monopoly on porcelain produc- tion for the Republic of Venice. Today they sell to the trade primarily, producing able porcelain reproductions of historical Nove ceramics, as well as items that appeal to modern decorators' tastes.

Ceramics Museum
Museo della Ceramica
Palazzo De Fabris
0424/829807
www.ceramics.it/museo.nove/

In addition to an impressive collection of ceramics from the eighteenth, nineteenth, and twentieth centuries, the local ceramics museum also carries a fascinating collection of *cuchi*, little terra-cotta whistles used since antiquity to catch the attention of people and animals, and fashioned into the like- nesses of birds, reptiles, and other creatures.

PADOVA

In the hinterlands about an hour west of Venice, the prosperous city of Padova reflects the prestige and historical importance of the Veneto region. Many of the crafts famous in Venice—glass, lace, paper, books, and so on— thrive here as well. You'll often find better deals and higher quality items by buying from a reputable dealer in Padova and other regional towns outside of the tourist main- stream of Venice.

LACE
Merletti

Patrizia Piccaluga
Via Polacco, 15
049/8021738
www.piccaluga.it

Patrizia Piccaluga crafts lovely reproductions of eighteenth-century Venetian designs. But that's just the beginning of the story. Browse for quality table linens, curtains, handker- chiefs, and other lace accent pieces.

TREVISO

Thirty miles west of Venice in the foothills of the Dolomite Mountains, Treviso is off the beaten track. It's well worth a detour, though, especially when the famous bitter green, the *radicchio di Treviso*, ripens, is harvested, and then is stirred into hearty risotto and other regional dishes. There is also a local tradition of engraved glass crystal, so if you're a fan of these wares, make a trek to Treviso.

CARNIVAL MASKS AND PUPPETS
Maschere e Marionette

Mangiafuoco
Via Riccati, 12
0422/541738

This shop is a fantasy-lover's dream. In addition to masks of every kind, marionettes, puppets, and a wealth of other papier-mâché objects cohabitate in this wonderful space. In addition to the traditional Commedia dell'Arte characters like Harlequin and Pulcinello, you'll find more menacing gnomes, demons, and other characters. Don't miss the miniature theaters. The owner, Paola Roella, recently moved the shop to a space three times as big as the old one on the via Roggia. They now showcase some 600 jaw-dropping carnival costumes. A dream for children and children at heart.

GLASS AND CRYSTAL
Vetro e Cristallo

La Bottega dei Maestri Incisori
Via Bomben, 2
0422/300698

The master engravers in this workshop—Raimondo Maddaluno and Gianfranco Rioda—specialize in incised glass mirrors, a tradition that can be traced back to seventeeth-century Murano.

La Bottega di Italo Varisco
Via Nervesa della Battaglia, 59
0422/300980
www.cristallivarisco.it

Italo Varisco trained with his father, a traditional Murano glassmaker, before transferring his shop to Treviso, and passing on the tradition to his son, Marco. Don't come here expecting to find the bright, fanciful colors you see all over Venice and Murano. The Varisco family specializes in very fine incised white glass and crystal that show off light in a spectacular way. Each one of their pieces is a unique work of art.

VENICE   *Venezia*

CARNIVAL MASKS
Maschere di Carnevale

Il Forziere
Calle dei Saoneri, San Polo 2720, 041/5223857
Via Rialto, San Polo 80, 041/5242887

These stand among Venice's most magical shops. Gorgeous carnival costumes, all handmade by the proprietors, decorate the walls of this boutique shop. The shops themselves are jewels of Venetian decoration, with mosaic floors and fancy woodwork behind a beautifully appointed shop window full of goodies.

Max Art Shop / Il Sole e La Luna / Venetia
Frezzeria S. Marco, 1232
041/5233851
www.ballodeldoge.com

This cluster of shops under the same ownership is tucked in a narrow alley just west of Saint Mark's Square. Though only in business since 1984, founder Antonia Sautter and her colleagues have distinguished themselves as one of the city's premier mask and costume outfitters, especially for the chic carnival party Il Ballo del Doge. They also offer a dizzying array of dolls, marionettes, lamps, pillows, paintings, and other decorative items in the rich fabrics and fantastical style only Venice could engender. Make arrangements one to two days in advance if you want to visit their magical workshop at Calle del Carro, San Marco 1628.

NAVIGATING VENICE

Venice wins the prize for the most confusing address system in all of Italy. That's saying a lot in this country, where nearly every city has its own way of denoting addresses and only the locals seem to understand it.

Venice is divided into several districts with distinct names (e.g. San Marco, San Polo, Dorsoduro, and so on). Within each district, addresses are numbered consecutively, so a typical address might read Dorsoduro 3567, meaning that it's building number 3567 in the district of Dorsoduro. Sometimes streets have a name, sometimes they don't, and sometimes they have more than one. Sometimes even and odd numbers are on the same side of the street, and sometimes they're on opposite sides. By all means buy a map, but be prepared to enjoy the adventure of being lost in one of the world's most beguiling cities.

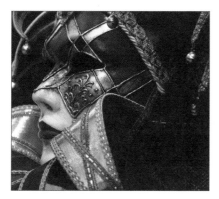

Mondonovo
Rio Terrà Canal
Dorsoduro 3063
041/5287344

This shop opened its doors in the late 1970s, when carnival in Venice began its rebirth, and it's become one of Venice's leading mask art shops. Today, you'll find hundreds of masks of every type, from classic Greco-Roman theater masks to the traditional Commedia dell'Arte characters. Make an appointment to see the masks made according to ancient traditions.

GLASS
Vetro

Carlo Moretti
Campo San Moisè
041/5231973
www.carlomoretti.com

This is the Venice showroom of the famous Murano family (see page 69) whose elegant works grace many of the world's museums, including New York's Museum of Modern Art and London's Victoria and Albert Museum. Expect to pay about 150 euros for a single goblet signed by a Moretti family artisan, or about 900 euro for a set of six. What delicious decadence!

Pauly
Piazza San Marco
041/5209899
www.pauly.it

Pauly runs three highly visible showrooms on the Piazza San Marco. Its showroom across from the facade of the Basilica di San Marco houses some of the most grotesquely ornate chandeliers I've ever laid eyes on, and I always pop in to gawk at the outrageous prices and outrageous designs this big-name glass designer produces. Pauly also has a factory overlooking the Bridge of Sighs at the end of the Calle Largo San Marco that caters to the tourist trade.

Venini
San Marco, Piazzetta Leoncini, 314
041/5224045
www.venini.com

Now we're talking. Alongside the north flank of the Basilica di San Marco, Venini has carved out an exhibition space that exudes the hallmark of Venini style: understated elegance. My favorite items are the *fazzoletto* vases meant to look like folded tissues. If you can't get to their main Murano showroom (see page 70), at least spend a few minutes here basking in the beauty of these sophisticated glasswares.

GONDOLAS
Gondole

Daniele Bonaldo
Dorsoduro 1547/a
041/5236673

Daniele Bonaldo is one of Venice's most experienced master boat makers. The semi-retired Bonaldo was one of many gondola makers in his youth, but is now just one of a few masters to continue this tradition.

Franco Furlanetto
San Polo 2768/B
041/5209544
www.forcola.it

Franco Furlanetto can be called nothing less than a master sculptor, specializing in the *forcola*, or wooden oarlock so important to the gondolier's trade. Once a simple wooden fork, the Venetian *forcola* evolved over the years into a complex and high-precision instrument that allows the gondolier to maneuver the single oar into thousands of different positions, and easily navigate narrow, crowded canals. *Forcola*-makers, or *remeri*, are specialized craftspeople apart from the *squeri* (gondola-makers); many connoisseurs collect and display these gorgeous carved pieces as works of art.

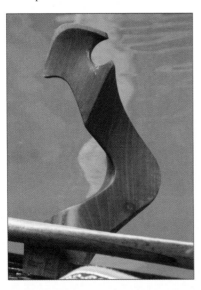

Gilberto Penzo
Calle Seconda dei Saoneri
San Polo 2681
041/719372
www.veniceboats.com

Gilberto Penzo, a historian of Venetian boats, crafts painstakingly accurate models of many of the historical canal and lagoon craft of Venice, including gondolas. His studio is a fascinating jumble of books, documents, boat models, blueprints, and other para-phenalia that any boat enthusiast will savor. Visit this *laboratorio*, located between the Campo San Polo and the church of the Frari, for a more portably sized gondola.

Saverio Pastor
Dorsoduro 341, Fondamenta Soranzo
041/5225699
www.forcole.com

Saverio Pastor is another mastero *remero*, or forcola-maker, who, like Franco Furlanetto, has mastered the sculptural possibilities of this traditional Venetian oarlock. You can purchase a scale model of an authentic *forcola* for about 100 euros (or even a *forcola* book-mark for 35 euros), or spend much more for a larger-than-life *forcola* sculpture for a garden or interior.

Squero Tramontin
Dorsoduro, Ognissanti 1542
041/5237762
www.tramontingondole.it

Roberto Tramontin learned the craft of gondola building from his father, Nedis. The junior Tramontin remembers the days when he and his father used to make three boats a month, but now he crafts only one or two a year.

Squero San Trovaso
Dorsoduro 1097
041/5229146
www.squerosantrovaso.it

This is Venice's oldest continuously operat-ing *squero*, where new gondolas are made and old ones come to be refurbished by a co-op of specialized artisans. It is owned by the city of Venice.

LACE
Merletti

Jesurum
Cannaregio 3219
041/5242540
www.jesurum.it

Founded in 1870, Jesurum employs artisans
who turn out expert reproductions of historical Venetian lace patterns, as well as new
designs. The showroom displays umbrellas,
gloves, baby clothes, bridal wear, hats, and
the traditional table linens. You'll fall for its
luxurious bedspreads and heavenly pillows.
Prices are commensurate with this producer's reputation.

PAPER
Carta

Biblos
Calle XXII Marzo
San Marco 2087
041/5210714
www.biblos-venezia.com

When I stay at my favorite hotel in Venice,
the Hotel Flora on the Calle XXII Marzo in
San Marco, I always stop at Biblos to pick up
leather albums and a few fountain pens made
with Murano glass. These stunning pieces
make great gifts.

Legatoria Piazzesi
Campiello della Feltrina
San Marco 2511
041/5221202
www.legatoriapiazzesi.it

This shop—one of Venice's leading paper
producers—is located behind the church of
Santa Maria del Giglio in the San Marco
quarter. The Piazzesi family started their
bookbinding business in 1904, and today it
is one of the few *legatorie* still producing by
hand. You'll find thousands of varieties of
marbleized paper, some of it used for wall-
paper and paper to decorate furniture. At
carnival time, Piazzesi also makes wonderful
papier-mâché masks.

Paolo Olbi
San Marco 3653
041 5285025

Paolo Olbi has been instrumental in
reviving the Venetian *legatoria*, or book-
binder's shop. In addition to his studio near
the piazza San Marco, Olbi also runs two
shops in the Cannaregio section of town,
a gallery-type space at Cannaregio 5478/A,
and a smaller bottega in the Campo
Santa Maria Nova. Upon request, you can
visit their *laboratorio*, and watch craftsmen
create gorgeous leather book covers and
marbelized papers.

Polliero
Campo dei Frari
San Polo 2995
041/5285130

Located across from the Frari church,
Polliero creates stunning leather-bound
books and albums that make fabulous gifts
if you want to splurge. There are also
smaller notepads, stamps, pens, and other
knickknacks.

ISLAND OF BURANO (VENICE)

LACE
Merletti

Dalla Lidia
Via Galuppi, 215
041/730052
www.buranolace.it

This is one of the best shops on Burano: in addition to new lace, it showcases genuine, handmade Burano lace from as far back as the 1500s. Check out the lovely shirts and vests with lace accents.

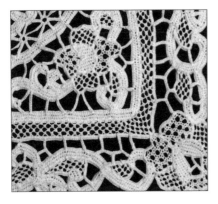

Lace Exhibition and School
Scuola di Merletti
Piazza Baldassare Galuppi, 4
041/730034

This is one of the few places to find genuine Burano lace made using traditional methods. The lace school, the Scuola di Merletti, is housed in the fourteenth-century Palazzo del Podesta. The school was founded in 1872 to revive the lace craft, which had nearly died out on the island. Over 350 pieces of stunning lacework are shown in rotating exhibits.

ISLAND OF MURANO (VENICE)

Chances are you'll arrive at the boat ramp on the south end of the island. When you disembark, move away from the area as quickly as possible, as hawkers will try to lure you into the more touristy glass factories that sell lower quality goods for top dollar. Head toward the glass museum and window shop along the way. The farther north you walk toward the museum and church, the more the prices fall.

GLASS
Vetro

Basilica Santi Maria e Donato

Don't miss this enchanting twelfth-century church, which displays centuries-old Murano glass shards used to make images of birds, animals, and creatures in the floor.

Glass Museum
Museo Vetrario
Palazzo Giustinian
041/739586

Before heading off to the glass factories, visit the museum to train your eye. I always thought that the miniature mice and horses crafted of Murano glass were a product of modern kitsch taste, but I was wrong. Artisans made them even in the seventeenth century, and you can see them in the museum's collection. Don't miss the incredible glass centerpiece made for what must have been an enormous dining table in the Palazzo Morosini in the 1700s. This intricate contraption resembles a garden, complete with glass shrubs, vases, and fountains!

After viewing this impressive collection of glass from the Roman era to the present, it's hard to imagine that today's glass artists could come up with anything new. Still, styles change continually, and rest assured that you'll emerge from the museum with plenty to see.

Barovier & Toso
Fondamenta Vetrai, 28
041/739049
www.barovier.com

This is one of Murano's big names, with
gorgeous vases signed by known masters
in the range of 300 to 500 euros. Another
specialty is stunning lighting, from traditional Venetian chandeliers to more
modern creations.

Carlo Moretti
Fondamenta Manin ICD
041/736272

Carlo Moretti (see also Venice listing) set up
shop along the main drag of Murano, where
he and his assistants craft elegant stemware at
steep prices.

Davide Penso
Art Studio Murano
Fondamenta Cavour, 48
041/5274634
www.artstudiomurano.com

Davide Penso's specialty is churning out stunning handmade jewelry incorporating Murano
glass beads and glass pieces. Some of his most
breathtaking pieces pair glass with incised
silver beads and other precious metals. For a
unique Venetian experience, sign up for one
of Penso's beadmaking courses.

Galliano Ferro
Via Colleoni, 6
041/739477
www.gallianoferro.it

The Ferro family has been making glass
in Murano for nearly 500 years, and its
workshop is one of the island's most
evocative. The family specializes in lamp
production, painstakingly reproducing styles
that decorated some of the Veneto's most
prestigious *palazzi*. Each lamp takes its name
from the mansion that the original came
from, and you'll find lamps in the shape of
flowers, candles, and even human figures.

Linea Vetro
Calle Bertolini, 6 (workshop)
Fondamenta Vetrai, 68 (showroom)
041/5274455
041/736266
www.simonecenedese.it

Young Simone Cenedese is a quick learner.
Born in Murano in 1973, he learned the old
techniques from his father and has made a
name for himself in the glass world, both in
Italy and abroad. Some of his most stunning
works are modern twists on classic Murano
glass forms.

Seguso
Fondamenta Radi, 20
041/5274255
www.seguso.com

Seguso stands alongside Venini and Barovier
& Toso as one of Murano's most esteemed
glassmakers. The family traces its glassblowing roots to 1300, when the Segusos are
noted in historical documents from
Murano. Its showroom is deceivingly modest
for the fabulous, elegant pieces on display.

Venini
Fondamenta Vetrai, 47
041/2737204
www.venini.com

This is my favorite Murano glass institution.
From vases to candlesticks, jewelry to tableware and even Venetian masks, Venini has
no peer. Venini has been a Murano tradition
only since 1921, when Milan lawyer Paolo

Venini traded the bench for a career in
glassblowing. With him, he brought a
Milanese taste for streamlined elegance and
refined simplicity. Be sure to check out the
cool vases designed for them by Gianni
Versace. If you can't get to Murano, be sure
to check out their Venice showroom (see
page 65). Venini is one of Murano's best
factory tours.

MIRRORS
Specchi

Artigianato artistico veneziano
Calle dietro gli Orti, 7
041/739518

In this workshop, located on a path known as
"the street behind the gardens," the Barbini
brothers craft some of the most stunning
mirrors you'll find in all of Venice. I know,
this is not really the colored Murano glass
that you came to see, but while you're on
Murano anyway, don't miss this no-frills
workshop, a fascinating collection of
gorgeous, fancy mirrors only a Venetian
could produce.

VERONA

GRAPPA

Fratelli Bolla
Piazza Cittadella, 3
045/8670911
www.bolla.it

You would never guess that there's a high-
tech grappa distillery behind the baroque
façade of the Bolla brothers' elegant villa
in Verona. The Bolla family owns nearly 37
square miles of vineyards in the region
around Verona, producing wines from
Merlot to sauvignon blanc. These are the
same guys who produce the ubiquitous
Valpolicella you find on supermarket shelves
across America, but don't let that deter you.
Their Grappa di Amarone is one of the most
intriguing grappas of northeast Italy, with a
nutty aroma and dry finish. Try it in the
onsite Bolla visitor's center.

VICENZA

JEWELRY
Gioielli

Adelina Scalzotto
Piazza Matteoti, 7
0444/327294

Adelina Scalzotto hand-creates bold, sculptural forms from gold and gems, with hammered effects and chunky lines. She's a brave soul, for she's one of the only artisanal jewelry makers in this part of town, which is full of more industrialized jewelry factories.

Laboratorio Orafo Nicolis Cola
Via Zamenhof, 587
0444/239474
www.nicoliscola.com

Renato Nicolis and his assistants handcraft 18-karat-gold jewelry, following in the footsteps of Renato's father, Giuseppe Nicolis, who founded the shop in 1954. They specialize in the chunky, chainlike bracelets and necklaces that have become a status symbol for Italian women, and that are worn with every imaginable outfit, including swimsuits.

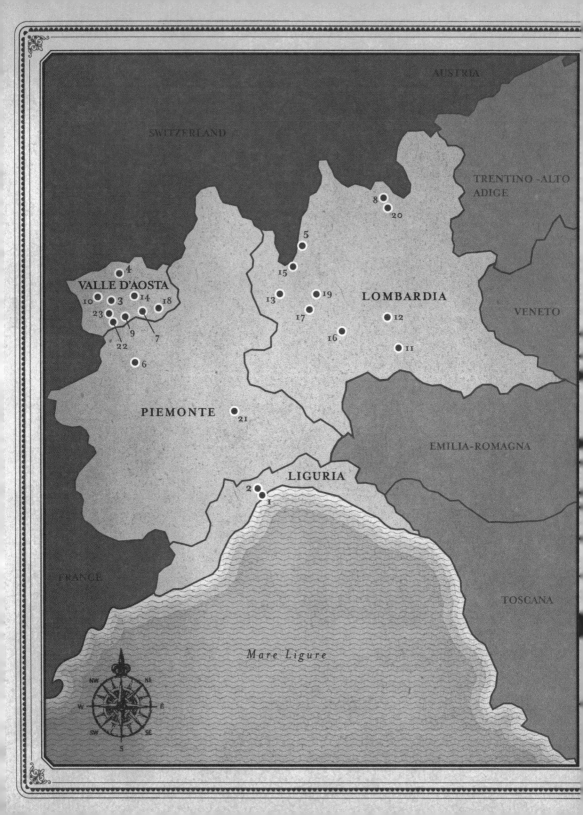

AUSTRIA

SWITZERLAND

TRENTINO - ALTO
ADIGE

8
20

5

VALLE D'AOSTA

4

15

10 3 14 18
23
9 7
22

13

19

LOMBARDIA

VENETO

6

17

12

16

11

PIEMONTE

21

EMILIA-ROMAGNA

LIGURIA

2
1

FRANCE

TOSCANA

Mare Ligure

NW NE
W E
SW SE
S

Chapter 2

NORTHWEST ITALY

LIGURIA · LOMBARDIA · PIEMONTE · VALLE D'AOSTA

WELCOME TO ITALY'S ECONOMIC POWERHOUSE. SINCE the Industrial Revolution, nearly all of the country's important industries—textiles, automobiles, fashion, pharmaceuticals, banking, telecommunications, and manufacturing of every incarnation—have claimed northwest Italy as their home. Milan and Turin—northwest Italy's principal cities—are the center of much of this commercial activity. Milan's industrial suburbs host corporate headquarters of international status. Ironically, landlocked Lombardy is even Italy's seafood capital: fish caught in Italian waters are brought here for distribution to Europe and the rest of the world.

With all this industry, is there any room left for handcrafted treasures? The answer is yes, but you have to look a little harder. Many of the regional artisanal trades—like furniture, shoes, and silk—have been largely industrialized in the last 150 years. Only a few dedicated artisans preserve the old techniques.

The town of Vigevano, southwest of Milan, is the shoe capital of the world—one company there even crafts shoes for the Pope—but although some of the work is hand-made, the process is mostly industrialized. Likewise, the lakeside city of Como, once a magnet for weavers working fabrics by hand on antique looms, today relies almost entirely on industrialized production. It remains Europe's silk capital, churning out luxurious patterns for Versace, Gucci, and other top designers in nearby Milan.

Another reason for the paucity of old-fashioned trades in the area is that Milan and Turin see only a fraction of the international tourists that invade Florence, Rome, and Venice each year. That means the market for unique souvenirs is smaller. Though the modern cities of Milan and Turin host a handful of old-fashioned artisans, you must look to the smaller towns—Aosta, Castellamonte, Cremona, and countless tiny villages—to see the Old World occupations of ceramics-making, woodcarving, wrought iron, glass, and metalsmithing in their most sublime forms. The tiny coastal region of Liguria, cut off as it was from the rest of the peninsula by formidable mountains and the sea—is like a cultural island with unique traditions of its own.

Finally, some of the most wonderful traditional products made in this region are those that end up in your stomach. Piemonte, which borders France to the west, rivals Emilia-Romagna as Italy's most cultivated culinary scene. Italy's best wines—Barolo, Barbaresco, and others—flourish on the lovely hillsides that define this picturesque region. Piemonte also boasts its own ceramics tradition and, like Trentino-Alto Adige, is known for its ceramic stoves, or *stufe,* that keep residents toasty during the cold winters.

The autonomous, bicultural Valle d'Aosta, which borders France and encompasses some of the Alps' tallest peaks, is extremely rich in woodcrafts, wrought iron, lace, and copper—in short, any kind of manual labor that can be done indoors during snowy winters. Aosta is the capital of this extremely interesting region. This Alpine city, with its fresh, clean air, mountain architecture, and French/Italian atmosphere, is also the center of a lively artisan tradition. Aosta is home to the administrative offices of the IVAT (Institut Valdôtain de l'Artisinat Typique), the organization that establishes quality standards for the local trades, recognizes artisans for upholding traditional crafts with a trademark, and promotes them on a national and international level.

The Lombard plain, which stretches across northern Italy from just west of Milan almost to Verona, is one of the only areas of Italy that is totally flat. It's home to the wet fields that produce rice for risotto—a sublime dish. The Alps, which form the northern rim of this region, rise abruptly and dramatically from the vapid landscape, their snowcapped glory a breathtaking vision on a clear day.

THE TRADITIONS

CERAMICS

Ceramiche

L ike the rest of Italy, the northwest boasts a thriving ceramic tradition. But nowhere else on the peninsula is ceramics-making so diverse.

First, there's porcelain. The major centers of northern Italy, including Lodi in Lombardy, produce designs that were originally inspired by Chinese export porcelain. Lodi is a quiet, picturesque medieval town just beyond the southern fringes of Milan's urban sprawl. Ceramicists have worked here since Roman times, but Lodi's ceramic heyday didn't begin until the late 1700s. At that time, several local families made a name for themselves by supplying noble courts of Europe with highly refined, delicate porcelain featuring elegant floral motifs against a largely white background—a style more akin to Limoges and Meissen than to *maiolica* pieces in central and southern Italy. So expect to see lots of frills, fancy doodads, basket patterns, figurines, statuettes, and ornate tea sets with a transparent white glaze.

Northwest Italy also boasts two other interesting ceramic traditions that have nothing to do with tableware. The first is the production of ceramic stoves, or *stufe*, that have been used for centuries to heat rooms in homes across northern Italy. These are based on the same concept as the cast-iron stoves that I remember from my childhood in Georgia; my parents and grandparents spent all winter long loading them with wood and carefully regulating the temperature. But Italian *stufe* are vastly more elegant, crafted from ceramic instead of iron, and decorated with traditional motifs.

Castellamonte, in Piemonte, is a major center for these fascinating and often beautiful ceramic objects. Many artisans craft *stufe* entirely of ceramic, raising these utilitarian objects to a whole new level of class and style. Locals in Castellamonte have been creating ceramics from the plentiful clay in the nearby hills since ancient times. Throughout history, they've produced primarily utilitarian objects such as jugs, plates, pitchers, and wall and floor tiles for a local audience. At some point—the first mention is in the 1500s, but it could have begun earlier—local artisans extended their ceramic skills to produce ceramic stoves to heat homes.

By the mid-1800s, Castellamonte had made a name for itself as an important center for the production of *stufe*. In recent years, these stoves have enjoyed a resurgence in popularity because of their reputation as environmentally friendly, economical sources of heat; some stove producers claim their products can heat up to 2,000 square feet of space, at half the cost of more conventional heating methods. Today, in addition to ceramic stoves, Castellamonte is also home to numerous more industrialized enterprises specializing in ceramic tiles and building materials. After all, this is Italy's manufacturing hub.

The third unique ceramics tradition of this region is the crafting of clay whistles, referred to as *cuchi* or *fischietti*. These terra-cotta whistles have been used in Europe since prehistoric times to call herds of animals or people, as the sound carried long distances. Many of them are made to look like whimsical birds, ducks, or chickens, presumably to visualize the chirping noise they make. They were also just for making music and fun. It is hard to find them today in shops, as they are collector's items and are traded actively in the Italian antiques markets. This is folk art at its best.

Finally, a limited tradition of *maiolica* ceramics exists on the narrow strip of a region known as Liguria, which borders the sea to the south of Lombardy and Piemonte. The Albisoles—two villages whose names are spelled differently, causing confusion—are twin towns clinging to the breathtaking coastline of Liguria. Albissola Marina lies to the south, and Albisola Superiore to the north. Both are known for the production of ceramics.

The sea seems to have been the driving creative force for ceramics in the Albisoles, as blue is the primary color. Ranging from deep royal blue to lighter hues imitating watercolors, this color is used against a white ground to bring images of people, boats, trees, and calligraphy to life.

Ceramics production began in the Albisoles in the fifteenth century, as locals began excavating clay from deposits in the dramatic, craggy hillsides that characterize the Ligurian landscape. Typically Renaissance forms—pharmacy jars, vases, plates—with Renaissance-style decoration characterize these early works, with blue and yellow decorative forms and heraldry. Local artisans became especially known for floor and wall tiles, which were exported to Spain and France by ship (Ligurians have been excellent seafarers since ancient times, as a formidable mountain range cut them off from the rest of Italy).

COPPER WARES

Rame

Copper mines are plentiful throughout Italy, and the metal has been mined since ancient times.

Since antiquity, copper has been prized for its properties. It's malleable and can be bent and shaped into many different forms without cracking. It can be rolled into sheets with a thickness of just a fraction of an inch. It's an excellent conductor of heat, and so was used in cooking and heating implements. Copper is also rust-resistant, tarnishing instead to a pleasant green patina in the presence of moisture.

Heat makes copper malleable, so copper craftspeople begin with fire. Some copper cooking wares are hammered into shape, leaving a characteristic mottled effect. Copper may also be cast, or poured into a mold in its molten, liquid state. Copper sheets are pressed, then hammered into pot or bowl shapes. It is then polished with abrasive pastes and soft fabrics. Handles of brass may be riveted on.

In the Valle d'Aosta and Piemonte, local chefs use these wares to cook scrumptious stews, *risotti*, and other local dishes. They also bring warmth to countless

homes of the region. Copper cookware paired with beams, stucco walls, and a roaring fire, all bring back memories of the wonderful places I have visited in Piemonte and the Valle d'Aosta during the fall and winter.

J E W E L R Y

Gioielli

Y ou'd never guess that the tiny, unassuming town of Valenza, in Piemonte, is one of Italy's gold capitals. But with nearly 1,000 jewelry companies in a town that measures little more than one square mile, there's no disputing it. Along with Italy's other jewelry mecca, Vicenza (see Chapter 1), Valenza is all about gold.

Valenza rose as a jewelry center in the mid-nineteenth century, but the city's reputation solidified during the export boom of the 1960s, when international demand for Italian gold began to skyrocket. Today, Valenza hosts an important trade fair that draws jewelry dealers from all corners of the globe, and numerous jewelers catering to the haute couture industry are based in Valenza. Businesses specializing solely in the manufacture of clasps, fittings, and jewelry-making machines and accessories also thrive here.

Although a few artisanal jewelry makers set up shop in Valenza, the vast majority of jewelers here feed the healthy wholesale export market for Italian jewelry that exists all over the world, especially in North America, Asia, and the Middle East. Therefore, while the overall quality of the work is high, it's often hard to find the more traditional, artisanal producers in this sea of gem and gold factories.

Milan is also an important jewelry center. This shouldn't come as a surprise, given the city's preeminence in the fashion world. Jewelry lovers and traders watch the catwalks every fall not only for the latest apparel trends, but also to see what models are wearing around their necks, in their ears, and on their wrists. Nor should it be a shock that Milanese jewelry tends to look forward rather than backward. If you need a chic accessory for this season's outfit, look no farther than Milan's jewelry artisans.

B E L L I S S I M A !
Lucky Gioielli in Milan (page 91) boasts oh-so-chic handmade adornments for men and women.

LACE AND TEXTILES

Merletti e Tessuti

Cogne, in the Valle d'Aosta, is a major center of lace production. Medieval nuns were the first purveyors of this art, which they practiced in quiet, snow-covered abbeys throughout the region. In small towns across the Valle d'Aosta, lace-making techniques using linen in its raw or bleached form have been passed down from mother to daughter. These intricate works of art are commonly sewn on as borders on tablecloths, bedspreads, towels, and other table linens. They also make up an important part of collars, sleeves, hats, and other traditional costumes of the region.

Not so long ago, the production of silk fabrics was also a major craft tradition of Lombardy. Silk making is one of those traditions that the Industrial Revolution transformed into an industry, replacing old-fashioned, hand-loom production with machines and giant factories. Today, the lakeside town of Como produces about 3,200 tons of silk annually, or about 90 percent of all silk produced in Europe. The handmade techniques have virtually all been replaced by machines, which crank out luxurious patterns to be fashioned into ties, scarves, robes, lingerie, and other gorgeous goodies for designers like Gucci, Versace, Armani, and Dolce & Gabbana.

BELLISSIMA!

If you want to experience the ancient art of Italian lace making firsthand, visit Les Dentellières Cooperativa in Cogne (page 95).

STONE CRAFTS
Pietra ollare

I n Lombardy, people have made crafts from stone, plentiful in the mountains above Bergamo and Brescia, since the Iron Age. In a valley known as Valmalenco north of Brescia, prehistoric residents extracted a hard stone from caves that pierce the mountains.

From this hard soapstone known as *pietra ollare*, they crafted bowls, plates, and utensils, presumably going to all that trouble because of the heat-retaining properties of this stone. (I guess it just goes to show that Italians will always go to great lengths when it comes to food!) It's perfect for making bowls and tableware that keep food warm for long periods of time. It's also been used to create works of art, utilitarian objects, and mysterious and whimsical human and animal figures. Many artisans mine chunks of the mountains themselves.

While you're in the area, check out the fascinating drawings of people and animals scratched into stones on the local mountainsides by our Neolithic ancestors. The national park of prehistoric carvings is located in nearby Capo di Ponte.

BELLISSIMA!
Stone crafter Silvio Gaggi (page 87) extracts the durable *pietra ollare*, or soapstone, from the mountains near his workshop.

VIOLINS
Violini

C remona's native sons put this town in central Lombardy on the map by crafting the world's earliest and best violins. In the 1530s, Andrea Amati began developing an early form of the violin, one that was solidified by around 1600 in Cremona. But it was Antonio Stradivari (1644–1737)—known as Stradivarius—who elevated this instrument to new heights. Stradivarius was born in Cremona and apprenticed with Amati. After the master's death, he began to experiment with new forms and new varnishes, which resulted in a perfected instrument. Even today, the Stradivarius violin remains the benchmark by which violins are measured.

Of the thousand or so violins that Stradivarius created himself, about half remain among the collections of museums and famous musicians around the world. They are known for their deep amber varnish, maple back, and stunning acoustic qualities. Throughout the eighteenth century, as Cremona rose as a violin-making capital, its artisan families jealously guarded their secrets, cultivating unique methods and techniques to make sounds better and different.

Today, Cremona's craftspeople look to the historical models for inspiration, and restore antique models, but they also put their own personal stamp on the works. Many of Cremona's violin makers were born and raised locally, but others have made Cremona their adopted home, drawn from as far afield as Germany, France, Colombia, and Japan by the international reputation of this town. For them, a diploma from Cremona's International Violinmaking School is a requirement for success, as is recognition from one or more of the world's most prestigious violin-making competitions.

The art of the *liutaio*, or stringed-instrument maker, begins with the right wood. Legend has it that Stradivarius hiked in the Dolomites in search of the perfect wood for crafting violins. Spruce is the standard wood for the top, or soundboard, while maple is preferred for the back of the instrument. While the inside workings of the violin are fairly standard, the exterior is a blank canvas, and artisans fill it with elaborate inlays, varnishes, and different kinds of woods, making each violin unique. It can take more than 200 hours to craft a single instrument by hand.

THE REAL DEAL

Even with years of study and the availability of modern technology, no one has improved upon the violin design that Stradivarius created some three centuries ago. The Stradivarius violin is still the benchmark for quality. This is truly craftsmanship at its best.

BELLISSIMA!

In a rotating exhibition set up in the headquarters of Cremona's Consortium of Violin and Bow Makers, you can "test-drive" one of the many violins crafted by the town's master artisans. The acoustics are great in this historic building, with its high ceilings and arcaded courtyard (page 87).

WOODCRAFTS

Legno

T he range of things that artisans craft from wood in northwest Italy is truly staggering.

First of all, there's the gamut of traditional wood products in the Valle d'Aosta. From cute toys to utilitarian tableware, wood is the material of choice for these artisans. One of their signature items is a wooden cup with a lid known as a *grolla,* or grail, a reference to the local legend that the Holy Grail is hidden somewhere in the snowcapped peaks.

But the real sacred drinking vessel of the region is a communal cup called a *coppa dell'amicizia* or "friendship cup." This shallow bowl with six or eight spouts is the perfect vessel for local *caffè valdostano,* a powerful mixture of espresso, grappa, sugar, and spices that is served flaming and passed from friend to friend.

Other woodcrafters of northwest Italy specialize in furniture. In the Valle d'Aosta and Piemonte, artisans create beautiful rustic pieces of pine, maple, and fir. Hope chests carved with folk art rosettes and geometric designs are the highlights of the region, but artisans also create chairs, dining tables, sideboards, and other pieces in stunning simplicity. Heading south toward Milan, furniture becomes sleek and modern, but is no less high quality. Lissone, northwest of Milan, is a furniture-making capital, though most of the enterprises near the Lombard capital tend to be industrialized.

Last but not least, the artisans of Cremona produce what are probably the most refined and sophisticated woodcrafts in the world: Stradivarius violins (see 82).

THE REAL DEAL

Legend has it that Saint Orso, an Irish monk who lived in the Valle d'Aosta in the sixth century, distributed to the poor sets of wooden sandals he made himself. That was just the beginning of a lively woodcarving tradition that would span centuries, and still brightens this Alpine region with lovely woodcrafts and rustic folk art.

BELLISSIMA!

The best place to buy traditional woodcrafts of the Valle d'Aosta are the local IVAT stores scattered through the region (pages 93 and 94).

THE LISTINGS

LIGURIA

THE ALBISOLES

The Albisoles feature picturesque walks through cobblestone alleys and along nice beaches and boardwalks. Albissola Marina, directly on the ocean, boasts the lovely *passeggiata degli artisti*—a sidewalk with pavement inlaid with ceramics by local artisans.

ALBISSOLA MARINA

CERAMICS
Ceramiche

MI-ART Ceramica
Bottega Artigiana
Via C. Colombo, 4
No telephone

Silvana Fazio and Michelle Bernat operate this small shop jammed full of ceramic fountains, plates, and jars, all in the blue-and-white style typical of the area.

ALBISOLA SUPERIORE

CERAMICS
Ceramiche

Ceramics Museum
Museo della Ceramica Manlio Trucco
Corso Ferrari, 193
019/482741

A nice collection of local wares from the fifteenth to the nineteenth centuries are the main attraction in a gorgeous modern building with lots of windows and light overlooking the Ligurian coast.

Ceramics School
Scuola di Ceramica
Località la Massa 17-18
019/485785

The school opened in the 1980s to help train professional and amateur ceramicists, and to promote local ceramic products outside the area. They operate three show-rooms and welcome visitors to watch the artisans work. Sign up to try your own hand at Italian ceramics-making.

Ceramiche Ernan Design
Viale Mazzini, 77
019/489916

Begun in 1974, this shop specializes in larger pots—some decorated with paint, some left natural in terra-cotta—with an eye to historical styles. They work on commission, and make limited-edition pieces for collectors.

Sandro Soravia
Via Colombo, 13
019/485202
www.soravia.it

The multi-talented Sandro Soravia paints images from fables and local stories in a folk art style. His work is not limited to ceramics, but extends to wood and other materials. Soravia founded a cultural club for the Albisoles, and he teaches ceramics and painting in the local schools. I love his cone-shaped ceramic vessels with stylized images of local people in traditional dress.

L O M B A R D Y *L O M B A R D I A*

B ELLAGIO

Bellagio is a gorgeous spot, worth a special trip from anywhere in northern Italy. Its picturesque setting on a point projecting out into Lake Como affords it sweeping vistas of the lake and the mountains surrounding it.

WOODCRAFTS
Legno

Pacio
Via Panoramica, 48
031/951866

In addition to a thousand utilitarian objects—spoons, bowls, napkin rings, plates, and so on—Giacomo Cranchi also creates mystical, bearded faces emerging from tree trunks.

C HIESA

STONE CRAFTS
Pietra

Pietra Ollare Gaggi
Via Roma, 2
0342/451283

Today, Silvio Gaggi is one of the only people still extracting the distinctive stone known as *pietra ollare* from the verdant and craggy mountains near his home. From it he crafts both utilitarian objects and more creative works of sculpture inspired by prehistoric art.

C REMONA

Most of the luthiers in Cremona operate small, private studios with little traffic. You should always call ahead to arrange a visit, whether you are a potential buyer or curious cultural tourist. The violin consortium (following) is a good place to start.

VIOLINS
Violini

Luthier's Consortium
Consorzio Liutai "Antonio Stradivari"
Piazza Stradivari, 1
0372/464490
www.cremonaviolins.com

The Cremona violinmaker's consortium displays special instruments in its evocative showroom, and can provide you with all manner of information about the town's famous craft. Here you can also arrange a visit to one or more of the private studios of the town's many master luthiers.

Violin Museum
Museo Stradivariano
Via Dati, 4
0372/461886

This is an impressive collection of Cremona instruments from the seventeenth century to the present, including some made by Stradivarius himself.

Violin Collection
Palazzo del Comune
Piazza del Comune
0372/22138

The town hall of Cremona boasts a small but impressive collection of violins and other stringed instruments.

Violin School
Scuola Internazionale di Liuteria
"Antonio Stradivari"
Palazzo Raimondi
Corso Garibaldi, 178
0372/38689
www.scuoladiliuteria.com

Anyone serious about becoming a violin maker need look no farther than Cremona's world-class Violin School, which has graduated the world's top *liutai*, from Italy and around the world.

Alfred Primavera
Corso Garibaldi, 207
0372/471238

Behind Alfred Primavera stands an impressive legacy of violin making, both in Italy and America. His grandfather, Giuseppe Primavera, emigrated from Italy and founded the well-known Casa Musicale Primavera in Philadelphia; he later passed the trade to his own son, Adolfo, Alfred's father. Alfred returned to Italy in 1972, attending the International Violinmaking Institute. Deciding to stay put in his ancestral home, he set up a workshop in Cremona, where today he turns out violins for an international clientele.

Francesco Bissolotti
Piazza San Paolo, 5
0372/34947

Francesco Bissolotti is one of Cremona's most illustrious violin masters, having crafted more than 500 instruments over a 40-year career. His early training as a wood inlay craftsman—an *ebanista*—prepared him for the painstaking techniques of violin making. He has passed on the craft to countless younger craftspeople, including his own three sons, who will carry on the family tradition.

Giorgio Scolari
Via Virgilio, 1
0372/34890

Since 1974, when he began teaching at the International Violin Institute, Giorgio Scolari has played a key role in the formation of hundreds of young *liutai*. In his workshop, he collaborates with his brother, Daniele, to produce some of the city's most acclaimed violins. His workshop is always busy with one or two eager apprentices working alongside these two masters.

Massimo Ardoli
Via Cadolini, 17
0372/26883

Born and bred in Cremona, Massimo Ardoli teaches at the International Violinmaking School of Cremona. The violins he crafts in his private studio are noted for their distinctive yellow-orange finish. Young Eros Barcellari, another master *liutaio*, works alongside Ardoli in the same workshop.

Riccardo Bergonzi
Corso Garibaldi, 45
0372/28445
www.riccardobergonzi.com

A passion for painting, and sculpture of wood and bronze, has brought a fine-arts dimension to the work of this prolific *liutaio*. In addition to crafting his own instruments in his workshop, he teaches at the International Violinmaking School.

Stefano Conia
Via San Giuseppe, 13
0372/25541
www.coniailgiovane.com

For more than two decades, Stefanio Conia, Sr. has inspired and taught a brigade of violin students at the International Violin School of Cremona. A workshop within a peaceful, verdant courtyard is where Stefano's son, young Stefano Jr. ("il giovane"), carries on the family tradition of his father.

VIOLIN BOWS

Giovanni Lucchi
Via Trecchi, 1/3
0372/491193
www.lucchicremona.com

In his workshop, Giovanni Lucchi and family specialize in producing and resorting bows for violins and other stringed instruments. The Lucchi pride themselves on using a special kind of horsehair that results in the best-quality sound.

DALMINE

PAPIER-MÂCHÉ
Cartapesta

Museum of Nativity Scenes
Museo del Presepio
Via XXV Aprile, 179
035/563383
www.museodelpresepio.com

I found this curious museum one day when I was taking my son to our favorite zoo in this town, just west of Bergamo. This is an odd location for a museum of nativity scenes—an art more prevalent in southern than northern Italy. But in the 1960s, the collector Giovanni Piazzoli founded this museum with a basic collection. It now holds over 800 examples of handmade nativity scenes from all over the world, most of papier-mâché. A fun and fascinating way to spend a couple of hours!

GALLARATE

JEWELRY
Gioielli

L'Artigiana Orafa
Via Giovanni Jacopo Rossi, 2
0331/785333

If you have a layover at Milan's Malpensa airport, have your cab driver whisk you over to this modest studio in nearby Gallarate, where all jewelry is handmade, mostly for resale in other retail shops. Sara Passerini has been working at this painstaking craft for 30 years and creates beautiful gold jewelry with natural stones. I particularly like the unique pendants on cords.

LIPOMO

WROUGHT IRON
Ferro Battuto

Mario Sampietro
Via Belvedere, 2
031/280357
www.sampietro.com

In Lipomo, just outside the lakeside town of Como, Pierfelice and Giampiero Sampietro continue the tradition their father began in 1927, creating luscious wrought-iron furniture and decorative items. Their selection includes some of the most refined and ornate gates, chairs, wells, arbors, wall décor, and beds I have seen in all of Italy. Many fall under the category of large-scale works or *grandi lavori*: gates, staircases, and other decorative pieces used in architectural settings.

LODI

PORCELAIN AND CERAMICS
Porcellana e Ceramiche

Civic Museum
Museo Civico di Lodi
Sezione Ceramica
Corso Umberto, 63
0371/420369

The museum holds an impressive collection of local porcelain chronicling the story of Lodi's great ceramics families.

Ceramica Artistica Lodigiana "Vecchia Lodi"
Via San Fereolo, 9
0371/32575
www.calvecchialodi.it

Vecchia Lodi nearly single-handedly carries on the historic tradition of *lodigiani* porcelain, with their ornate forms, creamy background, and limited color palette.

Their workshop, located in a nondescript, industrialized area southwest of Lodi's center, nonetheless carries an excellent range of their fancy wares. I love the multi-piece plates that fit together to form a floral or decorative design; they make great serving plates for parties.

Ceramiche Gino Franchi
Via San Colombano, 10/12
0371/432542

Luigi Franchi and company produce tableware based on historical prototypes from Lodi, as well as innovative, modern ceramic plates, vases, and other wares in bold colors.

MILAN *MILANO*

Welcome to Italy's most cosmopolitan city. Milan is about today and tomorrow, not yesterday. Sure, there's the breathtaking Duomo, a few Roman ruins, and some other impressive vestiges of Milan's long history, but browse the streets and it won't take you long to figure out that Milan is all about now: what's hot, what's trendy,

what's in season, and what's to come. High-fashion store windows set the tone for the whole city, and young people from all over the country flock here to seek their fortunes among the prosperous businesses that populate the city and its suburbs. Still, it's possible to discover some Old World craftspeople diligently carrying on traditions in the nooks and crannies of this sprawling metropolis.

GLASS
Vetro

Venini
Via Montenapoleone, 9
02/76000539

This is the sleek Milan showroom of the famous Venetian glassmaker (see Chapter 1). A good selection of Venini's best works, and convenient if you can't get to Venice.

JEWELRY
Gioielli

Mario Buccellati
Via Montenapoleone, 23
02/76002153
www.mariobuccellati.com

Jewelry just doesn't get more chic than this. Milan's Via Montenapoleone is probably the world's most impressive street of big-name designers and this historic firm competes with the best of them. Founded in

1919, Buccellati has been creating stunning jewelry and silver designs for several generations. They also have an elegant showroom in Florence (see Chapter 3).

Lucky Gioielli
Viale Sondrio, 3
02/66984802
www.luckygioielli.it

I flipped for the cool, modern silver jewelry crafted by artisans in the workshop of Antonella Calso. The chunky bracelets, earrings, and pendants—some set with precious stones such as garnets, emeralds, and rubies—are inspired by Calso's travels throughout the world, especially in India, but their designs are unmistakably Milanese: sleek, elegant, understated, and chic.

NJA Gioielli
Via Medegino, 39
02/8437340

Now under new ownership. NJA Gioielli specializes in high-quality, handmade jewelry made of a stunning combination of pearls and coral. This is one of the best places outside Sicily and Sardinia to buy coral jewelry.

METALWORK
Metalli

Artstamp
Via Bramante, 22
02/344836

This unique family business crafts ink stamps of metal, but these aren't just any old ink stamps. They are painstaking reproductions of famous Renaissance paintings, engraved in infinite detail. If you want to add a personal touch to stationery and envelopes, this is the place to find that reproduction Raphael or Michelangelo. They work mostly on commission, so call in advance to visit their studio.

PROSTO DI PIURO

STONE CRAFTS
Pietra

Roberto Lucchinetti
via alla Chiesa, 5
0343/35905
www.pietraollare.com

Roberto Lucchinetti excavates the hard local soapstone, *pietra ollare*, directly from deposits in caves around his home, just outside of the mountainous village of Chiavenna. In addition to utilitarian pots, pans, and even ovens, he crafts more creative, sculptural works from the ashy black stone. His wife, Paola De Pedrini, is an expert weaver with her own studio in the same complex.

SONDRIO

STONE CRAFTS
Pietra

La Pietra Ollare
Via Venosta, 5
0342/212005
www.ollare.com

Floriana Palmieri crafts innovative household decorative objects from this material, looking to the past for inspiration. Her relief sculptures of human and animal figures recall the prehistoric cultures that roamed the northern Italian mountains. From horses to figures, bulls on bowls, vases, and other vessels, her carvings seem like mystical evocations of primeval spirits.

PIEMONTE

CASTELLAMONTE

CERAMICS AND STOVES
Ceramiche e Stufe

Ceramiche Savio di Elio & C.
Strada Preie 35/A, Torre Canavese
0124/513788
www.ceramichesavio.it

This father-and-son business on the outskirts of Castellamonte was founded in 1957 to produce the handmade ceramic stoves that put Castellamonte on the map. These square, rectangular, or cylindrical stoves on castiron feet display rich relief patterns of rosettes, scrolls, and other motifs in the spirit of the local folk art tradition in Piemonte.

Ceramica Castellamonte di Elisa Giampietro
Via Educ, 20
0124/581560
www.ceramichecastellamonte.it

This is the in-town showroom of Elisa Giampietro and company, who will craft just about any kind of decoration you please on their signature ceramic stoves. Their specialty is painted and engraved decoration. Choose from a nineteenth-century reproduction, or one of their more modern, whimsical designs. Their *stufe pazze* ("crazy stoves") collection will make you smile.

Ceramica Castellamonte
Via Educ, 50
0124/513885
www.lacastellamonte.it

Roberto Perino and Silvana Neri produce many ceramic items but specialize in the *stufe* used in the region since the 1700s—square, rectangular, or cylindrical. Many have brass doors—the ultimate heat conductors.

Ceramica Antica Castellamonte
Via Educ, 51
0124/582642
www.ceramicaanticacastellamonte.it

This factory was founded in 1814, making it Castellamonte's oldest maker of ceramic *stufe*. They pride themselves on making stoves according to the old traditions, using clay hand pressed into molds of wood or plaster. Cylindrical or rectangular models can be had in many colors and styles. They run a sideline business in terra-cotta garden pots.

Giose Camerlo
Via Costantino Nigra, 28
0124/515160

Stop by this showroom for a taste of the household ceramics that have been created for centuries in Castellamonte. In his studio on the outskirts of town in the Sant'Anna Boschi district, Giose Camerlo crafts pots, trays, boxes, and vases using folk decoration in geometric forms, for home decorating and gardens.

VALENZA

Some of the larger jewelry factory showrooms are open to the public, so keep your eyes out for those. Here I have listed a few of the artisanal producers who still rely on handmade techniques.

A HOT IDEA

Toward the end of the eighteenth century, the Reasso family of Castellamonte began marketing an open ceramic stove they dubbed a *stufa* Franklin, after Benjamin Franklin, who patented the idea in America.

JEWELRY
Gioielli

Arco d'Oro
Via Carducci, 9
0131/947667

Bruno Vicini and his assistants at Arco d'Oro can realize your dreams. Just bring in a sketch of a design and they will create it, using gold and gems of all types. They make absolutely gorgeous rings dripping with colored stones.

Grilloro
Via Cavallotti, 63
0131/945956
www.grilloro.com

Grilloro specializes in handcrafted, funky designs that appeal to a young and trendy audience. From sleek rings and bracelets to headbands made of jewels, this is one of Valenza's more innovative jewelers.

Guido Vaccari
Via Cavallotti, 12
0131/953777

Animals—lizards, turtles, elephants, horses, and more—provide the inspiration for some of the designs of Guido Vaccari and his artisans. Specializing in white and yellow gold with precious stones, these pieces are fanciful and fun, a nice change from the more serious and important feel of many of the jewels in Valenza.

Harpo's
Via Oddone, 5
0131/953671

Harpo's makes the understated but chunky rings that are popular in Milan these days. The Gastaldello family founded this company in 1979, specializing in innovative designs in white gold. Although they export around the world, Harpo's relies on old-fashioned artisanship in these beautiful adornments. Call in advance to arrange a visit to the workshop.

VALLE D'AOSTA

AOSTA

GENERAL CRAFTS

IVAT
Piazza Chanoux, 11
0165/41462
www.ivat.org

This is the Aosta retail store of the IVAT. Wood crafts, textiles, and copper line the walls and display cases of this great shop on Aosta's main Piazza Chanoux.

WROUGHT IRON
Ferro Battuto

Piero Nigra
La Salle, Località Santa Barbara
0165/861758

Piero Nigra has a deep understanding of tradition yet still achieves a contemporary feel in his wrought iron works. In his Aosta studio, he creates large wooden templates with designs sketched in chalk. Sleek crucifixes cohabitate with six-foot

AUTHENTIC TREASURES

The IVAT, the official organization that promotes traditional crafts in the Valle d'Aosta, runs several wonderful retail shops full of the treasures the IVAT-approved artisans create. If you want to be sure you're getting an authentic, high-quality craft typical of this region, head to one of the IVAT stores listed here.

candleholders and fireplace tools. Nigra works mostly on commission in his large, utilitarian workshop.

AYAS

GENERAL CRAFTS

IVAT
Hameau Antagnod
rue de l'Eglise
0125/306767

A cozy room with beams and a wood-burning stove welcomes you to the Ayas home of the IVAT. Wooden *grolle*, "friendship cups" or *coppe dell'amicizia*, copper pots, and hand-made rugs are stacked on the shelves of this warm, homey shop.

CHAMPORCHER

TEXTILES
Tessuti

Cooperativa Lo Dzeut
Chardonnay
0125/37327

In the village of Chardonnay, outside Champorcher, a small cooperative of 12 textile artisans weave articles characteristic of the Valle d'Aosta, using threads of hemp to create delicate linen. If you want to see the old-fashioned wooden hand loom in action, this is a great place to watch it done by people who learned from the experts—their mothers and grandmothers. The curtains, table and bed linens, towels, and other cloths are finished with lace typical of the region, and many are also finished with embroidery using colored or neutral threads. A great place to buy these beautiful textiles.

COGNE

It's a pleasure to walk around the center of this small town, which lies in the heart of one of Italy's most spectacular national parks, the Parco Nazionale del Gran Paradiso. This is the Valle d'Aosta at its best: stunning views of snowcapped peaks, roaring fires, comfort food, and world-class local craft traditions.

GENERAL CRAFTS

IVAT
rue Dr. Grappein, 32
0165/74322

A spray of delicate, long-stemmed flowers—yes, they are made of wood!—greets you at the door to this retail outlet of the IVAT. This is the town's best selection of wooden toys, rustic religious objects, and the "friendship cups" or *coppe dell'amicizia* typical of the region.

Private Craft Collection
Hotel Bellevue, Cogne
Rue Grand Paradis, 22
0165/74825
www.hotelbellevue.it

Signor Roullet, proprietor of the four-star Hotel Bellevue, has amassed a stunning private collection of local crafts, thoughtfully arranged throughout this spectacular hotel that is part of the luxury Relais & Chateaux chain. Many of these treasures are antiques, like the fabulous wooden medieval saint that originally stood in one of the region's churches and now adorns one of the hotel's recreation rooms. Then there's the nineteenth-century wine press in the restaurant and the antique wooden toys so typical of the Valle d'Aosta that populate the kids'

THE GRANDDADDY OF CRAFT FESTIVALS

My favorite time of the year to visit Aosta is the end of January, when the Fiera di Sant'Orso draws more than 1,000 artisans from this craft-rich region who show off their wares (see Calendar of Events, page 211).

playroom on the lower level. Each guest room is unique, decorated with local treasures. It's worth a visit and a stay.

LACE
Merletti

Les Dentellières Cooperativa
Rue Grappein, 50
0165/749282

This lace cooperative in the heart of Cogne is set up to accommodate several crafters—women in austere, traditional black dresses ornamented with glorious lace collars and cuffs so delicate they appear to have been spun by a spider instead of a human being.

Experts in bobbin lace, the women's hands whip around with a speed you would only expect from someone who has practiced this craft for decades and knows all the moves by heart. They lay out some 50 or so bobbins of thread pinned in place on a black velvet, spool-shaped cushion. Then they weave wooden bobbins into wildly intricate patterns that emerge from the other side as complex floral, animal, and geometric forms.

The great irony of this craft is that the frenetic pace of the work—they make hundreds of stitches per minute—produces only a fraction of an inch of lace per hour. A single project can take months, and even years, to finish.

WOODCRAFTS
Legno

Atelier d'Art et Metiers
Rue Grappein, 103
0165/74296

This is the Cogne showroom of the acclaimed woodworker Dorino Ouvrier, whose home and workshop lie in Epinel, outside of town. For Ouvrier, woodworking is more than a trade, it's a passion. He is one of the best-known artisans of the region because of his whimsical human characters, which seem to embody the spirit of the people of the Valle d'Aosta. These "wood people," crafted in a rustic, almost medieval style using dark walnut and other local woods, carry out traditional agricultural and artisanal activities—riding horses, gathering bread, carrying fruit on their backs, and working wood.

COURMAYEUR

GENERAL CRAFTS

IVAT
Rue de l'Eglise
0165/846227

In the heart of this Alpine ski resort popular with rich Milanese visitors, the IVAT shop overflows with typical wares of the Valle d'Aosta. This, the most evocative of the IVAT stores, is in an old building with stone arches and wooden beams.

GRESSONEY SAINT-JEAN

IVAT
Monte Rosa Waeg, 5
0125/356343

Gressoney Saint-Jean hosts one of the retail outlets of the IVAT. Inside this tiny shop, lined with warm wooden paneling and hand-hewn display cases, are the typical crafts of the region—handmade woolen blankets, copper pots, wooden tableware, dolls with regional costumes, and more.

PONT-SAINT-MARTIN

STONE CRAFTS
Pietra

Fratelli Ferrari
Via Nazionale per Carema, 34
0125/804166
www.ferrariollare.it

Brothers Claudio and Fabrizio Ferrari, natives of the Valle d'Aosta, use the local stone to craft rustic figures, tables, basins, and even stoves (*stufe*). The most interesting are stoves with relief sculptures depicting scenes from local life, such as mountain climbing, woodworking, agricultural work, and more, all done by hand.

VALGRISENCHE

TEXTILES
Tessuti

Les Tisserands
Chef Lieu, 3
0165/97163

In the wintry Valle d'Aosta, woolen blankets and textiles are prized for their warmth and beauty. In this cooperative of local weavers, you can watch artisans operating enormous, antique hand looms to produce colorful bolts of woolen fabrics. Large rolls of yarns in green, red, gold, and black lie scattered around the workshop. The fabrics are then turned into everything from blankets to shawls, curtains, and upholstery for rustic wooden furniture. Smaller items for sale include scarves, totes, and adorable little dolls made of wool.

VILLENEUVE

WOODCRAFTS
Legno

Bruno and Thierry Fusinaz
Località Champagne, 34
0165/903636

An unbelievable mishmash of small treasures greets you when you enter this little father-and-

son workshop. Wooden objects are haphazardly hung from the walls and strewn on shelves and tables. If you can get past the clutter, you'll see that Bruno and Thierry Fusinaz craft some of the region's most well-made *grolle* and *coppe dell'amicizia*, along with hundreds of other wooden objects such as clocks, kitchen utensils, and butter churns, all in the rustic spirit that characterizes this Alpine region.

Dario Gontel
Frazione La Crête, 16
0165/95092
www.falegnameriagontel.it

Dario Gontel remembers watching his great-grandfather making wooden furniture and says that it was the inspiration for his own career. Using mostly chestnut, he makes the characteristic rustic sideboards, tables, beds, and other pieces that adorn the sparse, tidy homes of this Alpine region. His rough-hewn doors—finished with antique wrought-iron hardware—are works of simple beauty.

Francesco and Ilario Béthaz
Cascina Champrotard
0165/95376

In their large, open workshop, Francesco and Ilario, a father-and-son team, craft the simple yet elegant furniture of the Valle d'Aosta. They've amassed an impressive collection of local pieces dating from the seventeenth and eighteenth centuries, and are able restorers of these old works. Working primarily with walnut and maple, they craft dining room tables, beds, hope chests, and more, showcasing the sparse, clean lines and rustic decorative patterns of this wonderful regional furniture tradition.

Fratelli Vairetto
Località La Crête, 301
0165/903741

Three brothers—Antonio, Enrico, and Sergio—create custom furniture in this family business begun by their father. Using mostly walnut, they pour their hearts into each item they craft, whether it be a small item like a chair or a large-scale project like cabinetry and staircases.

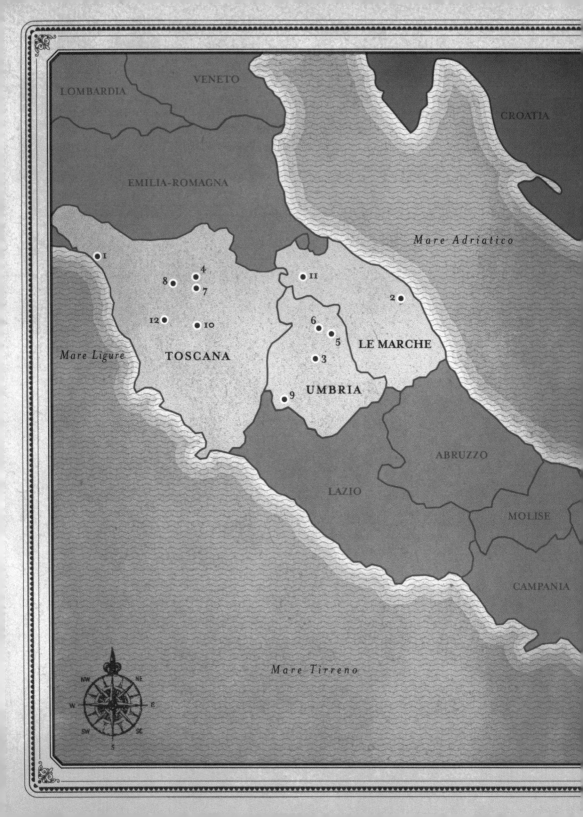

Chapter 3

CENTRAL ITALY

LE MARCHE · TOSCANA · UMBRIA

CENTRAL ITALY—MADE UP OF THE MARCHES, TUSCANY, and Umbria—boasts craft traditions as unique as each town, and a fiercely independent spirit—a strong sense of "us" and "them"—that still characterizes the people of this rich, picturesque region. In the Middle Ages and Renaissance, many prosperous towns functioned as autonomous city-states. The Florentines and Sienese, just a short distance apart, waged war for centuries. It's how the town of Deruta created a veritable ceramics empire on a small Umbrian hilltop. And it's how it came to pass that a particular type of embroidery is known even today as the "Assisi stitch."

By 1400, craftspeople of all stripes worked diligently to supply the needs and whims of nobles and burghers in these small empires. A lucrative international silk trade filled the coffers of Florentine merchants and inspired artisans to craft luxurious designs for clothing, church vestments, and more (see Silk, page 113). Noblemen commissioned ceramic artisans to craft "his" and "hers" plates ornamented with the elegant profiles of the bride and groom to decorate newlyweds' homes. The artisans of Deruta and Montelupo Fiorentino created commemorative vases with coats of arms to mark important political alliances between families. The wives of rich Florentine bankers shopped for gold earrings and bracelets on the Ponte Vecchio.

Some of the first artists and craftspeople to break through the veil of anonymity that characterized medieval art hailed from central Italy. The Sienese artists Simone Martini, the Lorenzetti brothers, and others, created impressive altarpieces, frescoes, and metalwork to decorate churches and civic buildings. They relied on the skills they learned watching their fathers, grandfathers, and the master craftsmen to whom they were apprenticed turn out small wonders day after day.

Of the three regions that make up central Italy, Tuscany has emerged as a mecca for North Americans. And who could resist this dramatic countryside of rolling red earth, pencil-like cypress trees, wispy clouds, and sapphire skies, not to mention its hearty stews, bold Chianti wine, and rustic breads? Anyone who appreciates Tuscany's cuisine and panorama will also enjoy its distinctive traditional crafts. From the ceramic shops of Montelupo Fiorentino and the terra-cotta ovens of Impruneta, to the alabaster mines of Volterra and the plethora of artisan studios that line the streets of Florence, Tuscany's craftspeople strike that unlikely yet perfect balance of the rustic and refined which characterizes the region.

Umbria, usually cast as the quiet sister of Tuscany, is growing in popularity among international travelers. Visitors find as much to offer in its rich craft traditions as in its alluring hill towns, varied terrain, and striking fields of sunflowers. Ceramics is king in Umbria, and it is home to a holy trinity of towns filled with *maiolica* masters: Deruta, Gubbio, and Gualdo Tadino. The red earth throughout the region is perfect for forming clay, and artisans have been turning out wares on the potter's wheel in Umbria at least since ancient Etruscan times. Artisans in Orvieto (see page 132) still carry on the tradition of fashioning the dramatic black wares of the Etruscans.

Le Marche is the quietest and most rural of the three regions of central Italy. It lies wedged snugly between the Appennine Mountains and the Adriatic Sea and, therefore, remains geographically and culturally isolated. The region was home to the powerful duchy of Urbino in the fifteenth and sixteenth centuries, so the Renaissance left a legacy of ornate, hand-painted *maiolica* ceramics destined for a noble clientele. Today, ceramic artisans in Urbania are seeking to revive this distinctive ceramic tradition. In Castelfidardo, musicians fill the air with the harmonious sounds of accordions, a craft that has put this little town on the map.

THE TRADITIONS

ACCORDIONS

Fisarmoniche

L egend has it that in 1863, an Austrian pilgrim on his way to a sanctuary in Loreto took shelter with Paolo Soprani, a peasant working the fields outside of Castelfidardo, in the rural region of Le Marche. In exchange for his hospitality, the pilgrim gave Soprani a peculiar instrument whose sound was produced by expanding and contracting a fanlike bellows. Soprani carefully studied and perfected it.

Today, this mountain village produces about 15,000 instruments a year. Many of them are still crafted exclusively by hand, making Castelfidardo the accordion capital of the world.

An accordion is nothing more than an aluminum skeleton covered with wood and celluloid. There are three basic types of accordions produced in central Italy today. The diatonic accordion is the simplest of the button accordions, usually with one to three rows of buttons. The chromatic model was developed in the 1850s to create a greater range of tonalities, and includes three to six rows of buttons. Finally, in the piano accordion, a keyboard replaces the buttons for easy playing, but the interior workings of the instrument remain more or less the same as other models. Today, the bellows is usually fashioned of heavyweight paper covered in fabric, and the keys are made of celluloid, or mother of pearl in the artisanal, luxury models.

Most of the two dozen producers of accordions active today in Castelfidardo are more or less industrialized, with large factories employing specialized laborers to produce specific components of the instruments. These high-quality pieces are exported all over the world. In addition to the mass-produced models, however, a handful of artisans still make the instruments entirely by hand according to the old-fashioned techniques.

PRICE POINTS

Prices for a handmade accordion in Castelfidardo range from 700 to 18,000 euros per instrument.

THE REAL DEAL

An entirely handmade accordion takes 40 to 100 or more hours to build. Nearly all artisanal accordions bear the name of their makers, usually as a metal trademark on the exterior shell of the instrument.

BELLISSIMA!

Fisart & Vignoni (page 118) is among Castelfidardo's most eminent handmade accordion makers.

MAIOLICA CERAMICS

Ceramiche Maioliche

The ruddy clay hills of central Italy are the source of some of the world's most coveted ceramics—primarily *maiolica*-style pottery, which features brightly colored pigments laid against a creamy white tin glaze.

The Renaissance distinguishes central Italian ceramics from those

made elsewhere in Italy. Michelangelo, Raphael, and countless other masters lived and worked in central Italy in the fifteenth and sixteenth centuries. Their spirit still breathes life into the scrolls, cupids, and idealized nudes that populate jars, plates, and other wares lining street stalls and shop windows in Florence, Siena, Deruta, Gubbio, and other towns.

Historically, wealthy Renaissance city-states like Florence and Siena kept most of the central Italian ceramics towns in business. For example, Montelupo Fiorentino (see page 130) emerged and thrived as a ceramics supplier to Florentine nobles and a rising merchant class. This wealthy audience commissioned ceramic artisans to create plates or even entire table services to commemorate engagements, marriages, political alliances, business deals, friendship, and more.

Eventually, an entire typology of ceramic forms emerged. Certain wares were destined for the table, while others were referred to as *da pompa*, or "for display." Pharmacies commissioned huge quantities of jars with lids to hold herbs and other medicinal concoctions. Often artists festooned these apothecary jars with refined decoration and a description of the contents in elaborate calligraphic script. My favorites are the so-called *coppe amatorie*, or "lovers cups"—trophylike vessels given as gifts to spouses, fiancés, and lovers. Today, ceramics artists reproduce these romantic pieces and use them as inspiration for more modern wares.

Even though Renaissance forms dominate central Italian ceramics production, other interesting types of wares flourish. Several artisans in Gubbio and Orvieto craft fabulous, dramatic ceramics based on ancient Etruscan designs. These all-black vessels, a type of ceramics called *buccheri*, are achieved by evacuat-

A CERAMICS MECCA

I recommend spending a week or two just in the towns of Deruta, Gubbio, and Gualdo Tadino. Each one boasts its own character and ceramics styles, and it takes a while to explore and appreciate all the nuances of each place. My favorite is Gubbio, with its quieter charm, spectacular views, and more evocative medieval quarter.

Deruta is the granddaddy of ceramics capitals. In addition to a rich historical tradition (its artisans had established major export routes for their wares by the fourteenth century!), the town counts some 300 active ceramics producers today, which means that the hardest thing to do in Deruta is make a decision.

ing the oxygen from the kiln, a technique the Etruscans seem to have discovered by accident around the seventh century B.C. In Gualdo Tadino, artisans reproduce incredibly ornate forms that were all the rage in the nineteenth century, with gilded edges and frilly designs.

Gubbio formed the center of a strong medieval ceramics tradition based on blue and green glaze against a white background, a technique imported from the East during the Middle Ages. In the 1500s, Master Giorgio Andreoli began a new tradition of historiated, or "storytelling," ceramics, with scenes from mythology and daily life, as well as new techniques for creating shiny lusterware. Along with Deruta and Gualdo Tadino, it gave birth to a style for which Gubbio is now famous.

Urbania, in Le Marche, also boasts an important ceramics tradition based on the Renaissance. In the sixteenth century, Urbania's ducal palace became a favorite seasonal home of the dukes of Urbino. About 40 regional artisans got to work creating ceramic wares befitting merchants and nobles in this place the pope wanted to transform into an idealized Renaissance city. Historiated ceramics—those that illustrate epic stories from mythology and religion—suddenly became all the rage. All the forms and themes that characterize central Italian ceramics of the Renaissance—pharmacy jars, "pretty lady" plates, cherubs, idealized nudes, flourishes of acanthus and swirls—began to appear in the villas of the local aristocracy.

The past is not the only inspiration for central Italy's ceramic artisans. Some modern masters like Franco Mari of Deruta (see page 134) breathe new life into the tradition by incorporating historical forms and colors into wares with a clearly contemporary spirit.

PRICE POINTS

Ceramics in central Italy are not cheap. In Deruta, arguably the most expensive of the central Italian ceramics towns, you can pay 150 to 250 euros for a high-quality decorative plate. In Gubbio and Gualdo Tadino, you'll pay a little less. The payoff? No matter the price, you'll still spend less here than you would for the same items at a retail store in the United States.

BELLISSIMA!

Attention, brides! Ubaldo Grazia (page 135) has staked a reputation on unique table services made to order.

LEATHER

Cuoio

For centuries, central Italy has been a capital of leather working. Today, central Italian leather production is divided into two sectors, industrial and handcrafted. The industrial leather business focuses on apparel, shoes, and accessories, while handcrafted production focuses primarily on bookbinding and the making of small trinkets such as boxes and desk sets.

Historically, the artisanal book industry made up a major part of Italy's leather economy. Medieval and Renaissance manuscripts relied on parchment paper made from cured sheepskins (if you look closely at a medieval manuscript page you can see the pores!). Leather covers were crafted to protect the books and provide a luxurious and beautiful showpiece.

Today, the industrial sector is enormous, representing a major force in Italy's domestic and export economies. Most of the Italian leather jackets, purses, belts, and shoes carried in chic apparel shops around the world are produced right here in central Italy.

Within this more industrialized leather sector, the Italian shoe industry is a world unto itself. Italians have been crafting leather shoes since antiquity; a few museums even boast examples of leather sandals from Roman times that do not look much different from today's fashions. Today, the area around Ponte a Egola, near Pisa, has nearly 900 businesses that produce 95 percent of the leather used in the soles of Italian shoes. While most of this production is industrialized, a few old-fashioned shoemakers keep the handcrafted tradition alive, such as Ugolini in Florence (see page 125).

The hides—cow, sheep, goat, and more exotic ones like ostrich and alligator—come mostly from India, Australia, Africa, and North America. In fact, Italy is Europe's largest importer of American hides. Some of these are dried, cured, and dyed before they enter the country, but Italy also boasts many domestic tanneries. Most are located in the north, where cattle are plentiful.

A few artisanal leather makers still use Italian hides, made and cured in Italy. The best ones, like Mastri Librai Eugubini in Gubbio and the top paper goods shops in Florence (see page 124), insist on natural hides with no chemical processing or dyes. One touch and you'll see the difference—supple, rich leathers that show natural grains and age gracefully. Artisans prefer natural vegetable dyes over chemical ones. The most authentic leather artisans use historical tools, or tools based on historical models, to stamp, punch, and burnish patterns into soft, natural leathers, creating wonderful results.

For tips on shopping for leather in Florence, see page 122.

PRICE POINTS

You will pay anywhere from 10 to 250 euros for a nice leather-bound album, depending on the size, number of pages, type of paper used, and laboriousness of the design.

THE REAL DEAL

Your sense of smell and touch will help determine the quality of the leather. The more supple the leather feels, the better. If an acrid, chemical smell assaults you when you enter the shop, chances are the goods are heavily dyed to disguise a lesser-quality product. A wonderful, earthy aroma characterizes natural leather.

MARBLE, STONE, AND ALABASTER

Marmo, Pietra, e Alabastro

"The more the marble wastes, the more the statue grows," wrote Michelangelo. The Renaissance master sought raw material from the marble quarries near Carrara, in Tuscany, for his *Pietà* and other sculptural groups. Since antiquity these quarries have provided an unending font of the famous translucent white marble. In fact, the ancient Roman quarries are still visible today and you can visit them, as well as the ones Michelangelo used.

For 2,000 years, men have plundered the Apuan Alps near Carrara for their precious white marble. The Romans chopped fissures into the stone, then inserted wet wood that, when it expanded, caused the marble to break off in giant pieces. Their mode of getting it down the mountain—a sledlike contraption on a wooden track—was used through the twentieth century.

While most marble and stonework in central Italy falls within the realm of the fine arts rather than craft (the Tuscan town of Pietrasanta is a mecca for marble sculptors, drawing masters from around the world), the skills and techniques of marble-working have been passed down verbally from master to student for centuries and involve a whole host of related crafts such as model casting and marble inlay that are fascinating to observe.

Specialized marble wizards like Simone Fiordelisi of Florence (see page 124) have turned the craft of marble inlay into a high art. Even in Italy, marble doesn't come

cheap, but there's no marble of higher quality anywhere else in the world. But marble isn't the only stone that artisans work in central Italy. The ancient Etruscan city of Volterra is a center of alabaster crafts (technically, alabaster is a mineral, not a stone). The streets of Volterra actually glow from the luminous effects of alabaster that fill the shop windows, making this ancient Etruscan town seem even more magical.

In Volterra, a move to industrialize alabaster crafts took hold after World War II. Luckily, a handful of diligent artisans preserve the handcrafted tradition, using high-quality alabaster excavated from nearby Castellina Marittima. Alabaster is an exceptionally hard material that occasionally contains little perforations and holes within it. The work is slow; it can take a month or so to craft a bust, for example. Some artisans do it part-time, relying on a second job to support themselves while they work diligently but slowly at this laborious craft.

Alabaster artisans in Volterra specialize. Some are strictly *ornatisti*, specializing in crafting ornamental and decorative objects. Others consider themselves strictly *animalisti*, crafting elegant horses and other animals. Finally, *scultori* focus solely on human subjects.

PRICE POINTS
Alabaster crafts are surprisingly affordable, considering the scarcity of the material and the laborious nature of working it. In the workshop of one of Volterra's top artisans, I picked up a handsome white vase streaked with black for about 150 euros. I carried it home in my hand luggage, secured in bubble wrap.

BELLISSIMA!
At the showroom of Alab'Arte in Volterra (page 131), alabaster vases with an ancient feel are stunningly displayed on lighted shelves, highlighting the beautiful streaks and colors of the material.

PAPER

Carta

Florence ranks second only to Venice for handmade paper (see Chapter 1). When marbleized paper became popular in the 1500s, it trickled down from Venice to Florence along with rich nobles and master craftsmen. At that time, the book trade was thriving and Florentine papers were used to line the inside covers of some of the world's first books printed with moveable type.

BELLISSIMA!

If you want to splurge in Florence, head directly to Pineider (page 125). This is the Rolls-Royce of Florentine paper producers. Their engraved stationery is an especially luxurious treat.

SILK AND FABRICS

Seta e Tessuti

The piles of silk ties and scarves that fill the shop windows of Florence today are vestiges of a thriving historical trade in silk and other fabrics. Florence was a silk and wool capital in the Renaissance, and the town's traders made a mint by doing business throughout the rest of Europe and Asia. Today, just a handful of fabric producers carry on the venerable tradition.

THE REAL DEAL

If you want to learn how people made fabrics in the Renaissance, take a course at the Casa dei Tessuti in Florence (page 125).

BELLISSIMA!

Antico Setificio Fiorentino in Florence (page 125) carries some of the most luxurious silk decorator fabrics in Europe.

TERRA-COTTA
Terracotta

Earth, water, air, and fire are all you need to make terra-cotta, so it's no wonder that humans have worked this material since the dawn of time. In central Italy, terra-cotta is a way of life. It paves countless floors in houses both humble and grand. As roofing, it keeps millions of Italians warm and dry. The ancient Etruscans used it to fashion everything from drinking vessels to funerary caskets. Terra-cotta tiles from Impruneta even cover the giant dome of Florence cathedral and were specified by the Renaissance architect Brunelleschi himself.

The process begins with collecting earth; there are several deposits around Impruneta, which is famous for its gray clay that tranforms into ruddy wares that last for centuries, resisting wear and the elements. Water then makes the impasto malleable. Most of the pieces are created on the wheel, using techniques passed down through the centuries. Decorative designs may be crafted using wooden or metal molds, or the hand of the artist. Then the pieces are left to dry.

Firing the giant kilns (*fornaci*) is quite a production, so terra-cotta artisans usually amass a large collection of pieces to be fired at the same time. The ovens themselves are works of art: giant, barrel-vaulted rooms stoked from fires under the floor. Entrances to the ovens are walled in with bricks, which can be removed and replaced to regulate air flow. The pieces are stacked on scaffolding sometimes 12 feet high. They may only fire the kilns once a month or so, and they cook the pieces at more than 1,800 degrees Fahrenheit for two days. This is the most delicate part of the process. It's the careful monitoring of temperature and airflow that oxidizes the pieces and results in the characteristic reddish color. After three days of cooling, the pieces are ready.

Decorative motifs include fruit swags, flowers, acanthus leaves, and geometric designs, all derived from the artistic vocabulary of the ancient world and translated by the Renaissance. Statues, fountains, and architectural motifs also emerge from the kilns. And terra-cotta floor tiles are produced by the thousands, to be exported throughout Italy and the world.

Impruneta is the terra-cotta capital of Italy. It boasts several deposits of high-quality gray clay, which is naturally waterproof and resists cracking. Through the centuries, its proximity to Florence made it an important source of architectural terra-cotta, used for roof and floor tiles, as well as countless household objects for the Florentine market. The nearby Greve and Ema rivers provided the perfect means for transporting wares to their destinations. In fact, as early as 1308, the terra-cotta artisans of Impruneta had already formed a guild to protect and regulate the production of their precious commodity.

PRICE POINTS

Prices in Impruneta can be steep. You can expect to pay around 150 to 350 euros for a large garden pot or vase, but rest assured it will last forever.

BELLISSIMA!

Ugo Poggi (page 130) is one of Impruneta's most venerable terra-cotta institutions and uses restored kilns from the 1500s!

WOODCRAFTS

Legno

I f I had to recommend a single traditional craft to buy in Florence, it would be one of the ornate, gilded woodcrafts that fills the dusty workshops of its narrow alleys. You won't find anything more unique in this city full of souvenirs.

Everybody knows that Florence is famous for painting, and it's no wonder that frame-making has been a big business in Florence for centuries. The town's many art museums, including the world-class Uffizi, keep the city's frame-makers and restorers busy. In the Middle Ages and Renaissance, Florentine craftspeople lavished gold on everything from altarpieces to jewelry and frames. Today, the art of gilding wood is still highly prized.

Lamps are another creative outlet for those trained in the art of woodcrafting and gilding. Florence is the only place in the world where you could bring in an antique candleholder—even an outrageously ornate, antique, gilded candleholder that stands six feet tall and belongs in a church treasury—ask for it to be converted to electricity, and order a custom lampshade to fit it. That's precisely what one man did while I was waiting in line at Il Paralume in Florence. Florence boasts some of the most unique, most wonderful creations in the world of lighting.

That mastery of wood also translates to furniture. While art and furniture restorers do not figure anywhere else in this book, for Florence I make an exception. Restoration is a major craft industry in Florence; unlike other places, you can readily see the masters at work. By all means go watch them work if you have a chance.

THE REAL DEAL
The Uffizi engages C. & S. Martelli (page 128) to restore frames for master-pieces by Botticelli, Raphael, and others.

BELLISSIMA!
If you only visit one craft shop in Florence, make it Bartolozzi e Maioli (page 127). I guarantee you will never see anything else like it in the world.

WROUGHT IRON

Ferro Battuto

A rtisans craft wrought iron all over Italy, but the blacksmith's art is strong in central Italy, and has been for centuries. Since the dawn of time, the blacksmith played a central role in the life of every town. In fact, he crafted objects that were key to everyday living: tools, swords, spears, knives, axes, agricultural implements, nails, cooking utensils, horseshoes, gates, locks, keys, and so on. An ancient Etruscan relief sculpture from the sixth century B.C. shows a wrought iron artist using tools very similar to the ones used today to craft works of art from this raw material that is mined from the earth.

Today, many wrought iron artists across Italy make their living from major commissions: a gate for a town hall or cemetery; a railing for balconies or stair-cases used in new construction or historical restoration; and park benches for municipalities. Mundane household objects like fireplace tools, tables, and chairs make up the rest of their work. But the best wrought iron artists depart from these assignments occasionally to let their creativity run free to produce writhing forms, abstract sculptures, and one-of-a-kind figments of their imaginations.

BELLISSIMA!
I will never forget the day I spent in the workshop of Tonino Scavizzi of Gubbio (page 138), watching, spellbound, as the artisans transformed nondescript metal rods into objects of exquisite beauty, using only fire and their blackened hands. During a break, we sipped local wine out of paper cups and they told me how they spent an entire month working on one table and how they fashioned the head of a snarling griffin from a single iron rod.

THE LISTINGS

THE MARCHES *LE MARCHE*

CASTELFIDARDO

ACCORDIONS
Fisarmoniche

Accordion Museum
Museo Internazionale della Fisarmonica
Via Mordini, 1
071/7808288

This is one of the world's most impressive
collections, with more than 500 accordions
from all over the globe, all displayed in
Castelfidardo's town hall.

Fisart & Vignoni
Via Garibaldi, 4/6
071/7822795
www.vignoniaccordions.com

Giancarlo Vignoni grew up in an accordion-
making family, and in 1980, founded his
own company to specialize in unique,
artisanal accordions. From piano and diatonic accordions to unique, custom models,
Fisart & Vignoni are intimately involved in
every stage of production from wood selection to putting the final decorative touches
on each model.

Fratelli Alessandrini
Via Verdi, 83
071/7823581
www.accordions.com/alessandrini/

For 50 years, the Alessandrini brothers have
been crafting some of Castelfidardo's most
impressive handmade accordions. They make
a range of traditional chromatic, diatonic,
and converter models, all by hand. In addition, they've combined the best of traditional and the modern, by creating a special
MIDI piano accordion that can be plugged
into today's sophisticated amplifiers.

URBANIA

Many locals still refer to this town as
Casteldurante, even though Pope Urban
VIII changed its name to Urbania some
400 years ago (who says Italians don't
cling to tradition?).

CERAMICS
Ceramiche

**Bottega Ceramiche d'Arte Ettore
Benedetti**
Corso Vittorio Emanuele II, 42
0722/318121

Ettore Benedetti has been at this craft since
1963, earning several regional and national
ceramics awards for his excellent reproductions of Renaissance wares. In fact, he keeps
several sixteenth-century fragments in his
studio, which he studies carefully and uses as
a point of departure for the grotesques,
human figures, and floral motifs that populate his works. Ettore's wife Claurisia also
assists in the decoration of countless pieces.

Bottega d'Arte in Castel Durante
Piazza San Cristoforo, 2
0722/317646
www.biaginiceramiche.it

In their small shop on Urbania's central
square, Silvio Biagini and his daughter, Elvira,
craft plates, jars, and other wares decorated
with forms typical of Urbania. Landscapes
flow onto plates with a painterly, watercolorlike effect. Happy cherubs (or *putti*) fly
effortlessly around the rim of a plate or jar.
Sign up to take one of their summer vacation
courses in the art of ceramic painting.

**Ceramiche d'Arte Violini di
Chiara Violini**
Via Bramante, 6
0722/312065

Chiara Violini is one of Urbania's youngest ceramics artists. Her father, Antonio, actively promotes the local ceramics tradition in the Italian media, and he produces his own works based on the ceramic technique known as *raku*, which imparts a crackled effect to the glaze.

Le Maioliche di Monal
Via Torquato, 8
0722/319673

Monica Alvoni infuses her otherwise contemporary works with a historical spirit. Sometimes, the reference to the past is clear: the use of specific decorative patterns from historical models, for example. Other times, they seem products only of our own age. Among her more interesting creations are pieces combining ceramics with wrought iron and basketry.

TUSCANY *TOSCANA*

CARRARA

MARBLE
Marmo

Carlo Nicoli
Piazza XXVII Aprile
0585/70079
www.nicoli-sculptures.com

Nicoli, Carrara's most famous marble-working cooperative, operates a studio in the center of town. For six generations, marble sculptors have trained and practiced here. Strewn around this light, dust-filled studio are full-sized reproductions of the masterpieces of Michelangelo, ancient Roman athletes, busts of royalty, and countless other treasures. Call ahead to arrange a visit.

FLORENCE *FIRENZE*

Rule number one: learn the Florentine address system. Businesses are marked with an "r" after their street number for "rosso" (red). Residences are marked with an "n" for "nero" (black). Unless you realize this at the outset, finding your destination can turn into a fool's errand, as the numbers quickly seem to become out of sync.

Historically, artisans occupied the poorer section of town, the Oltrarno, or southern bank of the Arno. Today, the majority of high-quality artisans still cluster here, especially around the Piazza Pitti and the Via Borgo San Frediano. I love this section of town, since it preserves the character of an Old World artist's neighborhood, similar to the Left Bank of Paris. It's full of *caffès*, hole-in-the-wall restaurants, and combination studio/living spaces.

Every second Sunday of the month, 50 or so artisans gather in the piazza Santo Spirito for a craft and antiques market. At the so-called *Arti e mestieri*, you'll find a bit of everything: junk, fine crafts, knickknacks.

One of the most wonderful things about Florence is that, even today, you can find a craftsperson to make just about anything your mind conjures up. From shoes to stationery, books, clothes, and furniture, a local artisan can turn your dream into reality. Just ask—it may not be as expensive as you think.

JEWELRY
Gioielli

The jewelers on the Ponte Vecchio cater to a lucrative tourist market, so I don't recommend buying here; many of the sparkling treasures you see in the windows are not even handmade. But it's fun to stroll the bridge and experience what most bridges in the 1400s were like: places to browse, barter, and people-watch.

In fact, some of the city's more interesting jewelry shops are located far from the Ponte Vecchio. I've plucked out a few of Florence's most interesting jewelry craftspeople, all of whom do their own production and offer unique creations.

Aprosio & Co.
Via Santo Spirito, 11
055/290534
www.aprosio.it

Like Gatto Bianco (see below), this shop is less traditional and more contemporary, but Ornella Aprosio's all-handmade goods are a feast for the eyes. The window display—in a minimalistic style that most Italians today equate with ultra-chic—drips with beaded belts, bags, earrings, and pins with gems, jewels, and sparkles.

Fiori del Tempo
Via dei Pucci, 3A, 055/2396443
Via del Corso, 31r, 055/284431
Via Porta Rossa, 27/R, 055/2658174

Walking into these workshops is like stepping into a jewelry box. In a space the size of an elevator, Francesco Deidda has created a fantasy world made of walls encrusted with jewelry confections of amethyst, crystal, pearls, and other stones. The prices are reasonable and the pieces are unique. Everything is handmade, including the business cards. The artisan/salespeople are friendly.

Gatto Bianco
Borgo SS. Apostoli, 12/r
055/282989

Designer Carla Tettucci's studio, conveniently located near the Piazza della Signoria, is less traditional but very unique. The entire shop is dark except for spotlights that dramatically highlight the treasures inside: chunky, sleek bracelets, earrings, and necklaces in sterling silver and semiprecious stones.

Buccellati
Via dei Tornabuoni, 71/r
055/2396579
www.buccellati.it

Buccellati stands alongside Gucci, Armani, and Ferragamo, and it holds its own next to these powerhouses of design. Founder Mario Buccellati himself designed the Florence showroom in 1929. This elegant showroom displays luscious examples of its creations in precious metals and jewels. The company has always designed and produced its own jewelry, distinct enough to be known as "Buccellati Style."

LEATHER
Cuoio

Pelletterie Fiorentine
Via Sant'Egidio, 31/r
055/245335
www.pelletteriefiorentine.it

This small, family-run workshop is a good bet for picking up handmade small items from cigar cases to change purses, desk accessories, and simple yet beautiful albums with oh-so-soft covers.

Scuola del Cuoio
Piazza Santa Croce, 16
055/244533
www.leatherschool.com

The leather school began as a collaboration between the monks of Santa Croce and the Gori leather-making family after World War II, with the mission of providing a marketable trade for young people. Today the school caters mostly to international tourists; a photo collection of famous visitors includes stars from Princess Diana to the golfer Jack Nicklaus. The shop sells purses, wallets, desk accessories, as well as a limited selection of apparel, but the main attraction here is the opportunity to watch craftspeople at work. If the experience sparks your own creativity,

CHEAT SHEET: FLORENCE

What to buy

• *Handmade paper and stationery:*
It's the ultimate Florentine souvenir.
• *Home décor:* Items crafted in metal
and wood—frames and lamps, for
example—are a great buy in Florence,
considering the quality and uniqueness.
• *Leather goods:* You can get some
good deals on not only garments and
shoes, but also handcrafted boxes, desk
accessories, and other small gifts.

What not to buy

• *Antiques:* If you are an antiques fan,
you'll find it hard to resist the plethora
of shops on the southern bank of the
Arno, but prices are high.
• *Ceramics:* You will pay top euro for
ceramic wares here, since nearly everything you see in Florence is produced
in the ceramic centers of Montelupo
Fiorentino, Sesto Fiorentino, Deruta,
or Sicily, and are marked up for the
lucrative Florentine tourist trade.
• *Anything not made in Florence:*
Buying Murano glass in Florence?
That's just, well, silly.

A GUIDE TO THE STREETS OF FLORENCE

• **Artisan workshops**: Via Borgo San Frediano, streets near Piazza Pitti
• **Antiques**: Via Maggio, Via Santo Spirito, Borgo Ognissanti, Borgo San Jacopo,
Via de Fossi
• **Art and furniture restorers**: Piazza Pitti, side streets off Borgo San Jacopo
• **Gold jewelry**: Ponte Vecchio
• **When money is no object**: Via Tornabuoni, Via Calzaiuoli

Leather Shopping in Florence

In Florence, leather shopping quickly can amount to an obsession. The city over-flows with quality handbags, jackets, belts, and accessories. The opportunities to buy leather are vast, from high-priced, full-service boutiques, to raucous street bazaars, to "private" workshops, to street-side trinket sellers. To make matters more confusing, things are not necessarily what they seem. You can find a reason-ably priced bag on the street whose quality equals an item in a high-end boutique. Other times, the same merchant may sell the same piece in a shop and on the street, at two different prices. Some pieces are made on an industrial scale, others on an artisanal one, and sometimes the same merchant sells both.

If you're serious about going home with a quality leather souvenir, you should know a few tricks of the Florentine leather-shopping trade. First, *what* you buy is more important than *where* you buy. Try to divorce the item from its setting, and focus on the quality of the individual bag or jacket itself. When it comes to judging leather qual-ity, let the buying environment fade out of focus, and use your senses instead:

• **Aroma**: The item should smell musky and natural. Steer clear of anything that smells like chemicals, which are used to treat the leather and cover up lesser quality.

• **Suppleness**: The leather should feel smooth, supple, and soft, not stiff.

• **Color**: The highest quality natural leather in tan or brown can stand on its own, without any added color, to reveal the natural grain and beauty of the material. Dyes, in red or green, for example, can mask lesser quality leather.

• **Stitching and other details**: The stitching should be tight and regular, with small stitches sewn close together. Loose, frayed, or irregular stitching can indicate lesser

quality. Look for bags, gloves, and apparel to be lined with a quality material (silk rather than polyester for purses, cashmere for gloves, for example). Examine the stitching of the lining, too.

The San Lorenzo markets attract leather-shopping visitors from Tokyo to Tulsa, with their pulsating rhythm, the chatter of bargaining merchants, the bustle of the crowd, and the musky aroma of leather wafting into the air. You will not necessarily find the lowest prices or the best quality here, but I have still scored some good-quality finds, including a classic brown jacket I bought a decade ago that still looks new. Many of these street vendors also have stores. Their street-side stalls are just another venue for generating sales, without the overhead of a shop (that's how you might find the same item with two different prices). Bargaining is the norm in the markets, and I have found that you can easily take off ten to twenty percent by simply asking, or by plying some tried-and-true haggling techniques such as offering to pay cash, buying more than one item at the same time, or just walking away. Talented hagglers might get the price down to half.

One of the market vendors may extend you an "exlusive invitation" to visit their "private" leather workshop. Yes, these are mostly gimmicks geared toward making tourists think they're getting the deal of a lifetime. Here's how it works: You follow a high-pressure salesman (OK, truthfully, it's usually a charming, handsome Italian man) to an unmarked door down a side street. There you encounter a no-frills, warehouse-type setting chock to the brim with leather apparel, and perhaps a few other handsome Florentines. They'll help you try on jackets before a mirror, all the while asking if *all* American women are as beautiful as you. Impressive sales tactics, no doubt.

What you pay depends on where you buy. I priced a medium-sized shoulder bag in several places around the city. A street vendor near Santa Croce carried the style I wanted and I bargained him down to 80 euros, but the stitching was beginning to fray and the leather felt stiff, so I passed. A similarly styled bag in a high-end boutique near the Duomo, this one of great quality with soft leather, silk lining, and fine stitching, was exorbitantly priced at 750 euros. In the end, I found a winner—the quality equal to the bag priced at 750 euros—at a mid-range boutique on a less-trafficked street in the Oltr'Arno section of town, for 225 euros.

As a general rule, leather goods in Florence are not cheap, but are usually less than similar-quality items in the U.S. If you want to buy something that is fully handmade, versus industrially produced, focus on small items—boxes, change purses, eyeglass cases, albums, desk accessories—rather than apparel. Many of these are completely handmade, and the prices are usually reasonable. They also make durable souvenirs and gifts that are easy to transport in your suitcase.

sign up for a course, anywhere from a half-day to nine months. To visit the workshops, buy a ticket for the beautiful church of Santa Croce, and include the leather school in your visit, or access the shop directly from its entrance at via San Giuseppe, 5r.

MOSAICS
Mosaici

Arte Decorativa di Simone Fiordelisi
Via dè Barbadori, 41r
055/215766

The sight of dust-covered Simone Fiordelisi laboring over a gorgeous inlaid marble mosaic tabletop drew me into his workshop. He patiently explained how he cuts out tiny fruits, birds, and geometric designs, and works them into a transparent disk of white marble that will become a beautiful tabletop. From conception to cutting, sanding, and polishing, it takes nearly two months to complete such a project; the cost is about 4,000 euros. Fiordelisi is one of those master craftsmen who can realize your dreams: custom orders are his specialty.

G. Ugolini
Lungarno degli Acciaiuoli, 66-70r
055/284969

Ugolini is one of Florence's most venerable artisan establishments, founded in 1868 and located along the Arno, near the Uffizi. Maria Lusia Antonelli, one of Giovanni Ugolini's descendants, continues this family business. Pick up hefty vases, bowls, and other objects made with an inlay technique called *tarsia*, virtually "paintings" made with colorful shards of hard rock.

MUSICAL INSTRUMENTS
Liutaio

Liutaio Jamie Lazzara
Via dei Leoni, 4r
055/280573

Italian-American Jamie Lazzara handcrafts violins and other stringed instruments for some of the world's most illustrious musicians. She crafted a perfect reproduc-tion of a 1714 Stradivarius for Itzhak Perlman. Lazzara trained at the world-renowned violin-making school of Cremona (see Chapter 2), and over the course of 18 years has made an indelible mark in the Florentine craft world. Today, Ms. Lazzara makes a handful of instruments per year, each painstakingly crafted, and upholds a lengthy waiting list.

PAPER
Carta

Alberto Cozzi
Via del Parione, 35r
055/294968

If you're lucky, you might find Alberto Cozzi hanging a sheet of marbleized paper to dry or stamping the binding of a leather-and-paper-bound album with a gold stamp. This tiny shop off the beaten track exudes a friendly family atmosphere; Cozzi's children do their homework on one of the desks in the back while their father crafts paper and their mother waits on customers. The shop carries individual sheets of paper, personal-ized stationery, albums, agendas, and more.

Bottega Artigiana del Libro
Lungarno Corsini, 38/40r
055/289488

Along with the usual suspects—marbleized papers, stationery, albums, agendas, pens, frames, and so on—this shop carries some well-done miniature chests of drawers covered in bright papers.

Johnsons & Relatives
Via Cavour, 49/R
055/2658103

Don't let the Anglicized name fool you: This bright shop located along the Arno is yet another of the scads of Florentine paper goods producers—this one affiliated with the artisan company Il Papiro—stuffed with sta-tionery, frames, pens, boxes, agendas, and other doodads. Their individual sheets of marbleized paper are particularly lovely.

ISOR-Lavorazione Astucci
Via Lambertesca, 11–13r
055/2382307
www.isor.it

This shop occupies a small space in what used to be a palace in the sixteenth century near the Piazza della Signoria. They produce an odd combination of items: paper boxes of all shapes and sizes, as well as specialty paper gift bags and their original specialty, watchbands and display boxes for Florentine jewelers. Their showroom is their workshop, so don't feel awkward when you interrupt their work.

Pineider
Piazza della Signoria, 13/14r
055/284655

If you can afford it, this is where you want to buy. Pineider is Florence's premier paper-goods store, founded in 1774, and its elegant atmosphere conveys its prestige and prosperity. It's an excellent place to buy a one-of-a-kind album or marbleized paper, but Pineider's specialty is customized engraved stationery. The quality of the paper and the work will outstrip anything you'll find elsewhere, in or outside of Italy.

SHOES
Scarpe

Roberto Ugolini
Via Michelozzi, 17r
055/216246

Roberto Ugolini is a bona fide, old-fashioned shoemaker crafting men's footwear from scratch right on the premises. His modest

studio displays a dozen samples of the kinds of shoes he crafts. The quality is breathtaking. Each shoe is a masterpiece of supple colored leather, hand stitching, and attention to detail. You can order from the samples, or describe what you want, and Ugolini will realize your dreams. All you need is about four months and 400 to 900 euro per pair.

SILK AND FABRICS
Silk and Tessuti

Antico Setificio Fiorentino
Via Bartolini, 4r
055/213861
www.setificiofiorentino.it

A lovely gravel courtyard and painstakingly restored Renaissance building form the setting for Antico Setificio Fiorentino. This workshop creates reproductions of historical Florentine fabrics with the same techniques and the same antique looms used by their forefathers. Interior designers can order fabric in bulk to create fabulous upholstery and draperies. Today, Antico Setificio Fiorentino mostly sells to the trade, but you can peek in their workshop for a glimpse into the past glory of Florentine silk making.

Casa dei Tessuti
Via dei Pecori, 20–24r
055/215961
www.casadeitessuti.com

The Romoli family is the guardian of the Renaissance tradition of fine fabrics in Florence. Today, Romolo and Romano Romoli carry on the business founded in 1929 by their father, Egisto. Their old-fashioned shop has become a museum of sorts, exhibiting precious fabrics from the Renaissance and other periods. They also run a school for designers, passing on secrets of textile design, weaving techniques, and the history of costume. Order a fully custom-made shirt or jacket for a one-of-a-kind souvenir.

Passamaneria Toscana
Piazza San Lorenzo, 12r
055/2396389
www.ptfsrl.com

Passamaneria Toscana was founded in the 1950s but remains faithful to styles and colors of the Florentine Renaissance. Tassels, fringe accent pillows, small-scale upholstered furniture, and other decorative items are all executed with attention to quality and detail.

SILVER AND METALWORKING
Argento e Metallo

Silver Museum
Museo degli Argenti
Piazza Pitti, 1
055/2388709

In the Pitti Palace complex, the silver museum displays the eclectic silver collection of the Medici family. The entrance is on the left-hand side of the imposing facade of the Pitti Palace.

Brandimarte
Viale L. Ariosto 11/cr
055/23041
www.brandimarte.com

Located next door to the Antico Setificio Fiorentino, Brandimarte produces stunning silver wares. Its sparse window displays masterpieces of silver, including bowls with fruit and beautiful hammered effects.

Lamberto Banchi
Via dei Serragli, 10r
055/294694

Lamberto Banchi, a bronze artist, continues the work of his mentor, Vasco Cappuccini, who opened this shop in 1925. Inside, Banchi crafts bronze hardware based on historical models, including door handles and frames, and also small objects like clocks, candlesticks, and tableware.

Ugolini
Via del Presto di San Martino, 23r
055/287230

In his workshop near the Piazza Santo Spirito, Sergio Ugolini crafts vases, bowls, and other ornate forms from hammered copper and bronze. He began his training as a restorer under his father's tutelage, but turned to making objects in metal based on the antique forms with which he was so intimate. Ugolini works with American clients on a regular basis.

WOODCRAFTS
Legno

Casa di Bambola
via Taddeo Alderotti, 26B
055/432660
www.casadibambola.com

You're greeted with a smile (a rarity in Florence) when you enter this warm shop along the Borgo San Frediano. Maria Concetta Milazzo trained in the fashion world before founding Casa di Bambola, and she fits and customizes each shade to each lamp as a dressmaker would fit a model.

Leonardo Cappellini
Via del Presto di San Martino, 20r
055/282935

Artists are well trained in Florence, and here you'll find the local talent painting historical Florentine scenes and motifs on antique furniture. Cappellini's specialty is scouring the region for armoires, chests, and other wooden furniture from the sixteenth, seventeenth, and eighteenth centuries, and lovingly restoring or reinventing the painted designs that originally adorned them. The results are stunning. Each piece goes for about 4,000 to 14,000 euros.

Luigi Mecocci
Via dei Velluti, 8r
No telephone

Since he set up shop here in 1954, Luigi Mecocci has set the standard for many Florentine restorers and artists. His restoration of furniture and antique works of art has earned him a reputation as one of the city's finest. Semi-retired, Mecocci runs courses to pass on his trade to the next generation.

Bartolozzi e Maioli
Via Maggio, 13r (showroom)
Via dei Vellutini, 5r (workshop)
055/282675
www.bartolozziemaioli.it

If you're in the market for fantasy, this is the
spot. Fiorenza Bartolozzi carries on the work
of her father, a restorer and dealer of unique
pieces of Florentine history. Visiting this
shop on the Via Maggio is like stepping onto
a theatrical stage set or a storage room of
relics. Painted wooden cupids swoop from
the ceiling and trail fabric drapes looped
over gilded scrolls. Ornate frames capture
images of Italian landscapes. Pilasters and
columns stand in the shadows. Saints with
hands missing and paint peeling from their
once-gilded robes preside over the scene.
If you want to take home a unique piece
of Florentine history, look no further.

Il Paralume
Borgo San Frediano, 77-79/r
055/2396760
www.ilparalume.it

If I had enough space, I would buy one
of each of the lamps produced by this outfit.

Their showroom occupies two spaces across
the street from each other on the Borgo
San Frediano. You can mix and match the
hand-painted wooden bases and the shades.
I ordered a pair of bedside lamps and they
crafted them for me within 48 hours. They
were a good deal, too! For under 100 euros
you can own a unique, handcrafted
Florentine lamp that you won't find anywhere else in the world.

Castorina
Via S. Spirito, 13/15r
055/212885
www.castorina.net

Details, details: that's the business of
Castorina. For more than a century, this
family enterprise has crafted wooden decorative accessories and furniture, specializing
in minutia. Their workshop is a fascinating
collage of scrolls, pilasters, frames, sconces,
table legs, columns, capitals, animal feet,
drawer pulls, angels, finials, posts, and doodads of every shape and size. Some are gilded,
some painted, and some in raw wood. The
array and amount are almost too much to
absorb in one visit. In typical Florentine spirit,

there is an emphasis on ornate, rounded forms. If you want inlaid wood, you can choose from ebony, cedar, cherry, mahogany, pear, walnut, maple, olive, and more, all laid flawlessly into geometric patterns in chairs and chests and polished to high sheen. Definitely worth a visit, if only to gawk.

Cornici Campani
Via dei Servi, 22r
055/216984

Founded in 1889 by the renowned Florentine art collector Gino Campani, this establishment upholds a legacy of producing quality, handcrafted frames. The shop is located near the Duomo.

C. & S. Martelli
Via Toscanella 18r
055/289415
www.oroecolore.com

There's nothing to buy here, but it's worth a trip just to stand in the doorway and watch Carlo Martelli work. This master craftsman, trained in the studio of his uncle, Giulio Martelli, stands amid a pile of sawdust and metal tools, hard at work putting the finishing touches on a frame that befits a Botticelli or a Caravaggio. His clients include the Uffizi, the Palazzo Pitti, and a smattering of other municipalities and museums. On commission, he'll execute a historical reproduction of an antique frame, using antique materials. Along with his cousin Stefania, Carlo operates a school for restorers with the wonderful name Oro e Colore ("Gold and Color").

Franceschi
Via Toscanella, 36-38r
Via Maggio, 15

Not long ago, Pier Luigi Franceschi was just one of a host of frame makers in the Oltrarno craft district, but today, he is among the last of this dying breed. His workshop on the Via Maggio, near the Piazza Pitti, occupies a fifteenth-century building.

Bini
Piazza Santo Spirito, 5r
055/282292

This is one of those businesses that will make you scratch your head and wonder how they make a living in today's world, but you have to hand it to them for carrying the torch of tradition. Bini was founded in 1887 as a maker of wooden forms for hats. Inside, artisans chip away at wooden blocks to create smooth, rounded forms on which hats could be proudly displayed, as in a shop window. More recently, the owners have added a few woodcrafts to their repertory, perhaps to create sales instead of curiosities and conversation pieces. They also claim to have created the world's first all-wood bicycle.

IMPRUNETA

You need a car to visit the terra-cotta producers of Impruneta, as the artisans need large spaces to work and store their wares, and are spread out around town. Kilns are scattered on the outskirts of town, often adjacent to the artisans' living quarters. Scouting them out is an exciting way to learn about not only the way Italians work but also how they live.

TERRA-COTTA
Terracotta

Cotto Chiti
Via Provinciale Chiantigiana 169, Ferrone
055/207030

On the main road linking Florence and Siena, Cotto Chiti occupies an evocative building constructed entirely of—what else?—terra-cotta. In addition to floor tiles and materials for architectural construction, they handcraft some lovely vases, pots, and other vessels for outdoor garden use.

Fornace Giorgio Pesci e Figli
Via Provinciale Chiantigiana, 36
055/2326285
www.terrecottepescigiorgio.com

Giant red pots, urns, planters, and window boxes litter the green slope that fans out from the humble headquarters of the Pesci family. Their kiln is located near the superhighway linking Florence and Siena, exit S. Casciano Nord. It's worth a detour if you're driving on the *superstrada* between Florence and Siena.

Mario Mariani
Via di Cappello, 29
055/2011950

Mariani and his three assistants are considered among Impruneta's top masters of terra-cotta. From his house/workshop, he carries on a tradition begun by his family in the 1860s. For the last four decades, the artist has been quietly creating tremendous pots entirely by hand and firing them in his old-fashioned, below-ground kilns, which constitute works of art in themselves. Mariani has been called on to restore the terra-cotta works of many old churches that dot the Tuscan countryside.

Masini
Via delle Fornaci, 57/59
055/2011683
www.fornacemasini.it

Since 1939, the Masini family has been hand-crafting giant garden pots and unique sculptures in their workshop, a restored nineteenth-century brickyard and kiln.

Poggi Ugo
Via Imprunetana, 16
055/2011077
www.poggiuggo.it

This is one of the oldest kilns in Impruneta, dating back to the 1500s. The Poggi family purchased the property in 1919 and restored the kiln to working condition. They produce basins, pots, vases, jars, and floor tiles following traditional methods. The Poggi pride themselves on crafting wares without the use of potters' wheels, templates, or molds; everything is produced solely by hand.

MONTELUPO FIORENTINO

Ceramics are the raison d'être for this Tuscan town; take away the kilns and workshops, and there would be nothing left. Even the street numbers in Montelupo Fiorentino are ceramic tiles with numbers painted in artistic flourishes of blue paint. The town itself is nothing special, but the selection and prices for high-quality Tuscan ceramics are second to none.

If you're lucky enough to catch Montelupo Fiorentino on the third Sunday of the month, don't miss the Mercatino della Ceramica. Artisans display their wares along the Corso Garibaldi, making for a delightful stroll and a feast for the eyes.

CERAMICS
Ceramiche

Ceramics Museum
Museo Archeologico della Ceramica
Via Bartolomeo Sinibaldi, 45
0571/51352
www.museomontelupo.it

The Museo Archeologico della Ceramica is the perfect place to begin your visit to Montelupo. The museum chronicles the history of local *maiolica* production. The quiet spaces showcase nearly 3,000 wares from the town's origins through the heyday of Montelupo Fiorentino, the fourteenth to the eighteenth centuries.

Ceramics School

You can take ceramics courses at the Scuola di Formazione Professionale per la Ceramica Artistica, ranging from a single weekend to a year-long curriculum. Call the town hall for more information: 0571/917527.

Bartoloni
Via Garibaldi, 36, 0571/51242
Via del Lavoro, 30, 0571/913569
www.ceramicabartoloni.it

If you're a fan of Renaissance art, you'll adore this shop. Bartoloni specializes in large plates, jars, and tiles featuring noble men and women, heraldic motifs, and regal animals, as well as mythical and religious scenes. The designs are well-executed and lively.

Maioliche Otello Dolfi
Via Tosco Romagnola Nord, 8/b
0571/910105
www.otellodolfi.it

Dolfi stands out from the industrialized producers along the main road leading into Montelupo because its facade features enormous ceramic plates incorporated into its exterior stucco walls. What great advertising! Dolfi is one of the leading producers in the area and boasts a thriving export business. The good news is that they also sell directly to the consumer. From busts of Renaissance noblewomen to jugs and pharmacy jars, they produce some of the most typical wares of Montelupo. They offer decent deals on great ceramics, and it's all tax-free for those outside the European Community. They have a showroom in the center of town as well.

IMA Ceramiche
Via Tosco Romagnola, 3/1
0571/910117
www.ceramicheima.it

IMA lies in the industrial outskirts of Montelupo. Their forte is grand-scale plates, jugs, and other large pieces with Renaissance motifs. I love their plates with young noblemen and women in profile.

SIENA

Long ago, royal courts across Europe sought Siena's metalworkers and altarpiece-makers. Alas, Siena's world-class medieval and Renaissance craft guilds have been replaced largely by artisans mass-producing junk for tourists who visit the famous horse race, the Palio, that takes place twice a year in this magical Tuscan town.

Today, you'll have to visit one of Siena's museums if you want to see examples of these stunning masterpieces of Gothic art, for you won't find anything close to it in the artisan shops of Siena's narrow alleys.

CERAMICS
Ceramiche

Tesori di Siena
Via di Città, 72
0577/46723
Via dei Fusari, 3
0577/289208
www.tesoridisiena.com

Ceramics with a modern sensibility crowd the two locations of Tesori di Siena. They are higher quality than much of the ceramics elsewhere in the city. The artisans will create a set of china for you in an array of pre-determined designs, or turn your dream into a reality with custom plates. They ship internationally via UPS or DHL.

FABRICS
Tessuti

Fioretta Bacci
Tessuti a Mano
Via San Pietro, 7
0577/282200

This is my pick in Siena. From an enormous antique loom that dominates this tiny cluttered shop, Fioretta Bacci crafts stunning knitted shawls, scarves, sweaters, and accessories. You can't help but touch the luxurious, soft loops of wool. Draping one of her gorgeous shawls over your shoulders is a taste of luxury.

VOLTERRA

ALABASTER
Alabastro

Alab'Arte
Via Orti S. Agostino, 28 (workshop)
Via Don Minzoni, 18 (store)
0588/87968
www.alabarte.com

The workshop of Roberto Chiti and Giorgio Finazzo, among the youngest of Volterra's alabaster sculptors, is a fascinating jumble of elegant female nudes, busts of ancient Greek gods and Jesus, lamps, and hunks of unwrought alabaster. Here, Aphrodite coexists with the Madonna and Child. Saints stare vacantly from translucent pupils. It's almost too much for the eye to take in at one time. Alab'Arte concentrates on the human figure, which it has perfected with idealized beauty.

THE BLACK DEATH

"One who did not see such horribleness can be called blessed." This is how the Sienese author Agnolo di Tura described the bubonic plague, the famous Black Death of 1348 that wiped out much of Siena's population. But this terrible calamity did not kill the craft industry. In fact, some historians believe that the Black Death only served to boost it—people became more pious and commissions for religious art and devotional objects skyrocketed throughout Tuscany.

Museo Guarnacci
Via Don Minzoni, 15
0588/86347

Many of the 600 or so Etruscan funerary urns in this impressive collection were crafted from local alabaster, some date as far back as 27 centuries ago. What a testament to the enduring qualities of alabaster!

Paolo Sabatini
Via Porta all'Arco, 45 (workshop)
Via Matteotti, 56a (showroom)
0588/81515
www.paolosabatini.com

Sabatini has a reputation as one of the last of a dying breed: Instead of slavishly copying designs of the past, Sabatini provocatively pushes the envelope with innovative designs in alabaster. In his workshop are apples, pens, candelabras, hats, and much more. Each one of his alabaster sculptures is a unique creation. He has challenged other alabaster artists, in Volterra and elsewhere, to think outside the box.

U M B R I A

D E R U T A

Ceramics have sustained Deruta for a very long time. In 1358 alone, the town exported over a thousand pieces of pottery to Assisi, and its ceramics guild was already among the strongest on the Italian peninsula. Deruta peaked in the 1400s and 1500s, but craftspeople have produced wares continuously since then, looking to the past for inspiration.

The old city of Deruta lies atop a hill, while the modern city snakes along the bottom of the hillside. In general, you will pay a premium in the shops in the historic town on the hill; prices drop slightly down the hill. A plethora of ceramics shops dot the cobblestone streets of Deruta's quaint historical center, but nearly all of these schlep their wares from larger workshops located along the Via Tiberina, which skirts the hillside. Less quaint but more extensive workshops cluster around the southern and northern ends of the Via Tiberina. Avoid the larger, more industrialized operations on the outskirts of town that advertise heavily along the highway. The prices are cheaper but so is the quality.

C E R A M I C S
Ceramiche

Ceramics Museum
Museo Regionale della Ceramica
Largo San Francesco
075/9711000

For over a century, this ceramics museum has chronicled the history of ceramic production in central Italy. Its location at the very heart of Deruta's old city makes it a great place to start your visit to Deruta shops.

Ceramiche Chiucchiù
Via Salvemini
075/9710747
www.ceramichechiucchiu.com

Patrizio Chiucchiù, with help from his father and his wife, operates a tiny shop chock-full of ceramics, ceramic accoutrements, and books. He still gathers the clay himself from the environs of Deruta, and makes painstaking reproductions of Renaissance works, even giving them an antiqued appearance.

CHEAT SHEET: DERUTA CERAMICS

Middle Ages (1100–1400): utilitarian objects like pitchers, bowls, flasks, tiles; blue or green against a white ground; stylized vegetal and animal motifs; very little figural decoration

Renaissance (1400–1600): more elaborate tableware, pharmacy jars, tiles; blue, yellow, and ochre against a white ground; acanthus leaves, peacock feathers, scrolls, geometric patterns, thorn patterns; saints, allegorical figures, idealized portraits, heraldry

Baroque (1600–1800): tableware, decorative plates yellow and blue, blue on white (an imitation of Chinese porcelain); animals, Raphaelesque decoration (lots of winged beasts or grotesques, swirls, flora) all-over decoration; saints, heraldry

Ceramiche Sberna
Via Tiberina Centro, 146
075/9710206
www.sberna.com

Since 1959, the Sberna family has been
producing a huge volume of ceramic pieces
with an excellent sense of tradition and gusto
for historical style. Despite the high quality,
the wares are often stacked haphazardly
around the shop. Sberna also runs a small
showroom in the center of town.

Fornace San Lorenzo
Via El Frate, 11
075/972356
www.fornacesanlorenzo.com

The Fornace San Lorenzo, in the heart
of Deruta's old city, is worth a visit even if
you don't come here for the ceramics. First,
their terrace offers a gorgeous panorama
of the Umbrian countryside from a high
vantage point. Second, the basement consists
of Deruta's only surviving ceramics kiln from
the Renaissance period which has been
painstakingly restored. Here you can see
the earthen floor, the giant vaults, and the
various chambers where artisans once stacked
their wares to be baked in a wood fire. It's
spectacular. The ceramics aren't bad, either.

Franco Mari
Via Tiberina, 69
075/9711224
www.majolichefrancomari.com

Franco Mari is related to the family that
runs the industrialized Fratelli Mari on the
outskirts of town, but that's as far as the
comparison goes. The uniqueness of Mari's
work lies in his ability to transform elements
of Deruta's past decorative vocabulary into
designs with a modern sensibility. Mari
studied in Perugia and in the United States
before returning to his hometown of Deruta
to make a name for himself. Mari works with
many American clients who appreciate his
more contemporary designs.

Fratelli Marcucci
Via Tiberina, 204
075/9711364
www.marcuccideruta.it

The size of the plate that fills the front window
of the Marcucci brothers' shop will make
your jaw drop and lure you inside. It's too
bad that they reserved the front showroom
for lesser-quality wares. If you really want to
see the goods, ask to descend into the seemingly endless corridor of basement-level
rooms. Marcucci pulls off one of the more
stunning table centerpieces in town, with
lively scrolls and animal motifs. Keep walking back—the work gets better and better.

Ceramiche Artistiche Gialletti Pimpinelli
Via Tiberina Sud, 300
075/972016
www.gpderuta.com

This is my favorite place to shop in Deruta.
What the showroom and studio lack in
charm, they make up for in the quality
ceramics that fill their shelves. In my opinion,
Prassede Gialletti, Graziano Pimpinelli, and
their assistants do the best job in executing
the historical figures, faces, and styles
on the objects. Don't be confused: the shop
next door is also called Gialletti; long ago
the families were related, but now there is
no connection between the two shops. GP
will ship insured to the United States.

Lombrici
Via Tiberina Sud, 293
075/9711272

Faustino Lombrici is one of Deruta's smaller
producers, excelling in high-quality tableware. This is one of the best places to buy
nice serving bowls, casseroles, and other
décor for your table.

Maioliche Originali Deruta
Via Tiberina Sud, 330
075/9711576
www.derutaitaly.com

This large operation is headquartered on
the south end of the Via Tiberina. On the
second floor, a brigade of ceramics painters
turns out delicate motifs on lamps, vases,
pitchers, bowls, and soup tureens. The
eccentric brother-and-sister team, Ivan
and Grazia Ranocchia, emerge from the back
office to help customers. The ground-floor

showroom gives the impression of being inside a tremendous warehouse, complete with dust and plain metal shelves. But don't be fooled by this spartan atmosphere: the prices are as stunning as the wares. Grazia Ranocchia is the author of a book on Deruta production in the twentieth century.

Antonio Margaritelli
Via Tiberina, 214
075/9711352

If you want to see what real historical Deruta ceramics look like, and don't have time to go to the ceramics museum, stop by this tiny shop along the Via Tiberina. Here Margaritelli displays precious shards of medieval and Renaissance ceramics in curio cabinets, as if they were expensive jewelry. Displayed nearby are breathtakingly faithful reproductions of the historical Deruta. Antonio Margaritelli studied with Ubaldo Grazia for 17 years before striking out on his own. He rediscovered, through trial and error, many of the rich, translucent glazes of the Renaissance. His own excellent work shows his love and deep knowledge of these original pieces. With only one assistant, the production is low, the prices are high, and the quality is top-notch.

Ubaldo Grazia
Via Tiberina, 181
075/9710201
www.ubaldograzia.com

Grazia is Deruta's most venerable ceramics producer, with a piece of landmark real estate to match its reputation. In a stone palazzo in the center of the Via Tiberina, their wares fill shelves and walls throughout a series of showrooms divided into themes. In the modern room are works inspired by Impressionist and modern masters. A historical room displays wares with designs representing the glory days of Deruta. My favorite is an enormous showroom with endless examples of the dinner services Ubaldo Grazia can custom-make for you. You can order entire collections, from serving plates to tea sets and salt and pepper shakers, in any number of patterns. For the bride-to-be with everything, this is the place. Grazia distributes through major

department store chains in the United States, but you'll pay less and have more fun if you come directly to the source.

GUALDO TADINO

Though potters have been working clay in Gualdo Tadino for centuries, the town is best known for two historic periods of ceramic production. The first was the 1500s, when a certain Master Giorgio, an innovative local craftsman, disseminated a technique in which pieces were fired three times to achieve a shiny, lustrous finish imitating metalwork. This so-called lusterware fills shop windows in Gualdo Tadino, catching and reflecting the golden effects of the sunlight.

Gualdo's second heyday was in the 1800s, when local artisans revived this Renaissance lusterware, but added to it very ornate forms that would be at home in a Victorian décor. The result: plates with lacelike edges and elongated pitchers with frilly spouts and handles that ended in flourishes. If your taste leans toward the ornate, this is your kind of town. It's why I affectionately call this town "Gaudy Gualdo."

Today, artisans maintain these two decorative traditions, reproducing the styles and forms that put this little Umbrian hilltop town on the map of art history.

CERAMICS
Ceramiche

Ceramiche Artistiche Passeri Giovanni
Via Flaminia, 1, Vaccara
075/9140089

Giovanni Passerini is one of Gualdo Tadino's most reputable artisans and has been working at the craft since the 1960s. He creates some fine reproductions of nineteenth-century lusterware, including highly ornate, delicate jewelry boxes and tableware with gilded edges.

Ceramiche C.R.
Via Fratelli Carioli
075/9143043

The C.R. stands for *ceramiche a riverbero*, which refers to a historical lusterware technique that this family enterprise helped rediscover in the

late 1800s. The current owners, Antonio
Paletti and Patrizia Cusarelli, are fourth-
generation artists born and raised in Gualdo
Tadino. The family business was founded in
1873, and over the years its wares have entered
important international collections, including
those of New York's Metropolitan Museum
of Art and Bulgaria's royal family.

Ceramiche Pericoli Graziano
Via Biancospino
075/910596
www.ceramicalustro.it

This is one of my favorite ceramics workshops in Gualdo Tadino. The artisans are
young and seem to breathe new life into
the old designs. Fancy vases with idealized
Renaissance portraits, decorative plates, and
shiny tableware are among their specialties.

Ceramics Museum
Museo Civico Rocca Flea
Piazzale Rocca Flea
075/916078

A small but impressive collection of local wares
from the sixteenth to the nineteenth centuries.

Vittorio Pimpinelli
Via Flaminia
075/9141306
www.pimpinelli.it

Pimpinelli is one of Gualdo Tadino's larger
producers, employing about 25 artisans in
their workshop on the outskirts of town.
However, they insist on handmade techniques and produce some lovely decorative
plates and vases. Their showroom on the Via
Flaminia displays just a fraction of their
extensive production.

GUBBIO

The picturesque hill town of Gubbio—one
of Umbria's highlights—exudes a medieval
flavor, and its shops capture the spirit of
the thriving craft guilds that formed the economic and social backbone of Old World
society. Many of the craft shops are located
along the Via dei Consoli, which climbs
toward the spectacular Piazza Grande and its
stunning vistas of the Umbrian landscape.

CERAMICS
Ceramiche

Ceramics Museum
Museo Comunale
Palazzo dei Consoli
Piazza Grande
075/99274298

The ceramics section of the town museum
exhibits a nice collection of regional ceramics
from the fifteenth to the nineteenth centuries.

Museo della Ceramica a Lustro "Torre di Porta Romana"
Via Dante, 24
075/9221199

In this museum you can see the real works
of Master Giorgio and his followers, as well
as other examples of regional lusterware.

Rampini
Via da Vinci, 94 (workshop)
075/9272963
Via dei Consoli, 52 (showroom)
075/9274408
www.rampiniceramiche.com

A pair of *biscotti* jars that Giampietro
Rampini made are two of the showpieces
of my kitchen. The Rampini workshop lies
beyond Gubbio's historical center, but it's
worth the trek. Here, Giampietro Rampini
carries on a tradition begun by his father.
This is a family affair; even the family cat
comes to work every day, gently skirting
the legs of Giampietro's assistants as they
paint graceful rabbits and scrolls on dinner
plates. Passion and tradition combine with
beautiful results. Rampini has also revived
the technique of lusterware. Pietro's teenage
son is in line to take over the family business; for now, he's the Rampini Webmaster.

Sebastiani
Via dei Consoli, 44
075/9271159

Sebastiani specializes in *buccheri*, dramatic
black wares inspired by ancient Etruscan
ceramics. These ceramics have an exotic
flavor and design borrowed from the ancient
Greeks. The authentic reproductions center
around a few basic shapes and styles.

CHEAT SHEET: GUBBIO

Gubbio's artisans look to historical wares from many periods for inspiration. Here are just a few of the historical styles you'll see reproduced throughout town:

• **Zaffera style** (*stile zaffera*): blue or green glaze over white, inspired by Moorish designs of animals and swirls, widespread in the 1300s and 1400s.

• **Lusterware** (*lustro*): There are many variations of lusterware, but all use a third firing to impart a slick, glossy finish, a technique introduced here in the 1500s.

• **Raphaelesque** (*a raffaellesche*): typically Renaissance motifs, popular in the 1600s.

• **Dark blue on light blue**: popular in the 1700s.

• **Neo-Renaissance**: reprises Renaissance motifs but with a Victorian decorative spirit, popular in the 1800s.

BARGAIN ALERT

Gubbio doesn't have the same world recognition that Deruta does, which means you can buy high-quality wares at better prices.

PAPER GOODS
Carta

Mastri Librai Eugubini
Via della Repubblica, 18
Via dei Consoli, 42
075/9277425

In addition to a tiny shop on the Via dei Consoli, these bookbinders operate a workshop tucked away on the Via della Repubblica. I was impressed with their successful combinations of marbleized paper bound into leather bindings. Their albums have lovely covers with impressions made with hot stamps, natural leaves and flowers, and checkerboard effects achieved by sewing together leathers of different colors. They ship to the United States.

LINENS
Tessuti

Paola Cainca
Via San Lazzaro
075/9275045

This cozy shop exudes warmth and Old World charm with its stone floors and walls and beamed ceiling. Handmade tables and personal linens are artfully displayed—a feast for the eyes. I set my sights on a gorgeous lace tablecloth, which I use for holidays.

Tele Umbre
Via Piccotti, 1
075/9271115

This shop is worth a visit just to see the antique hand loom exhibited in the shop. But you'll want to stay to survey the lovely fabrics, lampshades, and handmade brocades.

WROUGHT IRON
Ferro Battuto

Artigianato Ferro Artistico
Via Baldassini, 22
075/9273079

Like many wrought iron workshops across Italy, this enterprise is literally a hole in the wall along one of Gubbio's rambling cobblestone alleys. Here, Tonino Scavizzi and two assistants forge works of art from a sooty, hard metal that turns their faces and hands ashen. Sparks fly, tongs glow in the coals, and flames lick the stone walls of their workshop. From this messy, hard labor, works of unspeakable beauty emerge. The day I visited, the artisans were making a gate for a mausoleum that a local cemetery had commissioned.

ORVIETO

CERAMICS
Ceramiche

Many ceramics resellers catering to the tourist trade cluster on the streets around the cathedral plaza. Quality varies; you're better off sticking to one of the shops in the listings.

Archeological Museum
Museo archeologico della Fondazione C. Faina
Piazza Duomo
0763/341039

I'm a huge fan of Etruscan art, so I relish browsing the small but impressive collection of finds rescued from tombs around Orvieto.

Mirella Cecconi
Via Montemarte, 30
0763/340366

Mirella Cecconi, one of Orvieto's better ceramicists, crafts reproductions of Orvietana wares of the Middle Ages and Renaissance. Signora Cecconi offers ceramics courses, where you can try your hand at Orvieto's traditions.

La Corte dei Miracoli
Piazza de Ranieri, 13
349/3156502

Alberto Bellini pairs his passion for medieval art with a love of fantasy. The result: whimsical, intriguing human figures and seemingly impossible castles, all hand-built in terracotta. Bellini is the head of the local artisans' organization, active in promoting Orvieto's craft industry.

Paolo Golia
Via Pedota, 3/5
0763/342022

These are probably the most stunning
reproductions of ancient Etruscan *buccheri*
I've seen in all of central Italy. The pieces
are also perfectly displayed, as if in an
exclusive art gallery, with dramatic lighting
and sparse furnishings. Mysterious and
stately, these wares stole my heart.

DOLLS AND MARIONETTES

Pupe e Marionette

Capra Ballerina
Via de Magoni, 4

Sometimes whimsical, sometimes creepy,
these wood and papier-mâché marionettes
dangle from the walls of this small studio
on the best artisan street of central Orvieto.

Studio Artistico di Natalina Ronca
Via de Magoni, 16

Precious, handmade dolls peer out of the
tiny shop window of Natalina Ronca's humble
studio. In addition to the dolls are scads
of lovely lace items—table linens, decorative
items, lamp shades, and apparel for humans
and dolls.

LEATHER

Pelle

L'arte del cuoio
Via dei Magoni, 6
0763/344800

The unmistakable aroma of leather lured
me into this warm and cozy workshop off
of one of Orvieto's pedestrian streets.
In the back of the workshop, you can watch
Aldo Fusco polishing hides and stamping
patterns into leather strips. The prices
are great, too. For under 100 euros you can
buy a rustic, handmade purse, or for about
8 euros, a cute little cow for your desk.

WOODCRAFTS

Legno

Michelangeli
Via Gualtieri Michelangeli, 3
0763/342660
www.michelangeli.it

Michelangeli is Orvieto's most well-known
artisan enterprise and it's easy to see why.
Large-scale toys and whimsical decorative
items—all handcrafted with different kinds
of wood—make this shop a wonderland for
kids from one to 100.

Patris
Via dei Magoni, 11
349/2966146

If you need something to take home as a
gift, this is a great place to find it. This
shop specializes in small items crafted of
inlaid wood, created by a native Corsican
transplanted to Orvieto. I especially love
their toys and frames, and the prices are
reasonable.

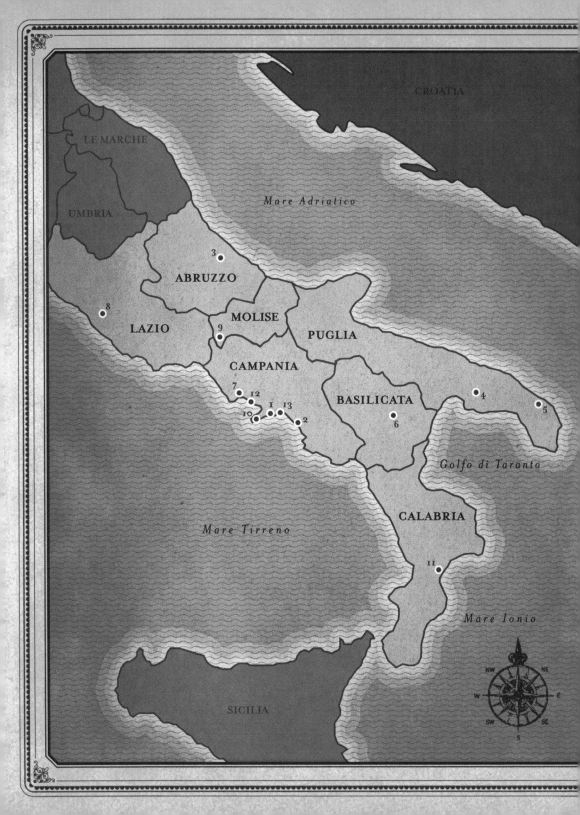

CROATIA

Mare Adriatico

LE MARCHE

UMBRIA

3

ABRUZZO

8

MOLISE

LAZIO

9

PUGLIA

CAMPANIA

7

12

BASILICATA

4

1 13

5

10

2

6

Golfo di Taranto

CALABRIA

Mare Tirreno

11

Mare Ionio

SICILIA

NW NE

W   E

SW SE

S

Chapter 4

SOUTHERN ITALY

ABRUZZO · BASILICATA · CALABRIA · CAMPANIA
LAZIO · MOLISE · PUGLIA

FOR PEOPLE LIKE ME, WHO HAVE A PASSION FOR traditional cultures, the south is one of Italy's most interesting regions. This is an intensely traditional area, where family, religion, and the Old World trades have formed the center of life for centuries. In shadowy doorways in villages like Scanno, in Abruzzo, elderly women in old-fashioned black dress work lace with their able hands. In small towns around Taranto, villagers still perform the Tarantella, the frenzied dance that has been curing the evil bite of the tarantula spider for 600 years. Fishermen who eke out a living from waters off this stunning coastline still make and repair their own nets, just as their ancestors have for centuries.

The crafts of southern Italy reflect the region's dependence on the sea. Jewelry made of coral is traditional here, as are cameos, which represent a major industry just outside Naples. The Church has also exerted a powerful influence on the crafts and visual culture of southern Italy. This is a profoundly Catholic region, and the Church's presence can be felt in countless street shrines, clergy walking the streets, and spic-and-span cemeteries festooned with fresh flowers and polished marble headstones. Artisan shops overflow with papier-mâché nativity scenes, multicolored rosaries in gold and silver, and wooden and plastic statues depicting the Madonna and saints both popular and obscure.

International visitors flock to Campania, which is the region where Naples, the island of Capri, the ancient cities of Pompeii and Herculaneum, and the stunning Amalfi coast are located. Others swarm to Rome but ignore the fascinating region of Lazio that surrounds the Eternal City. The rural regions of Molise and Abruzzo—cut off from the rest of the peninsula by formidable mountain ranges—remain undiscovered by most international travelers, but are a haven for traditional crafts such as lace, wood carving, and handmade bagpipes. Basilicata, Puglia, and Calabria form the foot of Italy's boot and are a great place to find deals on exquisite ceramics and papier-mâché works.

Outside of Naples and Rome, tourists are few and far between in the more remote areas of southern Italy, a region still maligned as the poor cousin of the more prosperous north. But if you look beyond the stereotype, you'll discover some of Italy's most important and fascinating cities, as well as hundreds of smaller towns brimming with significant local color and traditions. Southern Italy holds rich rewards for those adventurous enough to veer off the beaten track.

THE TRADITIONS

BAGPIPES

Zampogne

Bagpipes? It's not what you'd expect to find in Italy, but the bagpipe, or *zampogna*, made in Scapoli—a mountain village of rural Molise—is thought to be the ancient ancestor of the Scottish instrument, allegedly introduced to Scotland by Roman soldiers. Centuries ago, Italian bagpipes filled the air with their eerie, solemn cries, but today, Scapoli is one of the only towns in the country that preserves this ancient tradition.

No one knows when locals began making these strange instruments, but their origins surely reach far back into antiquity. Just 30 years ago, nearly 20,000 sheep grazed the mountain grasslands outside of Scapoli, providing skins for making bagpipes. They formed a quiet audience for the shepherd, who heard his own haunting melodies repeated back to him as echoes off the mountains. Today, just a few herds dot the verdant hillsides, and the *zampogna* is played mostly at Christmastime rather than daily.

The Scapoli bagpipe is a type known as a double-chanter, or with two sets of finger holes for producing its distinctive sounds. The instrument is a complicated contraption made of sheepskin bags, pipes of cherry or olive wood, and reeds made of cane. A handful of artisans residing in the Fontecostanza section of Scapoli preserve and pass on the ancient tradition and techniques for making these instruments.

If you want to see bagpipes in action, visit Scapoli at the end of July. A popular international festival draws bagpipe enthusiasts from all over the world (see Calendar of Events, page 215).

PRICE POINTS
Prices for Scapoli bagpipes run between 200 and 800 euros, depending on how they are outfitted, what types of wood are utilized, and their decoration.

BELLISSIMA!
Visit the Museo della Zampogna in Scapoli (page 172) to learn more about this ancient instrument.

CAMEOS AND CORAL JEWELRY
Camei e Gioielli di Corallo

S ituated halfway between Naples and Pompeii, Torre del Greco is the undisputed capital of Italian coral and cameo jewelry.

Seashells and corals were carved in ancient times; thousands of cameos with busts of Roman emperors and beautiful women fill the collections of museums around the world. In 1805, a royal cameo-making enterprise was established in Torre del Greco, and over the course of the nineteenth century, private coral and cameo businesses set up shop.

Historically, coral fishing was a major enterprise and coral boats (*coralline*) sailed daily from Naples to the major coral reserves, from the Neopolitan coast to the south of Sicily. Today, only scuba divers gather coral off the Italian coast, but many producers also import it from Asia.

Cameos are crafted from seashells, many of which have layers of different colors or tones. First, the external layer of the shell is sanded away. Next, the artisan sketches the image he or she wants to create with a pencil on the transparent, light layer underneath. The artisan then grinds the edges of the piece down to the darkest layer, which serves as a background for the light image that emerges from the top. Details of the figure are then engraved. The end result is stunning.

Coral and cameo jewelry making is a major industry here, employing no less than 5,000 people. Many of the larger producers in Torre del Greco cater to the trade only (a thriving export business sends many of these pieces to Japan, Australia, the United States, and northern Europe). There are also a lot of souvenir shops selling junk to tourists who arrive on escorted bus tours. Stick to the more well-known, reputable producers, and you'll come home with a beautiful, high-quality souvenir you'll treasure and proudly wear.

PRICE POINTS
The price range for coral and cameo jewelry is vast. However, you can expect to pay between 40 and 450 euros for a cameo mounted into a ring or pendant, depending on size and detail.

BELLISSIMA!
Basilio Liverino in Torre del Greco (page 166) is the region's premier producer of coral jewelry.

CERAMICS

Ceramiche

Southern Italy produces the most diverse range of ceramic styles of all Italy's regions, including everything from the delicate porcelain of Capodimonte to the serious and somber tones of Castelli and Squillace and the bold shapes and fun colors of Vietri sul Mare and Grottaglie. The one thing all of these ceramic traditions share is drama.

Two of southern Italy's ceramic towns—Grottaglie and Squillace—trace their ceramic roots to antiquity. Grottaglie, located on the heel of Italy's boot near Taranto, served as an outpost for the ancient Greeks, who left behind giant ceramic jugs for archeologists to unearth. Several ceramic families made a name for themselves by the 1500s, and over the course of the next few centuries, ceramics rivaled agriculture as the town's major industry. A ceramics school has graduated artisans over the last 150 years.

There are two major types of ceramics in Grottaglie. The first traces its origins to the local popular culture: rustic wares decorated with lively, sketchy scenes of peasants, agriculture, and daily life. Weird and wonderful shapes are the hallmark of this tradition, including characteristic pitchers called *sruli*. Bulbous on the bottom and wavy on the top, they exude a rustic, folk quality that is far from the sophistication of Castelli or Capodimonte, but is no less impressive. Anthropomorphic vessels—especially bottles shaped like females with bared breasts—are another favorite of Grottaglie's artisans. The second type of ceramics revolves around the noble taste of the Renaissance and this more refined tradition that shows knowledge of other Italian ceramics centers. One is not better than the other; they are just different.

The roots of the ceramics of Squillace can also be traced to the ancient world. Squillace is in Calabria, the toe of Italy's boot, a region that has been touched by many Mediterranean cultures over the centuries. For eons, artisans in this rural town have been decorating ceramic wares with an impressive *graffito*, an incised effect, probably brought to the region by Byzantine traders sometime in the late Roman or early Christian period. By the 1500s, Squillace was already renowned in the Mediterranean for the technique.

The *graffito* technique involves scratching an intricate design into the clay with a sharp tool after the glaze has been applied. When the piece is fired, the incised design turns white, making a stunning contrast against the ruddy plate or vase. The result: intricate floral and animal decoration, with rich compositions of decorative elements.

One of southern Italy's most important ceramic traditions is practiced in the town of Castelli, in Abruzzo. Castelli is considered the birthplace of one of Italy's grand ceramic traditions, and examples of these wares are prized in the collections of the Metropolitan Museum in New York, the Louvre in Paris, and other international museums.

Sometime during the Middle Ages, the Benedictine monks of San Salvatore of Castelli began teaching locals how to pull clay from the mountains and turn it into pottery. Ever since then, these mountain-dwelling people of Abruzzo have lived and breathed *maiolica* ceramics. By the 1500s, this town was famous for its sophisticated ceramic production, and it was widely exported throughout the peninsula as a luxury item. Their bell-shaped vases, pot-bellied jugs, and flasks with large handles were distinctive compared with wares from Deruta, Faenza, and other central Italian ceramics centers.

CASTELLI CHEAT SHEET

- **Forms:** flasks with handles, bell-shaped vases, pot-bellied jugs, pierced edges that create a basketlike effect, elaborate tableware ensembles
- **Themes:** dreamy landscapes; watercolorlike, painterly effects; classical nudes; winged *putti*; saints; sun, moon, and stars with serene faces
- **Colors:** basic palette of five colors—blue, ochre, yellow, green, and white
- **Tradition:** well-defined dynasties and styles since the Middle Ages; one of the only ceramics traditions of Italy to focus on landscapes

In the 1600s, Castelli made a name for itself by producing historiated, or story-telling, ceramics, with popular scenes from religion and mythology. Watercolorlike landscapes that treated the white ceramic like a blank canvas also delighted the noble classes who bought these objects. As tastes changed in the 1700s, Castelli's artisans began producing ornate, delicate white pieces that imitated Chinese export porcelain.

Though Castelli eventually built a reputation for its designs on fancy tableware, early ceramic artisans used the whole town as their canvas. The ceiling of the church of San Donato in Castelli is paved with ceramic bricks from the fifteenth and sixteenth centuries. Ceramic altarpieces, fonts, and streetside ex-votos in ceramic display saints and Madonnas lovingly painted by artisans of Castelli's most important ceramic dynasties: the Pompei, Grue, Gentili, Cappelletti, de Martinis, and Fuina.

In the 1500s, Castelli's artisans were commissioned to create a set of ceramics to celebrate peace between the Orisini and Colonna families. These wares—many of them bulbous vases and jars with handles, and busts of noblemen and women—inspired many imitators. Today's artisans still reproduce many pieces from this famous Orsini-Colonna collection.

Many of Castelli's ceramicists cluster around the artisan district known as the Villaggio Artigiano. In all, some 50 ceramic enterprises operate in Castelli today. Electric potters' wheels and gas-fired kilns have taken the place of the manual tasks that were, for centuries, so grueling to Castelli's artists, but the best ceramacists still capture the historical styles and spirit that characterize this town.

Nothing could be further from the serious tone of Castelli ceramics than the whimsical, bright ceramics of Vietri sul Mare, a village perched on what must be

FUNNY FORMS

Here are some of the typical forms you'll see in Grottaglie:
- **Acquasantiera**: basin for holy water, usually hung on the wall
- **Bambola**: "doll"; often a bottle in female form with bared breasts
- **Capasone**: monumental jars based on ancient models
- **Ciarla**: jar with lid and broad handles
- **Srulo or brocca**: a pitcher with a bulbous bottom and wavy top
- **Zuppiera**: soup tureen

Italy's most beautiful coast. Storefronts, houses, numbers, church domes, and pavement throughout the town are made of ceramic. Instead of using the classical motifs of the Renaissance as their point of reference, Vietri's artisans looked around them for inspiration. There is a passion for sea scenes and local color—people in costumes, mothers and children, fanciful boats, fish, and other maritime themes.

Vietri has earned a reputation as a producer of floor and wall tiles, but these are not simple terra-cotta squares. The most luxurious bath I remember is one I enjoyed in my suite at the Hotel Santa Caterina in Amalfi, which was surrounded by gorgeous tiles decorated with scenes of the rocky coast. Vietri artisans paint scenes that continue from one tile to the next, as if the wall were a gigantic canvas. The Amalfi coast is replete with breathtaking tile ensembles in architectural settings, all decorated by Vietri artists.

The last of the ceramics styles in southern Italy is Capodimonte, the delicate and ornate porcelain historically produced outside of Naples, based on tiny pastel flowers, sprays of buds, baskets, and elegant figurines. In the eighteenth century, porcelain tableware and figurines were all the rage among royals and nobles, and they remained inaccessible to the lower classes. In European capitals, the upper classes coveted little figurines of peasants, delicate flowers, and other decorative porcelain wares.

The Neopolitan origins of this fancy porcelain lie in the royal court of Charles III, who ruled from Naples in the eighteenth century. His queen, Maria Amalia Valpurga, was the niece of Augustus III, the creator of the Meissen factory. Charles's palace outside of Naples was built as a hunting lodge, and today this palace, on over 300 acres, houses the family's important collection of paintings. In the 1740s, the king added to it the Real Fabbrica. His goal was to produce porcelain that would vie with the famous royal porcelain manufacturers like Meissen. The king moved the factory to Spain when he left Naples in 1759, but his son, Ferdinand VI, reopened it in the 1770s, and it remained active until the French took Naples in 1806. In the 1800s and 1900s, artists continued to imitate the royal porcelain style, but the production became more mass produced, adapting to the taste of modern collectors.

Capodimonte porcelain was prized from the start for its luminous quality, a result of the soft clay pulled from the earth in Calabria. It absorbed the paint and had a reflective appearance. Flowers became one of the most popular subjects of Capodimonte porcelain because, according to legend, Charles was allergic to flowers; porcelain flowers were the only ones he could enjoy.

Today, Capodimonte ceramics are collector's items, and the value is all in the marks on the undersides of the pieces. Original items from Charles's Real Fabbrica were signed with a blue fleur-de-lis, but museums and exclusive private collectors are the only owners of these pieces. Those of Ferdinand were demarcated with a crown and the letter "N" above it. Today's artisans have their own individual marks. Authentic, antique pieces of Capodimonte sell for several thousand dollars at auction. Capodimonte-style works go for much less.

PRICE   POINTS

Of all the southern Italian ceramics centers, those of Castelli command the highest prices; you'll pay anywhere from 60 to several hundred euros for a decorative plate. In contrast, for under 100 euros, you can buy several pieces of Capodimonte or fun designs from Vietri sul Mare.

BELLISSIMA!

My picks for the best ceramics shops in southern Italy are:

Castelli: Ceramiche Mercante (page 158)

Grottaglie: Ceramiche Giuseppe Patronelli (page 173)

Naples: DEA Capodimonte (page 164)

Squillace: Cooperativa Ceramisti Vasai "S. Agazio" (page 161)

Vietri sul Mare: Solimene (page 168)

LIMONCELLO

Limoncello

P eople all over Italy make *limoncello*—I have even seen versions of it made and bottled in the Alpine regions. But ask any Italian, and they'll tell you that lemons from Sorrento make the best *limoncello* in the world. The famous "Sorrento oval," or *ovale di Sorrento*, is the giant lemon variety that makes this alcoholic elixir both sweet and tart. The variety grown in Amalfi, the *sfusato amalfitano*, is also considered excellent for making this special liqueur.

According to legend, Arabs brought the first lemons to the Sorrento peninsula in the tenth century. These tart fruits flourished along the hillsides of this volcanic earth, rich with sunshine and salt air. Many southern Italians grow lemon trees in their yards to make their own homemade *limoncelli*. The Amalfi *sfusato* lemon is the star of Amalfi's famous *limoncello* liqueur, as well as a zillion different types of pastries made with lemon and sold in the wonderful *pasticcerie* in town. Many of the Amalfi lemons are harvested from the trees in the nearby Valle dei Mulini, also famous for its paper production (see page 153).

The trees clinging to the cliff sides of the beautiful Amalfi coast hang heavy with giant lemons, sending a heady scent into the Mediterranean air. One of my favorite walks is along the meandering paths of the grounds of Amalfi's luxurious Hotel Santa Caterina. The paths are lined with lemon trees trained into arbors that provide refuge from the sun.

Limoncello begins with fresh lemon peels, free of the bitter white flesh that covers the fruit. For 40 days, they marinate in pure alcohol in a dark place. The mixture is strained and then combined with water and sugar. The whole mixture is filtered and corked. It's a simple process but producers boast their own *limoncello* secrets; for example, some use only the rinds, while others marinate the pulp and seeds. Taste and quality can vary tremendously from producer to producer and from bottle to bottle. Bad *limoncello* tastes like window cleaner; good *limoncello* tastes pure, refreshing, and oh-so-lemony—the perfect way to end a great meal on a summer day.

PRICE POINTS
Even great *limoncello* is relatively inexpensive, ranging from 5 to 20 euros a bottle.

BELLISSIMA!
I love Andrea Pansa's bakeshop in Amalfi (page 161), where you can buy bottles of homemade *limoncello* and fill up on scrumptious lemon pastries at the same time.

PAPER AND PAPIER-MÂCHÉ
Carta e Cartapesta

rtisans in Amalfi's Valle dei Mulini, or Valley of the Mills, have been producing luxury papers like handmade engraved stationery since the thirteenth century. The techniques remain virtually unchanged. Paper begins with cotton, linen, and hemp, which are wetted with waters from the nearby Canneto River and placed in stone basins. The pulp is mixed with minute strands of bronze or other metals, and then meshed and pressed into flat sheets with giant wooden handpresses.

There were 16 operating mills in Amalfi at the end of the sixteenth century, and only a few exist today. Visiting the old mills is a fun and easy excursion from the center of Amalfi, so when you've tired of the pool, take a cab to the nearby Valle dei Mulini.

Papier-mâché—known in Italy as *cartapesta*—is southern Italy's other fabulous paper product. Artisans began crafting statues in papier-mâché on a wide scale in the 1600s as a cheaper alternative to marble and wood. In addition to its economy, papier-mâché also provides infinite creative possibilities, as it is easy to add to and modify as you work. By the 1700s, papier-mâché figures filled churches, civic buildings, and homes throughout southern Italy.

Saints and Madonnas make up the bulk of figures crafted in *cartapesta*, but artisans also make animals and pastoral characters—shepherds, peasants, workers, and others—from traditional daily life. Their typically baroque forms, with bright colors, dramatic poses, and a love of heavy, billowy drapery, appealed to the fancy, ornate taste of the 1700s and 1800s.

Techniques for making papier-mâché figures have remained unchanged for hundreds of years. Sculptors form the body by making a skeleton of iron or aluminum that is covered in straw. Heads and hands are crafted of terra-cotta, wood, or papier-mâché, and are usually painted with great realism. The artisans then pose the figures and begin layering them with thin papers attached with *pommula*, a homemade glue made with flour. Then the garments are built, often growing to impressive proportions. When finished, angels seem to swoop down from the heavens, their gowns trailing behind them in billowing folds. Royal blue robes gilded along the edges adorn a crowned Madonna and Child. Peasant figures wear realistic breeches and vests, their white shirts soiled with earth.

You can discover fabulous *cartapesta* figures on the Via San Gregorio Armeno in Naples, throughout the town of Lecce, which lies on the heel of Italy's boot in Puglia, and in numerous smaller towns throughout the southern part of the peninsula.

PRICE POINTS

Generally, the less well-known the place and the artisan, the lower the price. I picked up a lovely angel in Lecce from a little-known artisan for about 50 euros. A stunning, medium-sized angel crafted by Ferrigno in Naples goes for about 400 euros, but is much more refined.

BELLISSIMA!

The Ferrigno brothers in Naples (page 165) are, hands down, the most important torchbearers of the southern Italian *cartapesta* tradition.

RELIGIOUS OBJECTS AND NATIVITY SCENES

Oggetti Religiosi e Presepe

A profoundly Roman Catholic region (after all, this is the home of the Vatican and the Pope), southern Italy's craftspeople turn out the world's largest selection of high-quality, artisanal religious items.

The streets surrounding the Vatican overflow with shops selling thousands of religious items, some for regular devotees and others strictly for the clergy. Whether you're in the market for a necklace with a cross or saint's pendant, a chalice, a devotional statuette, a nativity scene, a crozier, holy vestments, or a rosary, you won't find a better selection anywhere else in the world.

But crafting religious objects is not limited to this capital of Catholicism. Throughout southern Italy, craftspeople demonstrate a passion for nativity scenes and dramatic groupings of saints and angels crafted of wood, papier-mâché, terracotta, and more. The Via San Gregorio Armeno in Naples is one of my favorite craft streets in all of Italy, because of its infinite variety of saints, angels, peasants,

NAPOLI'S NOVELTIES

- **Presepe**: nativity figures made of terra-cotta and/or papier-mâché
- **Pastori**: stereotypical figures (peasants, politicians, farmers, bakers, and so on) made of terra-cotta and/or papier-mâché

farm animals, holy children, incredibly elaborate manger scenery, and grottoes piled with real rocks, fountains, and moss.

Naples—with its love of unrestrained funeralizing, the baroque, the macabre, and the melodramatic—is the home of extravagant nativity scenes. In the Middle Ages, elaborate religious groupings crafted of wood, terra-cotta, papier-mâché, and other materials began cropping up in the city's churches. Whether representing the birth or death of Christ, or any number of other well-known religious subjects, each one was more elaborate than the next. Guido Mazzoni's *Pietà*, created around 1500 in Naples's church of Monteoliveto (Piazza Monteoliveto), features eight life-sized terra-cotta figures with writhing bodies and grief-stricken expressions powerful enough to astonish even the MTV generation.

PRICE POINTS

It's not hard to break the bank once you get hooked on collecting *presepe* and *pastori*. Quality, handcrafted figures range from 80 to 450 euros, depending on the craftsmanship and size. Nativity sets and grottoes are almost always priced individually so that you can mix and match. Small accessories for these scenes go for as little as 1 or 2 euros each.

BELLISSIMA!

The town of Lecce (page 173) is a refreshing, off-the-beaten-track haven for people who want to shop for authentic *cartapesta* crafts outside the tourist mainstream.

THE LISTINGS

ABRUZZO

CASTELLI

Many of Castelli's master ceramicists cluster in the town's Villaggio Artigiano, a beautiful and evocative medieval quarter.

CERAMICS
Ceramiche

Ceramics Museum
Museo della Ceramica
0861/979398

This is a great place to start your foray into Castelli's ceramics history.

Ceramics School
Istituto Statale d'Arte per la Ceramica
0861/979126

Years ago, people learned the techniques of ceramic production and decoration in their family workshops but today, they are more likely to learn from the state art school in Castelli. The front stairs of the school are paved with—what else?—ceramic tiles.

Art e Decor Atelier Ceramico
Piazza Roma, 4
0861/979214

Since 1975, Nadia Maria Mancini has looked to the past glory of Castelli ceramics for her inspiration. She crafts lovely reproductions from the typical Orsini-Colonna vessels to fonts and astral decorations—the cool suns and stars with tranquil faces.

Raffaella Calvarese
Corso da San Rocco
0861/979541

Raffaella Calvarese achieves painterly effects in her dreamy landscapes and mythological scenes, deftly executed on plates and other wares.

Ceramiche Artistiche Censasorte
Via Grue, 1 (showroom)
Via Scesa del Borgo, 15 (workshop)
0861/979206

Antonio Mancini began his business as a restorer of antique pottery, and this understanding of historical models informs his crafting of modern pieces: plates, pharmacy jars, fonts, and tableware, all in historical Castelli styles.

Ceramiche Dina di Francesco
Corso da San Donato
0861/979383

When you walk into Dina di Francesco's beautiful showroom, you won't be surprised to learn that she worked as a decorator before changing careers and becoming one of Castelli's most interesting ceramic artists. Her eye for stylish ensembles is evident in her beautiful centerpieces for the table and plates with basketlike effects.

Ceramiche Mercante
Via Scesa del Borgo
0861/970652

This is the oldest continuously operating ceramics firm in Castelli, founded in 1840. Today, Lucia di Camaione and assistants turn out some of the more authentic reproductions of historical Castelli pieces.

L'Arte della Majolica
Villaggio Artigiano
0861/979551

Antonio di Luca completed a degree at Castelli's art school in the late 1960s, then set to work in the artisan village doing ceramics. His tea and coffee sets are among the nicest in town.

Maioliche d'Arte
Piazza Roma, 1
0861/970676

Giovanni Leonetti, born and bred in Castelli, has a good sense for the shapes that make the town's wares so distinctive: bulbous pots with big handles, deep soup tureens, and disklike flasks with multiple handles.

Maioliche Tradizionali Romao di Egidio
Via Scesa del Borgo
0861/970746

Along with his son and pupil, Graziano, Romao di Egidio crafts some of the best landscapes in town. The two have made it their task to study the antique fragments in Castelli's museum; their attention to detail is astounding.

Simonetti
Villaggio Artigiano
0861/979493
www.ceramichesimonetti.it

Simonetti is one of the larger operations in town and also one of the most traditional. The company was founded in the 1960s. The family renovated an old, abandoned pottery studio with old-fashioned kilns and wheels. Inspired by the ceiling of the church of San Donato, Giovanni Simonetti and company began producing *maiolica* bricks that can be used in architectural construction. I'd love to use these in my kitchen or bath!

Vecchia Bottega Maiolicara
Via del Giardino, 10
Via Fonte Vecchia, 20
0861/979003

In an evocative stone building with antique wooden doors, Vincenzo di Simone and his son Antonio have their work cut out for them—there are endless stacks of terra-cotta wares waiting to be painted. The family team crafts plates, tableware, and other ceramics in traditional Castelli colors and styles. They excel at reproducing the ornate wares of the eighteenth century.

BASILICATA

MATERA

Matera is an unforgettable treat for those adventurous enough to rent a car and tackle the mountains of Basilicata.

Matera consists of both an old and new city. The old town was formed not by building up but by digging out: its structures are a haphazard jumble of caves dug out of this soft, volcanic stone. The result is one of the most spectacular, curious sites you will ever see. In fact, the characteristic habitations, or *sassi* (literally, "rocks"), are recognized by UNESCO as part of the world's artistic patrimony.

A few craftspeople in the area use the characteristic volcanic stone known as *tufo* to create one-of-a-kind sculptures.

GENERAL CRAFTS

Il Bottegaccio
Via Madonna dell'Idris, 10
0835/311158
www.ilbottegaccio.it

The *sassi*—the mysterious rock habitations that make up Matera's old city—have long captivated Mario Daddiego. This local artisan has recreated the volcanic formations of Matera, both natural and man-made, in vast conglomerations of terra-cotta and papier-mâché.

Pietro Gurrado
Via Duomo, 3/5
0835/330447
www.pietrogurrado.com

Versatile sculptor Pietro Gurrado crafts ponderous, almost abstract figures of men and women from the *tufo*, the volcanic stone that characterizes the landscape of central Basilicata.

From terra-cotta, he creates fabulous little *fischietti* or *cuchi*, handheld whistles that make a loud chirping noise, which have been used by shepherds in southern Italy since ancient times. Also among his works are also impressive nativity scenes of papier-mâché. No matter the medium, his work is of exceptional quality and he often crosses the line into fine art.

CALABRIA

SQUILLACE

CERAMICS
Ceramiche

Bottega artigiana "La Tarracotta"
Corso Pepe
0961/912526

Self-taught, Nicola Aiello excels in the traditional *graffito* technique of Squillace but also creates some stunning all-black wares reminiscent of ancient Greek pottery.

Bottega d'arte "Il Tornio"
Viale Fuori le Porte
0961912440
www.ceramicheiltornio.com

Beatrice Russomanno and Claudio Panaia have set up a small work area in their Squillace showroom where you can watch them incise incredibly detailed decorative patterns into jars, pots, and plates. In addition, they craft reproductions of ancient Greek-style, black-figure pottery, which was widely made throughout southern Italy in ancient times.

Cooperativa Ceramisti Vasai "S. Agazio"
Via Rhodio
0961/912678

This artisan co-op was founded in 1978 by graduates of the state art institute of Squillace. One of the specialties of this group of enthusiastic potters is the reproduction of authentic museum pieces representative of Squillace's ceramic history. Their shop is full of gorgeous red and white plates that have an unmistakable air of antiquity.

Ideart Bottega Artigiana
Via Pepe
333/3166257

Antonio Commodaro traces his ancestry to Tonino Commodaro, mentioned in a 1756 document as an important ceramicist in Squillace. Commodaro honors his roots by crafting lovely incised wares typical of the area but also lets his creativity loose by creating stunning contemporary pieces splashed with color.

CAMPANIA

AMALFI

LIMONCELLO AND LEMON PRODUCTS
Limoncello

Andrea Pansa
Piazza Duomo, 40
089/871065

Enjoy tangy lemon tarts while you view the beautiful ceramic dome of Amalfi cathedral shining in the sun. This is a fourth-generation *pasticceria* that prides itself on some of the best homemade *limoncello* in Amalfi. Try some!

PAPER
Carta

Paper Museum
Museo della Carta
Via delle Cartiere, 23
089/8304561
www.museodellacarta.it

The paper museum is housed in one of Amalfi's antique paper mills.

Cartiere Amatruda
Via delle Cartiere, 100
089/871315
www.amatruda.it

This is one of Amalfi's most venerable paper institutions, occupying an old, evocative building and retaining many of its antique, hand-operated paper presses. Rosa Amatruda, with the help of her daughter, is one of the valley's only surviving torchbearers of this old tradition. This is some of the most elegant stationery I've seen outside of Florence!

Cartiere Cavaliere
Via del Giudice, 2
089/871954

Vita Cavaliere has recently taken the reins of this historic paper-making shop from her late father, Antonio. Their signature paper with pressed flower petals is stunning.

CAPRI

The island of Capri—so seductive and magical in its natural beauty—is unfortunately

filled with many tourist traps, including several exorbitantly priced ones. The most traditional crafts of the island, as well as its best values, include limoncello and hand-made leather sandals.

SANDALS
Sandali

L'Arte del Sandalo Caprese
Via Giuseppe Orlandi, 75, Anacapri
081/8373583

In his Anacapri shop, Antonio Viva offers a lower-cost alternative to Canfora (below). You can buy a simple, off-the-shelf pair of handmade sandals for just 30 euros, or commission Antonio to make a specially designed pair for up to several hundred euros. A personalized souvenir!

Canfora
Via Camerelle, 3
081/8370487
www.canfora.com

Sofia Loren, Jackie Kennedy, and many other fashionable ladies have made a stop at the humble workshop of Amadeo Canfora to pick up a pair of handmade sandals with colors and styles that seem to capture the soul of Capri. Colorful leather with sea-inspired motifs, from shells to starfish, embellish these beautiful sandals. Today Amadeo's daughters carry on the legacy of their father, updating the styles but still making everything the old-fashioned way. This shop is a breath of fresh air on a street crammed with luxury brands and tourist kitsch. A unique pair will set you back around 200 euros.

NAPLES *NAPOLI*

Italians have a wonderful expression—"*Che dramma napoletano!*" ("What a Neopolitan drama!")—and I can think of no other word that's more perfect than "drama" to sum up this city.

On my last trip to Naples, I was browsing through dozens of papier-mâché angels in a shop on the Via San Gregorio Armeno when I was abruptly ushered out the door by the insistent owner. Suddenly, all the shop owners on the street were closing their doors and battening down the hatches. It was too early for the sacred lunch hour, and I couldn't figure out why everything had just come to a screeching halt.

Then I saw it: hundreds of people walking solemnly and silently down the street toward me in a procession, carrying huge palm leaves and outlandish bouquets of flowers. Behind the first wave of people, some of them children dressed in white, came an old-fashioned, open hearse with its engines off, coasting down the cobblestone hill. Mountains of gaudy flowers surrounded the casket and a separate flatbed vehicle followed, bearing more floral arrangements and sprays of palm fronds. Elderly women and men stretched their arms out to touch the passing vehicles, and many of them wailed openly, lifting their arms in supplication and fluttering white handkerchiefs before their faces. Shop owners and browsers made way for the crowd, crossing themselves and muttering prayers as the group progressed. More funeral-goers passed. As the group finally turned the corner at the bottom of the hill, it was as if someone flipped a light switch, and as suddenly as it stopped, the bustling commercial activity resumed as if nothing had happened.

This is Naples, a city of pure spectacle. I love it more than any other city in Italy. My Milanese friends laugh and tell me I'm crazy, but I'm nuts about Naples. Maybe it's my Southern upbringing, my love of the sea, or my appreciation of dark humor that made me feel so at home here, but whatever the reason, I relish Naples's chaos, its rhythm, and its fascinating nooks and crannies.

Nearly anyone who's ever visited Naples has a story, and some of them, unfortunately, contribute to its reputation as a city full of shady characters and mafia types. Still, pickpockets are ever on the watch for tourists, so it's a good idea to keep your money on your body, stay aware, and duck into a crowded street or store if you feel you've aroused someone's curiosity. Above all, don't let Hollywood stereotypes dampen your enjoyment of this wonderful city, which embodies all the sophistication, originality, and unbridled exuberance of Italian culture.

NAPLES'S CRAFT NEIGHBORHOODS

If you only have time to see one craft neighborhood, I recommend the Via San Gregorio Armeno and the amazing "doll hospital," the Ospedale delle Bambole, down the street at Via San Biagio dei Librai.

Antiques restorers: Via Martucci

Baskets and wicker: Vicolo del Fico

Cameos: Torre del Greco, on the outskirts of town

Capodimonte porcelain: Capodimonte, on the outskirts of town

Copper and Wrought Iron: Rua Catalana, Via Basile, Vico Graziella

Jewelry: Via San Biagio dei Librai

Nativity and religious figures: Via San Gregorio Armeno, Via San Biagio dei Librai

CERAMICS
Ceramiche

Bottega di Ceramiche
Via Carlo Poerio, 40
081/7642626

Most of the ceramics in this chic boutique
hail from Caltagirone in Sicily (see Chapter
5), but they're all high quality, so if you can't
get to Sicily this time, this is where to buy.
They also carry locally crafted nativity scenes.

Ceramics Museum
Museo di Capodimonte
Via Miano, 1
081/7499111

In addition to the great Farnese collection
of European paintings, the Capodimonte
museum holds an important collection of
porcelain from Naples's royal heyday.

Capodimonte Fullin Mollica
Via G. Amato, 10/12
Casoria (outside Naples)
081/7587648

This is one of the higher-quality producers
of Capodimonte, specializing in little bouquets and sprays of pastel flowers, each bud
individually painted by hand. This company
does a healthy business in the wholesale trade.

DEA Capodimonte
Via de Filippo, 44, Calvizzano
081/7121714
www.deacapodimonte.com

Giovanni di Martino and company run a
relatively large enterprise on the outskirts
of Naples, but still insist on handmade
techniques and high quality in their work.
They focus on the hallmarks of Capodimonte
style—flowers, baskets, chandeliers, and
Christmas ornaments. They also have a
showroom in Florence (see Chapter 3).

DOLLS
Bambole

Ospedale delle Bambole
Via San Biagio dei Librai, 81
081/203067
www.ospedaledellebambole.it

It's just what it says: a hospital for dolls,
where antique, broken, or worn-out dolls
in wood, wax, terra-cotta, and papier-mâché
are brought back to life by the loving hands
of Gigi and Tiziana, founders of this enterprise. This is a magical wonderland of dolls
and doll parts, great for gawking and browsing. Their Website is cute.

NATIVITY SCENES AND PASTORAL FIGURES
Presepe e Pastori

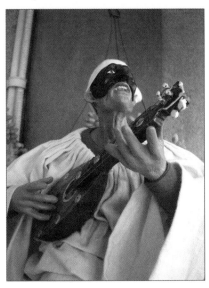

Annunziata Mercogliano
Via San Gregorio Armeno, 56
081/5523352

Annunziata Mercogliano and company craft
intricate scenes of wood, tree bark, and moss,
all of which can be finished off with dramatic
lighting. Fill them up with any combination
of peasants or shepherds, or, perhaps, a
Madonna con bambino.

Concetta Fusco
Via San Gregorio Armeno, 7
081/5516221

Stop in Concetta Fusco's tiny shop to see,
firsthand, how the terra-cotta heads of
presepe figures are crafted.

Ferrigno
Via San Gregorio Armeno, 8
081/5523148
www.arteferrigno.it

There's no comparison between the work of Giuseppe and Marco Ferrigno, and the artisans on the street. Since 1836, the family has created incredible lunging angels, elegant saints, and pastoral figures—all with stunning realism and the highest quality, and based on seventeenth-century models. They incorporate silk fabrics and wooden limbs in their best works. Prices range from about 20 euros for a small angel with a terra-cotta body, up to 300 or 400 euros for a large one crafted in wood and silk and hand-painted, suitable for the top of a Christmas tree.

Fulvio Forte
Via San Gregorio Armeno, 26
081/210302

Fulvio Forte can turn your dreams into reality. Just come in with an idea and he will create a custom-made nativity or pastoral scene according to your specifications. The shop has some nice angels and humorous peasant figures.

Gramendola
Via San Gregorio Armeno, 3 and 51
081/4206034
www.presepinapoletani.it

Matteo Prencipe and assistants create some of the most elaborate scenes on the street: houses on hills, horses pulling wagons, children doing a village dance, lovers in an embrace, people roasting meat on a spit, and more. This is one of the higher-quality producers.

Nativity Museum
Museo Nazionale di San Martino
Largo di San Martino, 5
081/5781769

With breathtaking views over the bay of Naples, this former monastery, now a museum, houses an impressive collection of Neopolitan *presepe*, some several hundred years old.

MASKS
Maschere

Nel Regno di Pulcinella
Vico San Domenico Maggiore, 9
081/5514171

The name of this store means "in the kingdom of Pulcinella" and refers to the classic comic character from the seventeenth-century theater troupe, the Commedia dell'Arte. The company makes impressive papier-mâché masks based on seventeenth-century forms.

VIOLINS
Violini

Liuteria Calace
Via San Domenico Maggiore, 9
081/5515983
www.calace.it

This old-fashioned violinmaker, or *liutaio*, crafts and restores violins, violas, mandolins, lutes, and other stringed instruments. You don't often find this quality outside of Cremona, Stradivarius's hometown (see Chapter 2).

WROUGHT IRON
Ferro Battuto

Pianese
Via Arco Mirelli
081/665561

From this tiny hole in the wall, beautiful works of forged iron come spilling forth onto the narrow street. Beds, coat racks, tables, lamps, and more clutter the space, as artisans forge iron from their hot workshop in the back.

SORRENTO

The specialty in Sorrento is *intarsia*, also known as marquetry or inlaid wood. In this technique, different woods—including orange, olive, and walnut—are painstakingly arranged into intricate surface patterns. Many shops carrying cheap trinkets line the streets around the Piazza Tasso; a couple along the via degli Aranci are among the best in town.

INLAID WOOD
Intarsia

Donato e Maresca
Via degli Aranci, 95
818/784497
www.donatoemaresca.com

In their workshop located in Piano di
Sorrento, Donato e Maresca employs a couple
of dozen craftspeople turning out furniture
and smaller masterpieces of intarsia. Although
they are one of the larger outfits, the craftsmanship and attention to detail is apparent,
particularly in their lovely chess sets.

Stinga Intars
Via degli Aranci, 102
via L. De Maio, 16
818/781130
www.stingatarsia.com

Two brothers, Franco and Roberto Stinga,
carry on the third generation of this family-
based artisanal business that stands apart
from the rest. Some of their inlaid furniture
is drop-dead gorgeous, but music boxes,
jewelry boxes, and Christmas ornaments
make more portable gifts for loved ones
back home.

TORRE DEL GRECO

CORAL AND CAMEO JEWELRY
Camei e Gioielli di Corallo

Ascione
Via Romano, 6
081/8811165
www.ascione.it

This is the oldest and one of the most
renowned of Torre del Greco's coral artisans;
it opened its doors in 1855. In addition to
cameos and coral, their elegant showroom
displays gorgeous jewelry in mother-of-pearl
and other stones. They also run a museum
dedicated to the history of coral-working.

Basilio Liverino
Via Montedoro, 61
0039 081 8811225
www.liverino.it

This is Torre del Greco's premier producer of
coral jewelry. Basilio Liverino heads up the
local school for cameo and coral artisans and
has authored a book about the tradition. The
company primarily caters to the trade, but
will sell major pieces to individuals (it's best to
make an appointment). Liverino also boasts
perhaps the world's most important private
collection of antique coral and cameo jewelry.
He even traveled to Sotheby's in London to
buy back a necklace he had made years before!

Giovanni Apa
Via E. De Nicola, 1
081/8811155
www.giovanniapa.com

Since 1848, the Apa family has been crafting
exquisite tiny masterpieces of shell, coral,

and agate. A small museum chronicles the history of this enterprise, with choice cameos and pieces of carved coral lovingly displayed in dramatically lit cases. A simple cameo starts at about 100 euro, but you can pay up to tens of thousands for special collectors' items whose beauty will make your jaw drop.

Vincenzo Garofalo
Via Sorrentino, 48
081/8813221
www.vingar.it

Vincenzo Garofalo has made a name for himself by creating stunning nativity scenes made from precious stones, including coral, turquoise, and ivory. His work has landed in several major private collections, including that of the Vatican.

VIETRI SUL MARE

CERAMICS
Ceramiche

Ceramica Artistica Falcone
Corso Umberto, 95
089/210046

Giovanni Falcone began this enterprise in 1940 and his sons, Carmine and Antonio, continue the family business. Their showroom on the Corso Umberto displays painted panels, vases, tableware, and other creations crafted in their workshop on the Via Mazzini, 89.

Ceramica CE.AR.
Piazza Matteotti, 172
089/211888

Siani Bruno and company specialize in the fabulous floor and wall tiles I love so much in Vietri—big, shiny pieces of ceramic with beautiful ocean scenes and bird life painted across them as if on a huge canvas. They also produce some outstanding mosaic works for floors and tables.

Ceramics Museum
Museo della Ceramica
Torretta di Villa Guarigla
089/211835

A great overview of ceramics production in Vietri sul Mare from the seventeenth century to today.

Ceramiche Pinto
Corso Umberto I, 21
089/210271
www.pintoceramica.it

The Pinto family is one of Vietri's oldest continuously operating ceramics clans, tracing their family art back to the seventeenth century. Today, Rosaura Pinto and her assistants uphold the tradition of Vietri ceramics: large pots, wall and floor tiles, and tableware, all with the traditional bright colors of this coastal gem.

Ceramica Vietri Scotto
Lungofiume Bonea, 56
089/210197
www.vietriscotto.it

The forte of Daria Scotto is stunning floor and wall ensembles that imitate designs from antiquity. From bold interlacing motifs to fish and floral patterns, the tiles are pieced together to form a cohesive design for floor and wall. If you're looking to turn your bathroom into something that looks like it belongs in a luxurious villa of ancient Rome, this is the place.

Kéramos
Via Giuseppe Pellegrino, 94
089/212573

Kéramos is a cool art gallery with changing exhibits featuring Vietri sul Mare's most innovative ceramics artists. This is where the locals break from churning out traditional wares and showcase the best and most experimental of their works, pushing the envelope of ceramic arts. Come here for a breath of fresh air when you've tired of the same old thing.

Solimene
Via Madonna degli Angeli, 7
089/210243
www.solimene.com

This is one of Vietri sul Mare's largest and most famous outfits, but despite the fact that about 40 people work here, Vincenzo

Solimene still insists on top-quality artisanship and the use of handmade techniques. The Solimene factory is an astonishing creation of ceramic architecture that resembles a gigantic beehive encrusted with mosaic. The architect Paolo Soleri designed this amazing building in 1951. Come here for fun dinnerware, decorative tiles, and more.

Vietritaly
Corso Umberto I, 45
089/211122
www.vietritaly.com

The Corso Umberto showroom of Vietritaly displays just a fraction of this large producer's gamut of ceramics. Their salmon-colored stucco factory outside of Vietri manufactures several lines of tableware, interior décor, giftware, and architectural tile. The contemporary designs feature animals, fruit, and flowers.

L A Z I O

R O M E *R O M A*

Nowhere on earth do past and present meld so perfectly as in Rome, and it's why they call this the Eternal City. Here, Roman ruins, baroque churches, ear-splitting mopeds, and self-righteous politicians coexist in relative harmony.

In Rome, the impressiveness and large scale of its monuments, statues, and other public works of art almost completely overshadow the smaller, less obvious crafts of wrought iron, glass, ceramics, and papier-mâché. Still, the most traditional of the city's crafts—religious objects and marble working—are also uniquely Roman. This is the heart of the Roman Catholic world, and shops spill over with rosaries, ex-votos, statues of saints, and a million other devotional objects. Marble crafters continue the traditions of their ancestors, creating stunning inlaid furniture, pavements, and decorative items that would be at home in any ancient Roman villa.

As in Florence, artisans of Rome historically lived and worked in the lower-class neighborhoods on the southern bank of the river. The Trastevere section of town has housed shoemakers, glass artists, sculptors, marble crafters, and other tradespeople since ancient Roman times. Today, the neighborhood retains the flavor of an old working-class neighborhood, with narrow alleys, pubs, homey *ristoranti*, and hole-in-the-wall workshops open to the public. It's far from Armani and Gucci, and its spaces are filled with art galleries, *caffès*, and yoga studios. This is a great place to shop for crafts, but be sure to check out shops and studios in other sections of town.

GENERAL CRAFTS

Museo delle Arti e Tradizioni Popolari
Piazza Marconi, 8/10
06/5926148
www.popolari.arti.beniculturali.it

This museum of Italian tradition has to be one of my favorite institutions on earth, dedicated to local craft from the Alps to the islands. An incongruous sight—folkloristic Sicilian horse carts displayed within a Fascist, Mussolini-era state building—greets you in the entry of this national museum on the outskirts of Rome. The interior galleries display everything from Tuscan ceramics to Sardinian costumes, regional nativity scenes, and many more fascinating objects. A must-see for fans of Italian craft traditions!

CRAFT NEIGHBORHOODS OF ROME

Antiques: Via del Governo Vecchio

Marble Crafts: Via dei Coronari, area between the Tevere and Piazza Navona

Unique Handmade Items: Trastevere

Religious Objects: The shops are clustered around the Vatican.

Straw and Wicker: Via dei Sediari

CERAMICS
Ceramiche

Maffetone Design
Via di Panico, 26
06/6832754

In their Tivoli workshop, ceramic artisans craft stunning decorative tiles based on designs from the ancient world. Many of these works are inlaid into wrought iron and wooden furniture, with spectacular effects. If you're looking for something unique, this is it. Their Rome shop is located where the Via di Panico meets the piazza dei Coronari.

GLASS
Vetro

Ars Vitri
Via San Girolamo della Carità, 67
06/6865984
www.arsvitri.it

In addition to lovely modern stained glass windows, Andrea Ribustini crafts glass plates, light fixtures, and pretty jewelry combining blown glass and metal.

Rita Rivelli
Via di Santa Cecilia 15 and 30
06/5812927
www.formesnc.it

Rita Rivelli is a master stained glass artist entrusted with glass restoration for some of Italy's most renowned historical monuments. Remarkably, she also finds time to run a refreshingly creative glass art studio along the nearby via Peretti, 29/b. Her restoration studio stands across from the façade of the church of Santa Cecilia di Trastevere.

HATS
Cappelli

Antica Cappelleria
Via degli Scipioni, 46
06/39725679
www.antica-cappelleria.it

Little has changed in this millinery since it opened its doors in 1936, the last artisan hat shop left in Rome. Today, Patrizia Fabri and her assistants craft each hat by hand, using the wooden hat forms stacked haphardardly around this old-fashioned studio. Each hat is exquisitely made on site, and will set you back around 100 euros.

JEWELRY
Gioielli

Negri
Via Campo Marzio, 36.
06/6871192
www.titonegri.it

On several occasions I've had the pleasure of watching Tito Livio Negri and his two assistants crafting his so-called "microsculptures"—a great way to describe the little jewels he lovingly creates, all by hand, in his closet-sized studio a stone's throw from the Italian Parliament building. Fluid and animal forms dominate his production, each one totally unique. At a minimum, spend a few minutes gazing at the lovely shop window display.

Quattrocolo
Via della Scrofa, 54
06/68801367
www.quattrocolo.com

If you're looking for an authentic piece of jewelry from the glory days of ancient Rome, this antique jewelry specialist can outfit you with an absolutely exquisite bracelet or necklace with a two-thousand-year-old history. In addition to their antiquities business, Quattrocolo's specialty is restoring nineteenth-century handcrafted jewelry made with miniscule mosaics representing ancient monuments of Rome. You have to see it to believe it; though prices are high, the quality is nothing less than breathtaking.

MARBLE CRAFTS
Marmo

Marmi Line Gifts
Via della Lungaretta, 90/90a
06/5814860

It is impossible not to reach out and touch the works so neatly displayed in this marble shop. In addition to life-size sculptures, they craft hundreds of small items, such as exquisite eggs, fruits, clocks, jewelry, and other decorative objects, all made of highly polished marble. Marmi Line (see below) has begun expanding its business of small marble objects, quickly opening several boutiques around Rome that specialize in these small treasures that are more portable than the company's architectural marble.

Franco
Via di Panico, 40
06/68802506
Via dei Coronari, 118
06/6833644
www.francoermarmista.com

With two showrooms on the same street, Franco flaunts his jaw-dropping mastery of marble. The shops glow with gorgeous mantelpieces, life-size reproductions of ancient sculpture, and much, much more.

Marmi Line
Via dei Coronari, 113
06/6893795
Viale Tor di Quinto, 171
06/33213833
www.marmiline.com

Stone and marble are the raw materials that Marmi Line artisans transform into works of art. They specialize in large-scale reproductions of ancient works of art, including busts, columns, bases, vases, fountains, and more.

RELIGIOUS OBJECTS
Oggetti Religiosi

Artechiesa
Borgo Vittorio, 64
06/68135145

Artechiesa makes among the highest-quality liturgical chalices in metal, as well as ecclesiastical ornaments, fabric for making vestments, and more.

Domus Artis
Via della Conciliazione, 48
06/6889284I
www.domusartis.net

Among the mass-produced items in this very slickly merchandized store are some nice handmade nativities and wooden statues.

Garey Lelli
Piazza Farnese, 104
06/6880189O

Lelli specializes in able reproductions of medieval and Renaissance icons, many gilded and bejeweled. The wooden angels and crucifixes are also well done.

Savelli
Piazza Pio XII, I/2
06/68806383
www.savellireligious.com

Displayed alongside high-priced kitsch for tourists are some lovely hand-carved statues and nativities. Next to the cash registers, you can fill out a request to have your purchase blessed by the Pope himself. Just drop your form in the box, and allow a few weeks turnaround time. If you're headed into Saint Peter's square, this shop is located at the top of the hill, on the right.

Mango
Via del Mascherino, 15
06/68308575
www.mangoreligious.com

Walking into this shop is like walking into a treasure chest. It glows with fabulous silver and gold objects, jewelry, chalices, crosses, and gorgeous jewel-studded crowns for statues of saints. All the jewelry and rosaries are designed by the shop's owner, Paola Mango, and her family.

Mar Statue Sacre
Borgo Vittorio, 61
06/6864554
www.marstatue.it

If you're in the market for life-size statues of Jesus, Mary, and the saints, you just hit the jackpot. This fascinating array of liturgical items includes life-size crucifixes; statues in gesso, wood, and plastic with crystal eyes; chalices; and beads for making your own rosaries. The shop has been in business since the early 1800s, and has been patronized by Pope John Paul II, Mother Teresa, and other religious big-whigs!

M O L I S E

S C A P O L I

BAGPIPES
Zampogne

Museo della Zampogna
Piazza Caduti in Guerra
0865/954002
www.zampogna.org

This is a small but impressive museum collection of *zampogne* from around the world.

Guido Iannetta
Via Ponte, 7
0865/954515

In addition to his day job, working as a park ranger in the nearby Parco Nazionale d'Abruzzo, Guido Iannetta crafts high-quality bagpipes. He also makes the *piffero*, an oboe-like instrument traditionally played along with the bagpipe. He plays in a local folk group known as Le Mainarde.

Luigi Ricci
Via Fontecostanza

Ricci has been crafting bagpipes in Scapoli for 20 years and is active in promoting the annual international bagpipe festival. (See Calendar of Events, page 215.)

P U G L I A

G R O T T A G L I E

Most of Grottaglie's ceramic artisans cluster around the Episcopio castle, along the Via Crispi, but be sure to venture off the main drag to discover some lesser-known shops and haunts of this sun-soaked town.

CERAMICS
Ceramiche

Ceramics Museum
Museo dell'Arte Figulina e delle Maioliche
Via Martiri d'Ungheria
099/5620222
www.museogrottaglie.it

Grottaglie's ceramics museum occupies what used to be the stables of the Castello Episcopio, a fourteenth-century feudal castle that dominates the landscape of Grottaglie. Its airy, vaulted spaces now house hundreds of pieces of pottery, attesting to a tradition that goes as far back as the ancient Greeks.

Ceramiche Artigianali Nicola Bonfrate
Via Crispi, 95
099/5661555
www.bonfrate.com

Nicola Bonfrate's workshop is located in a rustic building dating back to the 1700s. His family has operated as a ceramics shop since 1850. Bonfrate's specialty is geometric decoration incised on plates, jars, and vases, which is then painted in bright colors. The technique is an old, local one, and Bonfrate is one of the only artisans of Grottaglie carrying on this tradition.

Ceramiche Antonio La Grotta
Via Leone XIII, 9
099/5661632
www.ceramichelagrotta.com

Antonio La Grotta is a fourth-generation ceramicist of Grottaglie and produces a fine selection of tableware, tiles, decorative plates, and other goodies. He also organizes ceramics courses for those who want to experience this town's traditions in action.

La Ceramica Vincenzo Del Monaco
Via Sofia, 2/4
099/5661023

This Pugliese artisan traces his ceramic roots all the way back to 1416, when his ancestor, Leonardo del Monaco, is mentioned in local records. Today, Giuseppe del Monaco carries on this tradition in his home and workshop, a modest building off one of Grottaglie's side streets. The del Monacos make some of the best *sruli*, or pitchers, in Grottaglie.

Ceramiche "Gaetano Fasano" di Francesco Fasano
Via Caravaggio, 8
099/5665092

Francesco Fasano's passion is crafting gigantic terra-cotta pots that capture the spirit of the ancient Greek vessels found in great numbers in Grottaglie. These human-sized vessels are coated in a shiny, red-orange glaze that makes a stunning contrast with Grottaglie's all-white buildings in the intense southern sunlight.

La Ceramica L'Assainato
Via Crispi, 12
099/5622510

Francesco L'Assainato's passion lies in creating small objects, especially nativity figures and lovely *acquasantieri*, or basins for holy water. Along with his daughter, Simona, he also creates nice sets of tableware.

Studio 2DN
Via Caravaggio, 23
099/5622787

Luigi di Palma and Giacomo D'Elia are undoubtedly Grottaglie's most innovative ceramics artists. Throwing the past to the wind, they've moved ceramics into the realm of fine art by crafting unique sculptural forms, textural panels, and abstract forms.

Ceramiche Giuseppe Patronelli
Via Crispi, 21/23
099/5628139

Giuseppe Patronelli is a third-generation ceramicist who works with his brother and sister in his shop, a restored mill on the Via Crispi. Giuseppe has won Grottaglie's annual competition for nativity figures (see Calendar of Events, page 202).

LECCE

PAPIER-MÂCHÉ
Cartapesta

Carmen Rampino
Piazzetta Riccardi, 6
0832/331070

From Carmen Rampino's shop window in the historical center of Lecce, angels, saints, dolls, and peasants peer out onto the sidewalk. These fabulous creations of papier-mâché seem to sum up the baroque spirit at its best: voluptuous, billowing forms, bright colors, and dramatic poses. The shop is located across the street from the equally baroque church of Santa Croce.

I Messapi
Via Umberto I, 20/a
0832/246469
www.imessapi.it

Costantino Piemontese creates and restores a whole host of shepherds, peasants, saints, angels, dolls, and more. The name of the shop, I Messapi, refers to the ancient Greeks who made Lecce a Greek colony more than 2,000 years ago.

La Casa dell'Artigianato Leccese
Via Matteotti, 20
0832/306604
www.artigianatoleccese.com

Around the corner from Carmen Rampino (see left), Antonio De Rinaldis, Maria Arcona Ratta, and their assistants craft a wide range of angels, saints, nativity figures, dolls, and more in this tidy, well-organized shop.

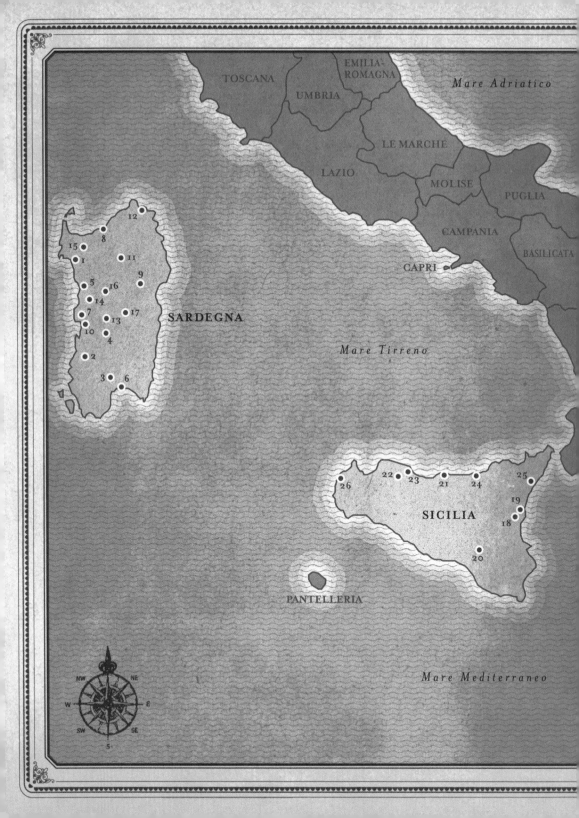

TOSCANA

EMILIA-ROMAGNA

UMBRIA

Mare Adriatico

LE MARCHE

LAZIO

MOLISE

PUGLIA

CAMPANIA

CAPRI

BASILICATA

12

8

15

1

11

5

16

9

14

7

13

17

10

4

2

3

6

SARDEGNA

Mare Tirreno

26

22

23

21

24

25

19

18

SICILIA

20

PANTELLERIA

NW   NE

W   E

SW   SE

S

Mare Mediterraneo

Chapter 5

THE ISLANDS

SARDEGNA · SICILIA

A h, island time. I grew up on an island in the United States, and I guess it's in my blood, but there's nowhere else I'd rather be than on an island, with its quirky ways, leisurely pace, and ever-present sea. So when vacation time rolls around, I always think of my two favorite places: Sicily and Sardinia. I love both of these Italian islands equally, but they couldn't be more different than if they were on opposite sides of the globe.

Sicily is like an onion. As you peel back layers of time on Italy's largest island, you find traces of Phoenicians, Greeks, Romans, Arabs, Normans, and, of course, the Sicilians themselves. Each culture and each era has made its own distinctive mark on Sicilian culture. From baroque church facades pockmarked by bullet holes to crumbling ruins of ancient temples and horse-drawn carriages still rattling through the streets of Palermo, traces of this rich but turbulent history are everywhere in evidence.

Sardinia couldn't be more different. Sardinia is like a time capsule from the prehistoric world, an idyllic Arcadia that has passed unnoticed by modern civilization. Untouched by invaders, and untouched even by the Renaissance, its prehistoric culture continues to be a culture based on agriculture, handicrafts, and ways of life that transcend time. From sheep grazing in the scrub brush along rocky hills to a sea so transparent it doesn't seem real and women dressed in black crafting lace in the shadows of stucco homes, Sardinia is another world.

The craft traditions of these two islands are as diverse as their cultures. Sicily's ceramics are splashy, fun, and colorful, in the style of ancient Greek pottery, a testament to the multicultural history of this island. Sardinia's ceramicists, on the other hand, craft bulls, chickens, and sheep in a stunning minimalistic style that recalls prehistoric cave paintings and sculptures. Sicily's artisans craft marionettes depicting famous knights of Norman fairy tales, while women on Sardinia's northern coast weave colorful straw baskets.

SARDINIA

T he ancient culture of Sardinia—Italy's second-largest island—has left last-ing traces in its contemporary life. This rural island boasts some of Italy's most time-honored and diverse linguistic, artistic, and musical tradi-tions. Since Paleolithic times, people have worked the land, fished its emerald seas, and made music and crafts on this island of stunning beauty. The island has always been cut off from the rest of the world, far from the riches and civ-ilization of Renaissance Florence. Agriculture and crafts have characterized the island's way of life since prehistoric times—the *nuraghe* culture, which left tangible vestiges on the island in the way of round, stone buildings and other monolithic creations. The result is a craft tradition that is totally unique in Italy.

Manual labor is at the base of the society and economy in Sardinia. This island has been populated since the Stone Age and as an isolated society, its people developed their own language and culture. Traditional crafts, including embroidery, metalwork, ceramics, wrought iron, and woodworking, follow practices used since antiquity. No other region of Italy boasts so many different costumes of diverse colors and fabrics. Each village preserves it own ceremonial dress lavishly covered with lace, gold, embroi-dery, and gems, which you can see if you attend one of the many festivals on the island (see Calendar of Events, page 212). This love of ornament also extends to fabulously ornate gold filigree jewelry set with corals and pearls. Shawls, table linens, rugs, and other textiles with traditional designs decorate the rustic rural houses of the island. Today, musicians incorporate centuries-old melodies into jazz and rock, forever breathing life into ancient practices and reinventing the island's timeless culture.

Sardinians are masters of what art experts refer to as the "minor arts"—jewelry, metalworking, textiles, weaving—and they are arguably the world's finest. When it comes to objects on a human scale—household objects—Sardinian craftspeople are second to none.

Sardinia boasts arguably the richest handicraft tradition in Italy and, luckily, its natives know. The organization known as I.S.O.L.A. (Instituto Sardo Organ-izzazione Lavoro Artigiano) has even developed a trademark, which it stamps on the works produced by artisans hand-picked and judged to be among the island's best and most traditional. If you look at the bottom of a ceramic pot or basket, you'll see the trademark. Not all of the region's good artisans are part of the I.S.O.L.A., but it's a pretty good guide for weeding out the tourist junk from the real stuff.

THE TRADITIONS

BASKETS

Cestini

B asket weaving is an important Sardinian craft that is closely linked to textile production. Like the working of rugs and costumes, basket weaving has been predominantly a women's art over the centuries.

For centuries people have used woven baskets, mats, rugs, trays, and vessels of every sort for the practical tasks of gathering a harvest, scooping up fish, and transporting bread. They're placed on floors, chairs, and tables throughout sparse, tidy Sardinian homes.

But these items are far from plain straw pieces. Artisans weave rush, reeds, straw, willow, and just about any flexible vegetable material to craft these items. They also color the pieces with bright hues using natural plant dyes. Some baskets and other straw items use color in decorative ways to create star, stripe, or other decorative patterns.

The seaside town of Castelsardo, on Sardinia's northern coast, is a major center of basket production. But you'll have to convince yourself that you haven't just arrived in the great American southwest; these rustic baskets with their bright geometric patterns and animal forms always remind me of the beautiful woven wares created by the Apache and Navajo.

All through the town's streets and shops, you can watch artisans—mostly women—busy at work weaving bright pink, green, and blue straw into lovely patterns. My favorites are the large, slightly curved baskets used to transport breads, sweets, and fruits and vegetables. Today, these traditional staples of utilitarian domestic life have been transformed into luxurious items for home décor.

PRICE POINTS
Sardinian baskets rank among the more affordable of the island's crafts, ranging from 7 to 50 euros on average.

BELLISSIMA!
To watch basket weavers in action, visit the northern Sardinian town of Castelsardo (page 190).

CERAMICS

Ceramiche

The ceramic tradition of Sardinia couldn't be more different from those of the great centers of the Italian mainland—Faenza, and Deruta, for example—or even that of Sicily. Untouched by the classical spirit of the Renaissance, Sardinian ceramics boast the same indigenous forms that inspire the gold jewelry and textiles of the island. The stylized birds, deer, and decorative motifs seem closer to the art of prehistory or the ancient Near East rather than to the classical tradition of the Italian mainland.

One of the most striking characteristics of Sardinian ceramics is the use of natural colors. Historically, artisans colored ceramics with natural extracts from the island's indigenous plants, leaving the pieces to dry in the sun. Greens, browns, ochres, and other earth tones characterize the most traditional Sardinian ceramics. Instead of rich and colorful painting, the decoration comes in the whimsical forms of the vessels themselves: chickens, sheep, birds, cows, vegetal motifs, and geometric forms.

Major ceramics centers include Oristano and Assemini, near Sardinia's capital city of Cagliari. Just outside of Cagliari, Assemini constitutes a small center for ceramic artisans. Its most commonly produced wares are casseroles, plates, pitchers, bowls, and other utilitarian objects, as well as whimsical pieces based on animal forms.

PRICE POINTS
I picked up some unique pieces from the I.S.O.L.A. store in Nuoro for under 70 euros each.

BELLISSIMA!
Giampaolo Mameli (page 189) is my favorite Sardinian ceramicist, known for his animal forms inspired by prehistoric art.

CORK

Sughero

I n the arid landscape around Calangianus, bark is rudely stripped from the lower trunks of gnarled trees that blanket the hillsides. Driving through this area—covered by parched earth, the occasional olive tree, and thousands of cork trees stripped of their bark—is like traveling on another planet.

Calangianus is Sardinia's major cork production area and numerous industrialized cork producers churn out wine corks, *tappi*, in breathtaking numbers. A single *sugherificio* can produce up to 50,000 *tappi* per day, many destined for the great wine producers of Tuscany and Piemonte. A few artisans also carve the material into frames, boxes, and even tea sets and jars.

The processing of cork begins with stripping bark from the trees, a process that does not harm them. The bark is seasoned in vast outdoor vats for up to two years. Then the cork is boiled and disinfected, dried, cut, and packaged.

A lot of the cork wares sold throughout Sardinia are aimed for the tourist trade, stamped with cheap scenes of Sardinia or silly sayings in Italian. Outside of Calangianus, your best bet is to purchase something in cork from one of the island's five I.S.O.L.A. stores, which are in Cagliari, Nuoro, Olbia, Porto Cervo, and Sassari.

PRICE POINTS
Cork crafts are relatively inexpensive. For under 20 euros you can go home with a unique souvenir.

BELLISSIMA!
Sugherificio Ambrosino (page 190) will stretch the limits of your imagination about what can be crafted from cork.

JEWELRY
Gioielli

T hroughout history, Sardinia has been known as the "land of metal." Silver and gold are abundant, worked with precious stones, including gems of the sea, coral, and pearls. Traditional gold jewelry used to embellish traditional costumes, contemporary women's costume jewelry, and religious objects all are typically Sardinian. In ancient Sardinian culture, certain metals and gems were believed to hold magic powers.

Traditionally in Sardinia, the woman of the house wears a large, ornate pendant known as a *domino*, usually crafted of gold filigree and precious stones. The larger the *domino*, the more important her place in local society.

Today, Sardinian craftspeople use the techniques of filigree (*filigrana d'oro*), embossing, casting, and welding to create unique brooches, pins, earrings, necklaces, chains, rings, religious objects, amulets, and a thousand other creations. Traditionally, these ornate jewels adorned local costumes that varied widely from town to town.

Artisans craft jewelry all over the island, but a large number of jewelers are concentrated in Cagliari. Alghero is the center of coral jewelry.

PRICE POINTS
Prices for Sardinian jewelry are competitive with other high-quality, handmade jewelry elsewhere in Italy. I picked up a unique pair of gold earrings for about 70 euros.

BELLISSIMA!
Salvatore Giannottu (page 187) ranks among Alghero's most original designers of coral jewelry.

MUSICAL INSTRUMENTS

Strumenti Musicali

O ne of the most moving local traditions of Sardinia is its music. The haunting melodies—made with stringed and wind instruments with vocal accompaniment—instantly transport the listener to the past. Wind instruments are made from cane, gourds, and other types of local wood. Reeds of different thicknesses and holes spaced a certain way create different sounds. The flutelike instruments known in Sardinian language as the *launeddas* and the *benas*—both handcrafted from local cane—fill the air with an unearthly sonorous quality. A bronze sculpture dating from the eighth century B.C. depicts a *launeddas* player blowing on a flute much like those produced by today's Sardinian crafts-people. Music historians consider the *launeddas* one of the oldest musical instruments in the Mediterranean. Today, the techniques for creating this ancient instrument are closely guarded secrets.

PRICE POINTS

If you don't want to spend a couple hundred dollars for an authentic Sardinian wind instrument, you can pick up a CD for less than 20 euros.

BELLISSIMA!

The musical instruments museum in Tadasuni (page 195) offers one of the most fascinating collections of the island's musical heritage.

TEXTILES

Tessuti

U ntil recent times, sheep outnumbered people on Sardinia, so it's no wonder that wool products and textiles emerged as a key industry. For centuries, coarse sheep's wool has been hand-woven on ancient looms. Rugs, wall hangings, bed linens, church vestments, costumes, and even saddlebags for carrying the harvest on the back of a donkey have been made. The costumes of Sardinia are among the richest in the world, and each town boasts a different tradition, so textiles are a major craft here.

Traditionally, Sardinian women were the weavers. Each area of the island boasts its own unique patterns and techniques. Colors and dyes from the island's indigenous plants, flowers, barks, and colored earth make striking geometric designs and stylized animal motifs. One of the most remarkable techniques is pebble fabric (*tessitura a grani* in Italian or *pibiones* in the local Sardinian language), in which the fabric is woven in bold geometric patterns with a relief texture.

I had the great privilege of spending an afternoon in the home of an 88-year-old weaver in Samugheo. With the help of my Italian translator (the woman spoke only the Sardinian language), she explained how her grandmother taught her to use the old wooden hand loom when she was just five years old. She had been weaving ever since on the same antique loom. Sitting at her loom on an upstairs balcony open to the scrubby hillside, she moved her hands swiftly back and forth, feeding white woolen yarn from a large basket on the floor. I marveled at how fast and able her hands were, and how she effortlessly created geometric patterns as she went, only half paying attention as she recounted to me how only a few women in town still carried on this tradition. She said her niece collected the blankets, rugs, towels, and other household linens she crafted from home, to be sold at the local weavers' co-op or at the I.S.O.L.A. stores.

The story of this weaver is the story of so many women in Sardinia. They practice an ancient trade based in the home, which passed from mother to daughter through the generations. Their art was a practical necessity; they churned out household linens and, more importantly, saddlebags and pouches for collecting the harvest.

Today, there are large concentrations of weavers in Dorgali, near Nuoro; Ittiri and Nule, in the province of Sassari; and Samugheo, in the province of Oristano.

PRICE POINTS

Sardinian textiles can run upward of several hundred dollars, which is not surprising considering the time required to complete a rug or blanket with a complex pattern. A lovely pillow sham costs about 20 euros.

BELLISSIMA!

The I.S.O.L.A. stores (pages 188, 190, 191, 193) are the best places to buy authentic Sardinian textiles, since most of the artisans work from home and send in their goods to be sold.

THE LISTINGS

ALGHERO

CORAL JEWELRY
Gioielli di corallo

Laboratorio Orafo Costa
Via Gilbert Ferret, 96 and 100
079/974198

For nearly 40 years, the Costa family has been crafting understated, beautiful gold and coral jewelry from these small shops in old Alghero.

Salvatore Giannottu
Via Arduino, 65
079/977441

Salvatore Giannottu specializes in combining gold filigree and coral in strikingly ornate designs for brooches, necklaces, bracelets, earrings, and more. Currently he heads up the consortium of Alghero coral producers.

ARBUS

KNIVES
Coltelli

Knife Museum
Museo del Coltello Sardo
Via Roma, 15
070/9759220
www.museodelcoltello.it

The Sardinian knife—a foldable, pocketknife-style instrument—has a long history on this island. Traditionally, these knives were crafted with handles made from the horn of mountain goats that once inhabited the formidable mountains of central Sardinia. Today, the best places to shop for authentic Sardinian knives are the towns of Pattada and Santulussurgiù (pages 191-4), but stop in to see an impressive collection in this small knife museum, the work of local artisan Paolo Pusceddu.

ASSEMINI

CERAMICS
Ceramiche

Antonio Farci
Via Sardinia, 113
070/944545

Along with Giampaolo Mameli (page 189), Antonio Farci is one of my favorite ceramic artisans of Sardinia. He crafts wonderful, whimsical queens and kings with a medieval flavor (the pair I have in my guest bathroom are always a conversation piece). He also crafts stylized animals familiar to the agricultural lifestyle of Sardinia: chickens, sheep, cows, and more. Farci follows in the footsteps of his grandfather in pursuing this traditional vocation.

La Fantastica Bottega di Ignazia Tinti
Via Cagliari, 195
070/944900

Is it bread or ceramic? That's what everyone asks when they peruse the display of curiosities in Ignazia Tinti's studio. Her forte is reproducing—in clay—the local breads of Sardinia, which for centuries have been crafted into all sorts of forms, from leaves to animals, sheaves of wheat, flowers, shells, and more. Tinti immortalizes what is normally a transitory art made of flour and yeast.

Giovanni Deidda
Via Pola, 70a
070/944632

Giovanni Deidda follows a family ceramic tradition that dates back to the 1830s. His signature style focuses on a limited palate of white and terra-cotta, etched with sharply defined geometric patterns—stars, rosettes, circles—as well as repeating leaf patterns that capture the spirit of prehistoric Sardinia.

ATZARA

TEXTILES
Tessuti

Cooperativa Sa Fanuga
Corso Vittorio Emanuele II, 9
0784/65382

This rural village near the mountain center of Nuoro is known for its rich textile production. This weavers' co-op displays the production of the town's best textile artisans. Atzara is known for producing striplike rugs or runners decorated with some of Sardinia's more delicate, ornate rug designs, in soft colors.

BOSA

JEWELRY
Gioielli

Laboratorio Orafo
Corso Vittorio Emanuele II, 84
0785/373148

Gold filigree jewelry inspired by the traditional designs of Sardinia make up the bulk of Giorgio Vadilonga's work. I love his cuff links that resemble little pointed hats studded with coral.

CAGLIARI

GENERAL CRAFTS

Archeological Museum
Museo Archeologico Nazionale
Piazza Arsenale
070/655911

This is a fascinating collection of objects from prehistoric to medieval times and provides proof that today's artisans draw from a primordial creative force that still pervades Sardinia.

I.S.O.L.A.
Via Bacaredda, 176/178
070/492756

This is one-stop shopping for the island's best crafts from the official organization that screens and promotes the island's most traditional and high-quality artisans.

CERAMICS
Ceramiche

Emilia Palomba
Via Abruzzi, 15
070/285255
www.emiliapalomba.com

Emilia Palomba is one of Cagliari's more innovative ceramicists, inventing a style based on terra-cotta wares dipped in gold. From whimsical porcupines with gold quills

to star-shaped frames for mirrors, Palomba infuses the ancient colors and techniques of Sardinian ceramics with a contemporary flair.

Giampaolo Mameli Ceramiche
Via Decimo, 107, San Sperate
070/9600411
www.giampaolomameli.com

Mameli is probably my favorite Sardinian ceramicist. His stylized animals—especially the three-legged bulls that look like they could be pulled straight from the ground of a prehistoric archeological dig—are to die for. I have two of them prominently displayed in my living room. His studio is located outside of Cagliari, but you can find his works at any of the I.S.O.L.A. shops on the island, as well as at the Tanka Village resort on the outskirts of Cagliari.

Raku di M. Cristina di Martino
Scalette Santa Teresa, 2
070/653989

Raku—the ceramic technique that renders a fine, crackled appearance to the glaze—forms the basis for Cristina di Martino's ceramic pots and fabulous doves, flamingos, and herons, all birds native to Sardinia's coastal wetlands.

JEWELRY
Gioielli

Bruno Busonera
Via Eleonora d'Arborea, 8
347/6527481

Bruno Busonera excels in creating reproductions of the antique filigree traditional in Sardinia. Giant brooches with lacelike, intricate designs are the stars of his collection, along with ornate rosaries incorporating silver, coral, pearls, and other precious stones.

L'Orafo del Corso
Corso Vittorio Emanuele II, 353
070/670329

Fancy, ornate gold filigree jewelry embedded with coral, pearls, and cameos comprise the bulk of Bruno de Agostini's production in this workshop in central Cagliari.

Oro Sardinia
Corso Vittorio Emanuele II, 109
070/659714

Gold filigree jewelry in highly ornate forms is the specialty of Giuseppe Lilliu and his assistants. His widespread use of pearls makes a striking contrast with the delicate gold filigree.

Paola Asquer
Via Sidney Sonnino, 30
340/2421811
www.bijouxasquer.it

Paola Asquer follows in her father's footsteps in this artisanal jewelry enterprise in the center of Cagliari. Her specialty is fine hammered gold with coral accents, many in vegetal and fruit forms. Earrings in the form of grape leaves, a brooch with a cluster of grapes, and heart-shaped pendants are lovely, unique pieces.

WROUGHT IRON
Ferro battuto

La Nuova Fucina
Via dei Carroz, 10
070/503707
www.lanuovafucina.it

Franco Fontanarosa crafts all the usual suspects of an Italian wrought iron shop, but one specialty sets him apart from his mainland colleagues: small iron statuettes reproducing the tiny pagan gods crafted by the prehistoric nuraghic culture that inhabited Sardinia. The little figures with scary masks, swords, and shields speak to us across the millennia as objects of mystery and power.

CALANGIANUS

CORK
Sughero

Sugherificio Ambrosino
Via Tre Monti, 8
079/660354

This *sugherificio* prides itself on creating varied and highly specialized corks for liqueurs, sparkling wines, and fine red wines.

CASTELSARDO

CERAMICS
Ceramiche

Serafino Loddo
La Marmora, 242
0784/96327

After inheriting his father's ceramics studio in the 1960s, Serafino Loddo set to work etching traditional Sardinian motifs—birds, leaves, and abstract geometric patterns—into white glazed pottery of all forms. His signature style includes soft pastel coloring of the etched areas, in blues, greens, and pinks.

JEWELRY
Gioielli

Cristian's Gold
Via Lamarmora, 131
0789/28337

Cristian Pattieri crafts extremely delicate filigree jewels—brooches, necklaces, pendants, rings, and earrings—all with elaborate gold swirls and coral stones.

KNIVES
Coltelli

Luciano Spanu
Via Deledda, 17
0784/94045

Luciano Spanu specializes in traditional Sardinian knives, with handles of bone, wood, and metal.

TEXTILES
Tessuti

Serafina Senette
Piazza Asproni, 22
0784/95202

Serafina Senette's specialty lies in incorporating all-over patterns of interesting, stylized birds and other animals into her curtains, pillows, table linens, and towels.

NUORO

The streets of Nuoro are filled with elderly women dressed from head to toe in traditional black dresses, occasionally ornamented with gold filigree jewelry on special occasions. Nuoro is the center of a folkloristic culture that is rich, even by Sardinian standards. The formidable mountains around it and the fierce independence of the people made the Romans call this region Barbaria. But that shouldn't scare you away from visiting this bustling mountaintop town steeped in ancient traditions that still live.

GENERAL CRAFTS

Folklore Museum
Museo della Vita e delle Tradizioni Popolari Sarde
Via Mereu, 56
0784/257035

This museum of Sardinian life and popular traditions is full of local jewelry, costumes, and other crafts.

I.S.O.L.A.
Via Monsignor Bua, 10
0784/33581

This I.S.O.L.A. shop has two floors chock-full of the island's best crafts. I picked up some lovely pillow shams, jewelry, and ceramics here, and finished my holiday shopping all in one place.

JEWELRY
Gioielli

Dario Marchi
Via Lamarmora, 11
0784/33155

Dario Marchi's work is a refreshing change from the more ornate filigree jewelry that characterizes the production of many of Sardinia's goldsmiths. Marchi uses pared-down, understated forms of hammered gold and precious stones. His chunky bracelets featuring two or three precious stones are stunning.

Salvatore Goddi
Via Gonario, 5/6
0784/230263

Salvatore Goddi crafts some of the most ornate of the traditional Sardinian gold filigree jewelry encrusted with coral and pearls. His pins, brooches, rings, and earrings make a striking contrast with the severe black costumes of elderly women in his hometown of Nuoro.

ORISTANO

GENERAL CRAFTS

I.S.O.L.A.
Piazza Eleonora, 21
0783/769005

This newest addition to the island's official chain of craft boutiques is one-stop shopping in Oristano for traditional Sardinian crafts, from ceramics to textiles.

CERAMICS
Ceramiche

Cooperativa Ceramiche Maestri d'Arte
Via Cagliari
0783/358103

This I.S.O.L.A.-sanctioned ceramics co-op showcases the best of ceramics production from this province on the southwest coast of Sardinia. Rich in vestiges from the island's prehistoric *nuraghe* culture, Oristano's artists prefer green glazes that recall tarnished bronze to create schematic animal motifs and striking, elongated flasks and amphora that seem as though they could have been pulled from an archeological dig. Others create finely incised geometric patterns against a monochromatic white glaze.

Margherita Pilloni
Via Crispi, 29a
0783/303980

Margherita Pilloni's stunning black pots with their squiggly handles blew me away. Her originality as a ceramicist is the unique forms and shapes of her wares, along with a dramatic monochromatic palette of black, white, or yellow.

PATTADA

KNIFE CAPITAL

Pattada has been a center for knife artisans for centuries. In fact, the word for knife in the Sardinian language is, simply, *pattada*.

KNIVES
Coltelli

Antonio DeRoma
Piazza Vittorio Veneto
079/754040

At just 30, Antonio DeRoma is already a master knife maker. Following in his family's footsteps, DeRoma crafts high-quality knives with handles of mother-of-pearl, ebony, and seasoned horn: the ultimate gift for the man in your life.

La Bottega del Coltello
Via Belvedere, 5
079/754137

The Fogarizzu family carries on a family tradition of knife making in this town famous for this craft. Most of the folding pocketknives are crafted with handles made from the horns of mountain goats, creating lovely transparent effects.

Raimondo Sistigu
Via Duca d'Aosta, 20
079/755410

Raimondo Sistigu is a third-generation knife artisan who crafts traditional Pattada knives with their lovely handles made of not only animal horn but also mother-of-pearl, coral, and luxury woods.

PORTO CERVO

Porto Cervo is the exception to the Sardinian rule. You won't find any traces of tradition or prehistoric culture here. Since real estate developers created this beautiful complex of shops, condos, and yacht yards in the 1950s, this oh-so-chic port town has been a favorite summer playground to top models and royalty. Don't be surprised if you recognize someone you've seen on TV.

I.S.O.L.A.
Sottopiazza
0789/94428

When you're tired of trying on Gucci sunglasses and Versace hot pants, head down to Porto Cervo's small but well merchandized I.S.O.L.A. store for a taste of tradition. It's located on the lower level of a shopping complex just a stone's throw from a marina with some of the biggest yachts I've ever seen in my life.

SAMUGHEO

TEXTILES
Tessuti

Textile Museum
Centro Museale dell'Arte Tessile Sarda
Via Bologna, 9
0783/64023

The town of Samugheo boasts a new museum displaying the textiles of this important weaving town. Town officials have knocked on the doors of nearly every resident, collecting heirloom rugs and antique linens that once stood in closets and wooden chests, but are now proudly displayed as a testament to

this craft, which has played a role in the life of all Samugheo's residents.

Cooperativa Medusa
Via Gramsci, 151
0783/64087

This weavers' co-op in the center of Samugheo displays the best of this town's renowned textile production: bedspreads, pillows, rugs, and saddlebags crafted of both mixed and single-colored yarns.

Grazia Pitzalis
Via Sardinia, 11
0783/64134

I own a few of Grazia Pitzalis's gorgeous off-white pillow covers featuring a rosette pattern in the center created with the technique known as *pibiones*, which has a nubby effect. She incorporates linen and cotton into towels, pillows, and bedspreads for rich, textured works.

SANTULUSSURGIÙ

This town with the strange-sounding name has two claims to fame. The first is its importance as a knife-crafting capital. The second is its well-known annual parade called *Sa Carrela e Nanti*, which takes place just before Carnival (see Calendar of Events, page 213). In this festival with ancient origins, horse riders donning masks and colorful costumes race through town at a frenzied pace to the delight of onlookers. To supply this festival, as well as horse enthusiasts across Sardinia, the town has also become an important center for the crafting of high-quality leather saddles and horse tack.

HORSE SADDLES
Selle

Francesco Piga
Piazza S'Eligheddu, 3
0783/550411

In his humble studio on a square near the edge of town, Francesco Piga makes beautiful horse saddles in light-colored leathers.

You can watch him stamp and cut decorative geometric and vegetal motifs into the soft leather and polish these masterpieces—each one unique—into shiny, soft, finished products.

KNIVES
Coltelli

Fratelli Salaris
Viale Azuni, 183
0783/550287
www.salariscoltelli.it

The Salaris brothers carry on a long family tradition of knife making, using old-fashioned techniques to craft knife handles from horn and bone with incredibly sharp blades. These are luxury knives at their best.

Vittorio Mura & Figli
Viale Azuni, 29
0783/550726

My father and brother are nearly impossible to buy for, but when I entered Vittorio Mura's workshop, I knew I'd hit the jackpot. These knives of exceptional quality are wonderful collector's items. All the blades are crafted on site, and the handles use horns

of goats, buffalo, and ibex, with silver or brass fittings. Some of the fancier ones have inlaid handles and even blades with inlaid effects. Mura can also provide a lovely gift box. They also make horse tack and some very impressive scissors that cut through leather.

SASSARI

GENERAL CRAFTS

Archeological Museum
Museo Archeologico Nazionale GA Sanna
Via Roma, 64
079/272203

This archeological collection displays stunning relics of Sardinia's prehistoric *nuraghe* culture. It's a good place to absorb the visual flavor of the island's past, which influences today's artisans.

I.S.O.L.A.
Via Taborata
079/230101

Sassari's open, airy retail space for the I.S.O.L.A., the island's craft-promoting organization, is located in the public gardens and offers a great selection of traditional wares from all over Sardinia.

CERAMICS
Ceramiche

Ceramiche d'Arte Silecchia
Via Luigi Pirandello, 24
079/250671

Sardinia's folk culture—peasants, agriculture, religion, animals, and daily life—provides the inspiration for Giuseppe Silecchia and his family of artisans. In fact, the artist holds a reputation for catalyzing the renewed interest in local historical traditions in the 1950s. I adore his little figures of Sardinian women in ceramic, complete with traditional costumes and headdresses.

JEWELRY
Gioielli

Laboratorio Orafo
Via Principe di Piemonte, 8/10
079/234687

Pietro Angelo Fiorino crafts gold and silver
filigree jewelry following the traditional,
ornate lines of Sardinian adornments.

TADASUNI

MUSICAL INSTRUMENTS
Strumenti Musicali

Musical Instruments Museum
Museo degli strumenti musicali sardi Don
Giovanni Dore
Via Adua, 7
0785/50113

Don Giovanni Dore is the local parish priest
of Tadasuni, a tiny village in the province of
Oristano. His passion for the *launeddas*, the
ancient woodwind instrument of Sardinia,
led him to collect and display impressive
examples of these instruments in his own
personal museum.

TONARA

BELLS
Campane

Carlo Sulis
Via Giovanni XXIII, 2
0784/63845

Tonara is Sardinia's undisputed capital of
bell making, and Carlo Sulis's family has
been making these so-called *campanacci* for
several generations. Most of them are simple
affairs of bronze, the kind of bells cows and
sheep wear around their necks so that shepherds can find them in the verdant, rolling
hills of rural central Sardinia.

SICILY:
THE TRADITIONS

CERAMICS
Ceramiche

I n Sicily, ceramic art is deeply rooted in time. The ancient Phoenicians and Greeks inhabited Sicily, creating amphorae, kraters, *kylixes*, and other typical ancient wares using the ruddy earth and painted with stylized black and red figures. These early artists left their masterpieces to bake in the hot Sicilian sun, which can create heat that reaches over 100 degrees Fahrenheit in the summer.

Ceramics are made and sold all over the island, but if you want to buy the real thing at the best price, head for one of the major ceramics centers. Caltagirone, Santo Stefano di Camastra, and Monreale are the most important centers, but Palermo has reemerged in the last two decades with its own particular style of decoration and production. Each town boasts a completely different ceramic tradition, so it's fun to visit them all and gain an appreciation for what each local tradition has to offer.

In Sicily, you won't find the refined Renaissance elegance so embodied by pieces from Deruta and Faenza in central Italy (see Chapters 1 and 3). Instead, you'll see bold patterns, bright colors, and brash, splashy decorations that capture the vigorous Sicilian spirit. The technique of laying saturated colors against a white tin oxide ground may have been introduced into Sicily by the Moors, who occupied the island

CALTAGIRONE STYLE

The Caltagirone style of ceramics is characterized by a white background and limited color palette.
- **Colors:** White background with bright blues, greens, and yellows.
- **Traditional forms:** Pharmacy jars decorated with busts of saints and nobles; amphorae; plates with vegetal motifs; tiles with fruit and animal decoration, heads of Moors, pinecones.
- **Modern inventions:** Planters, animal figures, lamps.

briefly in the Middle Ages and had been for centuries imitating Chinese porcelain. The term *maiolica* is recent, but refers to earthenware painted with tin oxide glazing enamels before firing at a low temperature to reach a reflective, hard finish.

Of the ceramics capitals of Sicily, Caltagirone holds pride of place. Just one look at the countryside surrounding Caltagirone and you'll understand why ceramics became the destiny of this hilltop town. The village rises above a parched landscape of sand-colored earth, with rolling hills and scrubby plants and olive trees eking out their existence alongside Sicilian potters. For two millennia, this clay has meant a living for the people of Caltagirone. In fact, the word Caltagirone derives from the Arabic phrase *Qal'at al Ghiran,* or Rock of the Vases.

The heyday of Caltagirone style was the seventeenth and eighteenth centuries. Most of the artisans crafting ceramics today in Caltagirone reproduce pieces from this era. Blue, yellow, and green predominate against a white background. Caltagirone is also known for large jars in the shape of human heads, popular in the nineteenth century. The crowned heads of queens and kings became common subjects, as are the more exotic depictions of Moors, which recall Sicily's history.

Sicily's most fun ceramics town is Santo Stefano di Camastra. Overlooking the sea on Sicily's northern shore, Santo Stefano di Camastra is the center of an uncomplicated, exuberant ceramics tradition. The designs are bolder, brasher, and less refined than those produced in Caltagirone, with a palette dominated by greens and yellows and big, bold lemons and other fruits, as well as profuse vegetal motifs. This pottery exudes a sense of warmth and cheer that could only exist in a Sicilian beach town.

A word of warning about Sicilian ceramics: Just because a piece is signed does not mean it's valuable, and many mass-market workshops hire untrained labor to churn out cheap wares for the tourist trade.

PRICE POINTS

Good news! In Sicily you can get ceramics of exceptional quality for a fair price. I picked up some lovely small pots in Palermo for under 20 euros each, then splurged on a huge planter made by Nicoló Giuliano (page 206) for about 250 euros.

BELLISSIMA!

The best places to buy quality ceramics in Sicily are:

Caltagirone: Alessi (page 204)

Monreale: Nicoló Giuliano (page 206)

Palermo: Tre Erre Ceramiche (page 207)

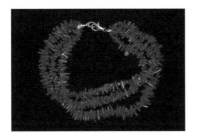

CORAL CRAFTS

Corallo

Trapani was once the center of a thriving coral-working industry and today, lovely jewelry in that distinctive color—not quite orange, red, or pink, but somewhere in between—abounds in the shops of Trapani, on Sicily's western coast.

Trapani's artisans were already working coral in ancient times, according to the Roman writer Pliny. By the end of the Middle Ages it was exported outside of Sicily. As most of the coral workers were Jews living in Sicily, production went down in the fifteenth century under repression from Ferdinand and Isabella of Aragon. In the sixteenth century there were only 25 artisan shops in Trapani, exporting mostly religious work and rosaries throughout Europe. The art all but died out by 1800, as coral began to be worked outside Sicily, but now there is a movement afoot to revive the craft in this place so rich with coral-working history.

Years ago, coral-fishing boats lugged thousands of pounds of coral to Trapani's shores using special vessels just for that purpose. Today, scuba divers harvest coral by hand, preserving the integrity of the reefs and selecting the pieces most well suited for crafting the jewelry and decorative items that today's artisans create.

PRICE POINTS

You can pay under 100 euros for a small piece and up to thousands of dollars for more complex jewelry ensembles.

BELLISSIMA!

Trapani's regional museum (page 210) houses some of the jaw-dropping coral creations made through the centuries.

DOLLS AND MARIONETTES

Pupi e Marionette

T he Sicilian marionette theater became popular toward the end of the 1700s and provided a major source of entertainment for people living in small towns across the island. The stories were based on the great legends of the Middle Ages and on battles between good and evil. Stock characters—kings, knights, princesses, sorcerers, and Moors—played predictable roles that audiences knew and loved. For example, the popular story *Orlando Furioso*, based on the book by Ludovico Ariosto, chronicles the trials and tribulations of a beautiful princess, Angelica, torn between the love of two knights, Orlando and Ranaldo.

The marionettes themselves are masterpieces of Sicilian craftsmanship. Each can weigh 65 to 85 pounds and stand up to four feet tall. Crafted of wooden skeletons covered in cloth and metal, then hand-painted, each one is different. The knights wear solid-brass armor, the weight of which the strong puppeteers must bear from the heights above the stage. Sicilian theaters are invariably family affairs, and both the art of making the marionettes and animating them on stage are passed down through the generations. The Cuticchio and Pasqualino families of Palermo are Sicily's leading artisans creating these impressive *pupi* today (see page 208 for more about them).

Nearly every town in Sicily has a marionette theater, or *opera dei pupi*, though Palermo and Catania are the best places to see them today. Although they don't hold the popularity with wide audiences that they did in the nineteenth century, a number of talented artisans continue this rich folk tradition.

PRICE POINTS

For authentic *pupi siciliani*, expect to pay anywhere from 40 to 650 euros, depending on the size and quality of materials and craftsmanship.

BELLISSIMA!

Don't miss a show at Cuticchio in Palermo (page 208), one of Sicily's most authentic marionette makers.

SICILIAN CARTS

Carretti Siciliani

O nly a little more than a hundred years ago, horse-drawn wooden carts were the main mode of transportation in Sicily. Throughout the streets of Palermo, Catania, and other towns, merchants and the public steered their horses through crowded cobblestone streets, pulling behind them wooden carts with enormous wheels, every inch covered with brightly painted decoration.

Automobiles have replaced these carts in the noisy streets of Palermo and Catania, and local collectors bring out their traditional Sicilian carts only for festivals and celebrations. But a few diligent artisans make sure the tradition of hand-painted Sicilian carts lives on.

No one knows the origin of painting stories along the sides of the carts, but by the middle of the nineteenth century, painters and cart owners were decorating their vehicles with elaborate decorations and stories from the Bible, mythology, literature, and popular culture. These scenes were often the same stories portrayed in the Sicilian theaters with marionettes—Romantic sagas of the Middle Ages, with knights, fair maidens, and sorcerers.

Each Sicilian cart is a group effort. Woodworkers create the frame, usually from walnut, then a carver makes elaborate figures on the wheels and the sides of the cart. Finally, painters create scenes all over it.

PRICE POINTS
A full-size Sicilian cart will set you back thousands of dollars, but you can pick up a miniature replica for under 100 euros.

BELLISSIMA!
Domenico di Mauro, whose workshop lies near the base of Mount Etna, is the torchbearer of the Sicilian cart tradition (page 204).

SWEETS

Dolci

I n artisanal kitchens, Siclian chefs raise the concept of *la dolce vita* to a new level. In fact, Sicily is world-famous for its sweets. A tour of Sicily's pastry shops and *gelaterie* will leave you hankering for more of the island's traditional pastries, candy, and frozen treats. Sweets are closely tied to local traditions and feasts, like the tiny lambs fashioned of almond paste that only appear around Easter time.

Almonds form the basis for many Sicilian specialty desserts. The island is one of the world's top almond producers, and the characteristic flavor and aroma are synonymous with Sicilian cuisine and pastries. Almond cake (*torta alla mandorla*), almond nougat (*torrone* or *torroncino*), and almond biscotti figure prominently in Sicily's pastry shop windows. Pastry shops overflow with *cannoli*—pastry crisps filled with ricotta cheese made with sheep's milk—and *cassata*—a traditional cake also made with fresh ricotta.

Sicily excels in frozen treats, and it's no wonder. I once spent the month of August on Italy's largest island and I can vouch for its intense heat. There's nothing like a cone overflowing with gelato, among the richest and sweetest in Italy when it's hot. But my favorite is *granita*, a shaved ice beverage made with sugar and a little fruit juice. *Granita* comes in every flavor imaginable, from kiwi to coffee,

HOME COOKING

Look for the words *pasticceria artigianale* or *produzione nostra* on pastry shop windows for the best quality homemade treats.

mint and strawberry. Nothing cools and refreshes better than *granita* on a hot August day in Palermo.

A favorite Sicilian *dolce* is Martorana fruits. Martorana fruits are not fruits at all, but masterpieces of marzipan. They are named for the Martorana Monastery in Palermo, whose monks began creating these *trompe l'oeil* creations in the thirteenth century. Martorana fruits were all the rage in the baroque period of the seventeenth and eighteenth centuries, when people sought to create imitations of luxury items and everyday objects, all with pastry.

It all begins with marzipan or "royal pastry" (*pasta reale*), that mixture of almond, egg white, and sugar that's been the star of Sicilian tables since the Middle Ages. This is then fashioned into pears, lemons, strawberries, kiwis, oranges, ears of corn, and more. The end product is limited only by the pastry chef's imagination.

Today, local and international competitions draw professional pastry chefs, home cooks, and even monks into the fray to take the prize of being the island's best Martorana fruit maker.

PRICE POINTS
This has to be one of the most pleasurable ways to spend your money in Italy. Pick up a Martorana fruit or a cup of *granita* for under 1 euro, and enjoy.

BELLISSIMA!
The Martorana fruits in the Pasticceria Etna in Taormina (see page 210) are some of the island's most lovely.

THE LISTINGS

ACI SANT'ANTONIO

CARTS
Carretti Siciliani

Domenico di Mauro
Via Tito, 8

In his humble studio on the southeast flank of Mount Etna, this master—now in his 90s and still going strong—keeps the tradition of Sicilian painted carts alive. One of his masterpieces graces the White House in Washington, a gift to President John F. Kennedy.

ACIREALE

DOLLS AND MARIONETTES
Pupi e Marionette

Opera dei Pupi Turi Grasso
Via Nazionale, 195
095/648035
www.operadeipupi.com

This marionette theater is located on the outskirts of Acireale in Capomulini. Here you can witness the stories and characters that have entertained Sicilians for over 200 years and admire the detailed workmanship of the marionettes themselves.

CALTAGIRONE

More than 100 ceramic studios make their home in Caltagirone, and it can be overwhelming. The best way to work the town is to park along the Via Roma as you enter the town coming from Catania. Make the ceramics museum your first stop, then browse your way to the impressive ceramic stairway, which is paved in tiles that were decorated by Caltagirone's modern masters.

Most of the ceramics studios are located along this main artery and on side streets branching off it. The crowning glory of Caltagirone is the breathtaking ceramic stairway that leads to the town's main square. The steep Scala Santa Maria del Monte had been a distinctive feature of the city for centuries, but in the 1960s, Antonino Ragona, director of the local ceramics museum and a ceramics promoter, organized an initiative for paving the entire staircase with ceramics painted by local craftspeople. The results are stunning.

There is tremendous variety in quality among the artisans of Caltagirone. Many of the ceramicists you see throwing pots and painting designs in the shops that litter the town are there just for show. Any serious artisan maintains a private studio full of assistants on the flank of the hill.

CERAMICS
Ceramiche

Alessi
Principe Amadeo, 9
0933/21967

My Sicilian friend Massimo Marchese led me to this fabulous shop. Signor Alessi and his assistants adhere more closely to the grand tradition of Caltagirone ceramics than perhaps any other practicing artisans in town. Pharmacy jars, vases, plates, decorative tiles, and a million other objects are all executed with a palpable taste for the past. Prices and quality are high. A must-see.

Ceramiche Artistiche Besnik Harizi
Via Gueli, 1
0933/24999
www.besnik-harizi.it

Besnik Harizi specializes in large-scale vases that resemble the heads of exotic Moorish kings, queens, and nobles. He also does a fine job with historical reproductions of Caltagirone ceramics of the 1700s and

1800s—pharmacy jars, plates with religious and mythological scenes, and decorative tiles. The studio is located next door to the local artisan trade group, the Confartigianato, across from the ceramics museum.

Ceramiche Artistiche di Martino
Via Roma, 88
0933/57729
www.ceramichedimartino.it

Giuseppe di Martino makes everything from important-looking decorative vases and tables to napkin rings, all using the historical color palette of the 1600s, 1700s, and 1800s. I particularly like his tiles, executed with crisp, clean designs and bright colors.

Ceramics Museum
Museo della Ceramica
Via Giardini Pubblici
0933/58418

If you're serious about ceramics, this should be your first stop in Caltagirone. This small but nicely displayed collection chronicles the history of ceramic production in the Caltagirone region from the seventeenth century B.C. through the nineteenth century A.D.

Ceramiche Nicolò Morales
Via SS. Salvatore, 17
0933/58472
www.nicolomorales.com

Nicolò Morales's talent is crafting ceramics that appear antique. Criseled paint and antiquing varnish give the surface a rich, old-world appearance. All of his works are lovely and refined, and would bring a taste of old Europe to any décor.

Ceramiche Sirna
Via S. Luigi Alto Basso
0933/57725

Francesco Sirna specializes in ceramic jewelry, combined with gold or silver. The works are not particularly refined but they're fun and unique.

Ceramiche e Terrecotte Artistiche
Corso Principe Amadeo, 26
0933/53399

Giuseppa Alparone and her assistants craft fine ceramics that adhere to the Caltagirone tradition. A good value for the quality.

Scarlatella
Scala Santa Maria Santissima del Monte, 2
0933/53887

The uniqueness of this shop is its specialty in terra-cotta nativity scenes and other historical figures. They also deal in historical pieces of Caltagirone ceramics from the 1700s and 1800s. The shop is located at the base of the monumental ceramic staircase in the center of Caltagirone.

Silva Ceramica
Piazza Umberto I, 19
0933/55707

This shop is located off the main square in a historic villa. You can watch artisans paint pots and tiles in the courtyard, then go upstairs to watch the more messy work of covering the wares in white slip. In addition to reproductions of historic ceramics of Caltagirone, Silva and his team create lovely table settings and decorative tiles for kitchen and bath. My choice for a place to buy wedding and anniversary gifts! The work is high quality and the staff is friendly.

CEFALÙ

In one of island's most evocative settings, Cefalù perches alongside a picture-perfect crescent-shaped beach, its medieval cathedral dominating the hillside. Cefalù is worth a day trip from anywhere on the island just to wander its cobblestone streets and explore its nooks and crannies.

CERAMICS
Ceramiche

A. Lumera
Corso Ruggiero, 176-182
0921/921801

Pure white porcelain and quality hand-painted ceramics line the walls of this tiny shop along a steep, cobblestone pedestrian path that climbs toward Cefalù cathedral.

WROUGHT IRON
Ferro Battuto

Piccolo Mondo Antico
Corso Ruggero, 154
0921/925001

This shop overflows onto the cobblestone sidewalk with old furniture, clocks, bric-a-brac, lamps, pictures, keys, and other discarded treasures. Among them are stunning pieces of forged iron made in-house, from plate racks to coat racks and chandeliers.

MONREALE

CERAMICS
Ceramiche

Elisa Messina
Piazza Guglielmo, Villa Belvedere
091/6404514
www.elisamessina.it

From a sea of tourist traps hawking mass-market souvenirs around the square of Monreale, Elisa Messina's studio rises like a star. In a warm, dimly lit showroom, Elisa and her assistants display two distinct types of wares: ceramics tastefully reflecting the styles and colors of Palermo, and delicate nativity scenes crafted of hand-painted terra-cotta.

Nicoló Giuliano
Via Circonvallazione, 25
091/6404393
www.nicologiuliano.com

After scourging Sicily for quality ceramics, this is where I finally dropped cash. Nicoló Giuliano and his family make some of the best ceramic pieces on the island.

Born in Santo Stefano di Camastra and transferred to Monreale, Nicoló Giuliano seemed to have ceramics in his blood. He founded a ceramics school, where he teaches the younger generation the techniques of his forefathers. Today his sons Daniele and Alessandro work with him to create beautiful, large-scale ceramic pots with individually painted fruits, fountains with Bacchus-like characters spouting water, and decorated tiles.

Giuliano is one of the most prestigious ceramics families in Sicily; Palermo's five-star Villa Igeia decorates its dinner tables—overlooking Palermo's harbor—with hand-painted cache-pots signed by Nicoló himself.

If you're making a day trip to Monreale from Palermo, you'll pass Nicoló Giuliano on the main road leading into the center of Monreale; it's best reached by car. They ship insured to the United States; request their catalog.

PALERMO

One of my most vivid Sicilian memories is a scene I witnessed from a taxi speeding through Palermo's hot, grimy urban sprawl. Inside a hole-in-the-wall off an industrial street, several men in heavy aprons were forging iron. Covered in dirt and sweat, they worked red-hot pieces of metal over sawhorses. Sparks flew, and the summer heat emanated from the tiny studio crowded with gnarled metal, tools, and raw sheets of metal. On the sidewalk outside the workshop, a stunning iron headboard—just one of the fruits of their labor—leaned casually against the crumbling stucco of the building.

This is Palermo, where, from an ugly, chaotic tangle of streets, emerge objects of breathtaking beauty. In the historic center, alleys bear names that recall the traditional arts that have flourished for eons: Via dei Candelai (Street of the Candlemakers), Via dei Biscottari (Street of the Cookie Makers), Via dei Bambinai (Street of the Doll Makers). Palermo crawls with creative passion.

Palermo is an enormous, far-flung metropolis, and artisans are scattered all over it. The largest concentration set up shop in the historic center. A number of artisans have clustered their workshops along the Via Bara all'Olivella, near the main shopping district, where La Rinascente department store is located.

Although it can't compete with Caltagirone and Santo Stefano di Camastra, Palermo has recently reemerged as an important center of ceramics production. Avoid buying from the shops in the immediate vicinity of the cathedral and the cruise-ship port. The prices are high and the quality low. Most are resellers of pottery from Santo Stefano di Camastra and Caltagirone. The one exception to this rule is Tre Erre Ceramiche (see right).

GENERAL CRAFTS

Museo Etnografico Pitrè
Via Duca degli Abruzzi, 1
091/7404893

This craft museum is located in the Mondello section of Palermo, in the park alongside Villa La Favorita. It treats crafts as ethnographic artifacts and holds an impressive collection of Sicilian marionettes, carts, ceramics, and other testimonies to the island's agricultural past. An intriguing place to spend a couple of hours.

CARTS
Carretti Siciliani

Franco Bertolino
Salita Ramirez, 2
091/580559

Franco Bertolino—a man as colorful as his creations—has single-handedly organized a bonanza of Sicilian crafts in his hole-in-the-wall shop behind the apse of Palermo cathedral. Hand-painted reproduction Sicilian carts

spill out onto the sidewalk; marionettes dangle crazily from the rafters. Quality reproductions lie alongside tourist junk. Brightly painted walls frame the theater of the mom-and-pop theater that stages productions of Sicilian marionettes.

CERAMICS
Ceramiche

Tre Erre Ceramiche
Via Amari, 49
Tel 091/323827
www.treerreceramiche.it

This is my favorite shop in Palermo. Lovely, high-quality pottery is artfully displayed in a beautiful stone-and-tile showroom with high ceilings and lots of light.

Since it opened in 1979, the Raffa family has been instrumental in reviving Palermo's ceramics production. They execute faithful reproductions of seventeenth- and eighteenth-century wares with religious and mythical scenes, as well as more decorative motifs like fruit and their distinctive logo, a sun with swirly rays and a serene face.

Prices are reasonable, and the works are of high quality. Most of the production takes place off site, but you might catch one of the artisans working at the potter's wheel or loading pieces into the kiln. The staff is very friendly and accommodating. They sent some pieces to my house in Milan by express mail, and the whole process was a breeze. They ship worldwide via DHL.

If you're visiting Palermo by cruise ship, keep walking up the Via Amari past the tourist traps, and you'll see Tre Erre Ceramiche on your right.

A PALERMO PRIMER

Best Craft Street: Via Bara all'Olivella
Carts: behind Palermo cathedral
Copper and Tin Wares: Via Calderai

Dolls and Marionettes: Via Bambinai
Silver and Jewelry: Piazza San Domenico and Piazza Meli

DOLLS AND MARIONETTES
Pupi e Marionette

Cuticchio
Via Bara all'Olivella, 52
091/323400

Mimmo Cuticchio follows in the footsteps of his father and grandfather, who dangled animated marionettes from the rafters of this small stage in central Palermo for years. Be sure to catch one of these shows featuring traditional Sicilian marionettes.

Museo Internazionale delle Marionette
Via Butera, 1
091/328060
www.museomarionettepalermo.it

I found it highly unsettling to be stared at by hundreds of pairs of eyes of antique puppets and marionettes, but for fans of puppet theater, this place is a mecca. The collection also includes other European and Asian puppets and marionettes. The museum was founded by the Pasqualino brothers, the undisputed marionette gurus of Palermo, whose passion is preserving and promoting this fascinating folk tradition.

Rose-Bud
Via Bara all'Olivella, 64
339/5416016

If you're a dollhouse collector, you won't want to miss the miniatures in this workshop on Palermo's historic craft street. Furniture, miniature people, pets, plants, and much more are crafted on site in this studio. They also restore antique dollhouses. Papier-mâché animals and other creations fill the shelves of this modest workshop.

SILVER
Argento

A.F.M.
Via Broggi, 4
091/6372950
www.afm.it

A.F.M. is one of the only silversmiths in Palermo that still creates pieces entirely by hand, without the help of machines.

Still, they are one of the larger companies, with about 40 artisans occupying a nondescript building in an industrial part of Palermo. From bowls to silver table services, they make lovely pieces.

Argenti Siddiolo
Via Materassai, 68/72
091/582669

Since 1836, the Siddiolo family has been producing handcrafted silver objects in Palermo. Turning ordinary household objects—pitchers, candlesticks, plates, tea services, vases—into works of high art is their mission. Among their clients are numerous churches and clergy, who commission chalices, patens, and other ecclesiastical accoutrements in this thriving Catholic community.

NATIVITY SCENES
Presepi

Sicily's Folk di Angela Tripi
Via Vittorio Emanuele, 450
091/6512787
www.tripi.it

Angela Tripi is one of the island's most well-known artisans for creating nativity scenes from terra-cotta figures dressed in fabrics. She made a three-dimensional model of Leonardo da Vinci's *Last Supper*, which is exhibited in Santa Maria della Grazie in Milan, near the original fresco by the Renaissance master.

The shop is tucked back in a courtyard that's worth seeing for a taste of old Palermo—an ornate baroque stairway and archway crumbling with time. You can watch Angela Tripi and her assistants turning out tiny masterpieces in the studio that adjoins the shop.

WOODCRAFTS
Legno

Giuseppe Vitrano
Via Bara all'Olivella, 42
339/4831074

If you're in the market for a lamp or a table with fancy legs, put in an order with

Giuseppe Vitrano. His studio is little more than a hole-in-the-wall along Palermo's most interesting craft street, but inside he creates treasures with hammers, chisels, a few low-tech machines, and his imagination. The wood can be gilded for more elaborate effects, or left natural.

Santo Lo Galbo
Via Bara all'Olivella, 32
091/587833

Neighborhood cats lounge and yawn at the doorway to Santo Lo Galbo's shop, oblivious to the hammering and chiseling taking place inside. Mr. Lo Galbo occupies another mere cranny down the street from Giuseppe Vitrano.

WROUGHT IRON
Ferro Battuto

Cusimano
Via Quinta Casa, 20
091/362051

During the summer, Signor Cusimano and his assistants only fire up the forge for an hour or so per day. If you're lucky, you'll get to see the sparks flying as they work over hot iron. They create headboards, hat stands, and unique sculptures. Their forge is off the beaten path, but convenient if you're staying at the Villa Igeia hotel.

L'Arte del Ferro Battuto
Via Messina Montagne, 13
091/492712
www.arteferromessina.it

Multiple generations of the Messina family have sustained this wrought iron shop, making everything from elaborate gates to more portable candlestick holders and lamps. Browse this exhibition space, which displays items representative of the workshop located on the outskirts of Palermo.

SANTO STEFANO DI CAMASTRA

Santo Stefano di Camastra is a trek from most other towns in Sicily, because the highway turns into a winding, two-lane coastal road. If you're looking for local flavor, small-town atmosphere, a coastal breeze, and fun ceramics, plan an overnight stop here. The town sponsors a nice outdoor exhibition in the summer in the park overlooking the sea.

Although many workshops lie on the outskirts of town, most of the town's ceramics artists have showrooms located along the Via Vittoria, which cuts a swath through town. It makes for a nice afternoon stroll with a gelato in hand.

CERAMICS
Ceramiche

Ceramiche Insana
Via Vittoria, 1B
0921/337223

In this otherwise dark workshop, lighting is reserved only for the ceramic pieces, giving the works in this space a mysterious and dramatic air. Nice quality, traditional wares.

Ceramiche La Spiga
Torre Castagna
0921/331822

This large-volume workshop on the outskirts of town occupies an evocative old building with a below-ground showroom chock-full of large painted plates, terra-cotta vases, and brightly decorated planters and pots.

Le Terracotte del Sole
Contrada Passo Giardino
0921/337244

This is one of the higher quality artisans of Santo Stefano di Camastra, and the shop is set up to insure and ship your purchase. In addition to the traditional fruit and floral motifs that characterize Santo Stefano di Camastra, they also produce unique terra-cotta baskets and vases with delicate painted flowers emerging from them.

Kebao
Via Vittoria, 79
0921/339423

From his workshop in the nearby town of Villa Margi, Maurizio Giglio and his assistants craft small-scale items with whimsical forms in a limited palette of blue, terra-cotta, and white. Giglio, along with Filadelfio Todaro (see page 210) and a few other local artisans follow this particular tradition of ceramics decoration. He has a small showroom on the Via Vittoria.

La Giara
Via Nazionale, 96
0921/331879
www.ceramichelagiara.com

Giovanni Patti and his assistants figure prominently in the annual outdoor exhibition of ceramics in the town park of Santo Stefano di Camastra. Their wares are characterized by rich, matte colors and carefully executed vegetal motifs on large-scale vases, amphorae, and bowls.

Modellati Filadelfio Todaro
Via Vittoria, 127
0921/335208
www.filadelfio.it

Filadelfio Todaro figures among a handful of local artisans who have departed from the fruit and floral motifs that dominate ceramics of Santo Stefano di Camastra. His wares are decorated with a limited palette of white, terra-cotta, and blue, with an emphasis on whimsical and curvy forms. From candlesticks to vases and lamps, his showroom on the Via Vittoria represents a good selection of the wares he and his assistants produce at their off-site studio in nearby Marina di Caronia.

TAORMINA

This ancient seaport in the shadow of Mount Etna beckons travelers from all over the globe with its breathtaking views, staggering cliffsides, and evocative cobblestone streets. Normally, I would not include Taormina in this book if it weren't such a popular Sicilian destination for international visitors. Its shops are mostly for the tourist trade but there are a few authentic artisans working diligently around town.

JEWELRY
Gioielli

Kamares
Via Pirandello, 16
0942/24909

A group of artisans based in Catania crafts unique jewelry incorporating ceramic beads and chunks decorated with motifs typical of Sicily. Mostly geared toward the tourist trade, but worth a visit.

SWEETS
Dolci

Pasticceria Etna
Corso Umberto I, 112
0942/24735

It's impossible not to stop at this pastry shop along the main pedestrian drag of Taormina. After a morning on the beach or at the pool, it's a great place to take the edge off with a *granita*, gelato, or one of the beautiful Martorana fruits for which Pasticceria Etna is famous. My two-year-old son thought that a banana never tasted so good!

TRAPANI

CORAL CRAFTS
Corallo

Regional Museum
Museo Regionale Pepoli
Via Pepoli
0923/553269

Among other coral works are some nativity scenes of unbelievable intricacy. They are fanciful and fabulous, making the trek to this museum worthwhile.

Platimiro Nicol Fiorenza
Via Osorio, 36
0923/20785

Fiorenza runs a school for coral working and has been an instrumental force in reviving this ancient tradition among artisans in Trapani.

A YEAR OF ITALIAN TRADITION:
CALENDAR OF EVENTS

One of the things that impresses me the most about Italy is the sheer variety and frequency of its festivals. These gatherings, which take place all over Italy all year long, are the perfect opportunity to soak up the country's rich local traditions.

It seems that just about anything can be cause for celebration—saints' days, religious and civic holidays, the ripening of lemons, the unveiling of the season's wines, the sprouting of truffles from the black earth, and thousands of remembrances of the past. Just about every food specialty, animal, saint, and historical event—literally anything with local significance—has its own festival, or *sagra*.

Traditional crafts often take center stage at these events, as they serve as a tremendous source of local pride and communal identity. Here are the major festivals in which local handmade goods play a key role.

JANUARY

FIRST SATURDAY

FAENZA, EMILIA-ROMAGNA
LA NOTT DE BISÒ
WINE AND CERAMICS FESTIVAL

Roughly translated from the local dialect as "wine night," this rowdy event culminates

in the liberal pouring of local wines from pitchers made of Faenza ceramics.

30-31

AOSTA, VALLE D'AOSTA
FIERA DI SANT'ORSO
FEAST OF SAINT ORSO

This has been the granddaddy of craft festivals for more than 600 years, filling the snow-covered streets of this Alpine town with giant horns of wood, handmade toys, farm tools, woolen blankets, dolls in local costumes, copper pots, wrought iron grates, rustic furniture, wooden bowls, and more.

FEBRUARY

FIRST WEEK

AGRIGENTO, SICILIA
SAGRA DEL MANDORLO
ALMOND BLOSSOM FESTIVAL

Almonds mean big business and big fun in Sicily, and this festival celebrates the first blooming of these highly valued plants with song, dance, costumes, and fireworks.

10 DAYS BEFORE LENT

VENICE, VENETO
CARNEVALE
CARNIVAL

This is the world's most famous carnival, and a great place to see the world-famous Venetian handmade masks and costumes.

MARCH

MID MARCH

TREVISO, VENETO
FESTA DELL'ARTIGIANATO DEL LEGNO
WOODCRAFTS FESTIVAL

This celebration of woodcrafts is a newcomer to the annual Italian crafts calendar, having just started in 2002 as a way to promote the work of local artisans.

APRIL

SUNDAY AFTER EASTER

FENIS, VALLE D'AOSTA
SAGRA DELLA FONTINA
FONTINA CHEESE FESTIVAL

This festival takes place when the cows are led into high-altitude pastures to graze on young grass, producing the best milk for this heavenly, melting cheese. An exhibition of local woodcrafts features hand-operated butter churners that turn this premium milk in butter and cream.

THIRD WEEKEND IN APRIL

BRESCIA, LOMBARDIA
EXA
FIREARMS SHOW

Artisans around Brescia handcraft knives, rifles, archery equipment, and replicas of historical weapons, showcased here for an elite clientele of collectors and sportsmen.

LAST WEEK OF APRIL

FIRENZE (FLORENCE), TOSCANA
MOSTRA MERCATO INTERNAZIONALE DELL'ARTIGIANATO
INTERNATIONAL EXHIBIT AND MARKET OF TRADITIONAL CRAFTS

One of the Italian craft industry's most important trade shows overtakes the historic Fortezza da Basso each year, with an emphasis on the trades of Tuscany—leather, wrought iron, gilded woodwork, antiques, painting, and more.

FOURTH WEEKEND IN APRIL

CORTONA, TOSCANA
FIERA DEL RAME
COPPER EXHIBITION

Cortona's Palazzo Casali and Piazza Signorelli host this exhibition of copper artisans from all over Italy, featuring giant cauldrons to practical cookware, decorative and gift items.

LAST SUNDAY

PONTI, PIEMONTE
IL POLENTONE
GREAT POLENTA FESTIVAL

This polenta festival includes a celebration of the fabulous copper pots that are a specialty of the region's artisans and considered the premier cookware for this creamy local starch.

MAY

1

CAGLIARI, SARDEGNA
SANT'EFISIO
SAINT EFISIO

Costume historians consider this event one of the world's most significant displays of local costumes, for the variety and authenticity of local dress. This stunning parade of Sardinia's colors, fabrics, and jewelry commemorates the local patron saint.

1

VILLAIOLA, EMILIA-ROMAGNA
SAGRA DEL PARMIGIANO-REGGIANO
PARMESAN CHEESE FESTIVAL

The streets of this little town fill with demonstrations and tastings to the delight of cheese lovers everywhere. Breaking a piece off the wheel as soon as it comes out of the seasoning houses is an incomparable experience.

FIRST SUNDAY

SESSAME, PIEMONTE
SAGRA DI RISOTTO
RISOTTO FESTIVAL

At this festival, if you want a heap of steaming, creamy risotto spooned into your plate, you first have to buy the plate: a ceramic one produced by a local artisan, that is.

7-10

NAPOLI (NAPLES), CAMPANIA
SAN NICOLÒ
SAINT NICHOLAS

For this local saint's festival, residents trot out gaudy puppets, papier-mâché angels, and handmade saints, all parading through the narrow streets of Naples's historic center. A feast for the eyes.

MIDDLE

MODENA, EMILIA-ROMAGNA
BALSAMICA
CELEBRATION OF TRADITIONAL BALSAMIC VINEGAR

Some of the world's most cultivated palettes convene for this premier event. Local producers of *aceto balsamico tradizionale di Modena* open their doors, and restaurants plan special menus in which every course features this syrupy condiment.

NEXT TO THE LAST SUNDAY

SASSARI, SARDEGNA
CAVALCATA SARDA
SARDINIAN PARADE

This folkloric parade features more than 3,000 pedestrians and horse riders donning traditional costumes and handcrafted papier-mâché masks.

JUNE

EARLY JUNE

TAORMINA, SICILIA
FESTA TRADIZIONALE
COSTUME FESTIVAL

Painted horse-drawn carts parade through the streets of this beautiful resort town, carrying people donning the best of Sicily's colorful traditional costumes.

EARLY JUNE

CAGLIARI, SARDEGNA
MOSTRO-MERCATO DELL'ARTIGIANATO SARDO
EXHIBITION OF SARDINIAN CRAFTS

In the Villa Siotto of Sarroch, outside the capital city of Sardinia, this annual festival promotes local craft production.

1-13

CERRETO SANNITA, CAMPANIA
FESTA DEL'ARTIGIANATO
CRAFT FESTIVAL

Ceramics, textiles, and woodcrafts take center stage in this town outside of Naples, which boasts a local ceramics tradition.

2

SANTULUSSURGIÙ, SARDEGNA
SA CARRELA' E NANTI
FAIR OF THE HORSES

In this rural town known for its high-quality metal horse tack and leather saddles, a daring bareback horse race through the town's streets features riders wearing handcrafted wooden and papier-mâché masks.

SECOND SUNDAY

AMALFI, CAMPANIA
SAGRA DEL LIMONE
LEMON FESTIVAL

The craggy cliffs of the Amalfi coast form the backdrop for a local celebration of everything imaginable produced with lemons, from *limoncello* to pastries, jellies, and other products.

MID-JUNE

ARBUS, SARDEGNA
SANT'ANTONIO
FEAST OF SAINT ANTHONY

A religious procession features the local traditional costumes of this town.

16-25

BEVAGNA, UMBRIA
MERCATO DELLE GAITE
NEIGHBORHOOD MARKET

For a week in July, the Umbrian town of Bevagna re-creates life in the Middle Ages, and artisans from every trade demonstrate their techniques along the cobblestone streets.

23

SPILAMBERTO, EMILIA-ROMAGNA
PALIO DI SAN GIOVANNI
BALSAMIC VINEGAR CONTEST

Nine hundred competitors vie for the title
in this balsamic vinegar competition. Tables
of judges—all with highly trained noses—taste
unmarked bottles of traditional balsamic vinegar
of Modena, some of which have been aged 25
years or more.

LAST WEEK

MONTELUPO FIORENTINO, TOSCANA
FESTA INTERNAZIONALE DELLA CERAMICA
INTERNATIONAL CERAMICS FESTIVAL

In addition to live demonstrations of ceramics
production and decoration that put this town
outside Florence on the map, you can enjoy
music, dancing, street theater, and great food.

LATE JUNE

ROMA (ROME), LAZIO
TEVERE EXPO
ARTS & CRAFTS FESTIVAL

This celebration of local crafts along the Tiber
River near the Castel Sant'Angelo is accompa-
nied by great food, wine, and fireworks.

END OF JUNE

FAENZA, EMILIA-ROMAGNA
FESTA DELLA CERAMICA
CERAMICS FESTIVAL

Faenza's summerlong Ceramics Festival showcases
the city's best artisans. The first week of the festival
kicks off Niballo, a medieval jousting tournament
in which the winner receives a ceramic trophy.

JULY

13-15

PALERMO, SICILIA
SANTA ROSALIA
SAINT ROSALIA

The feast of the town's patron saints brings local
crafters out to strut their stuff in street stalls
throughout the city.

MID-JULY

CARRUBA DI RIPOSTO, SICILIA
SAGRA DEL LIMONE
LEMON FESTIVAL

In this tiny town near Catania, locals celebrate
the lemon in all its glory. Artisanal liqueurs and
lemon pastries are stars of the show.

THIRD SUNDAY

VENICE, VENETO
IL REDENTORE
FEAST OF THE REDEEMER

This procession of the city's historic gondolas
commemorates the end of a bad plague epidem-
ic that struck Venice in the sixteenth century.

LATE JULY

PATTADA, SARDEGNA
MOSTRA-MERCATO DELL'ARTIGIANATO
CRAFT EXHIBIT

In the northern province of Sassari, artisans
demonstrate their prowess in crafting
magnificent knives of bone and wood.

LAST SUNDAY

CHAMPORCHER, VALLE D'AOSTA
ARTIGIANI AL LAVORO
ARTISANS AT WORK

Stroll the too-cute-to-be-real streets of this little
Alpine village, and witness woodcarvers, lace
makers, copper artisans, blacksmiths, and other
local masters demonstrating their arts.

END OF JULY

CASTELLI, ABRUZZO
FESTA DELLA CERAMICA
CERAMICS FESTIVAL

Local ceramics artisans bring out their best
wares for this annual, summer-long event.
On August 15, producers amass the year's
rejects, and smash them in a dramatic
communal event.

END OF JULY

THE ALBISOLES, LIGURIA
BIENNALE DI CERAMICA
BIENNIAL EXHIBITION OF CERAMICS

Every two years, arts organizations in this seaside
ceramics center host an arts exhibition showcasing
the region's characteristic blue and white wares.

END OF JULY

MOGORO, SARDEGNA
FIERA DEL TAPPETO
RUG FESTIVAL

This is a wonderful opportunity to watch this
community of rug-makers, mostly women,
work patterns, colors, and designs unique to
this area on antique handlooms as they pass
on their craft to daughters and granddaughters.

END OF JULY

SCAPOLI, MOLISE
MOSTRA MERCATO DELLA ZAMPOGNA
BAGPIPE FESTIVAL

Three days in July transform the quiet town
of Scapoli into a cacophony of screeching
bagpipes. Demonstrations of artisanal techniques provide a unique look at this ancient
craft, and local goat's cheese and black olives
complete the event.

AUGUST

END OF JULY, EARLY AUGUST

AOSTA, VALLE D'AOSTA
FOIRE D'ETÉ
SUMMER CRAFT FAIR

This fair is the little sister of the monster Fiera
di Sant'Orso, which takes place in January.
It began in 1954 as a competition for sculptors,
but has grown to include 500 artisans practicing
regional crafts: woodworking, wrought iron,
copper, lace, furniture, and more.

14-17

DORGALI, SARDEGNA
MESAUSTU
FEAST OF SAINT JOSEPHM

A fabulous display of crafts blankets the street
stalls in this remote mountain town of northeast
Sardinia, which is renowned for its rich traditions
of weaving, woodcarving, leather, and ceramics.

MID-AUGUST

GUALDO TADINO, UMBRIA
*FESTA INTERNAZIONALE DELLA
CERAMICA*
INTERNATIONAL CERAMICS FESTIVAL

This festival includes a heated competition for
the best wares among artisans in this ceramics hub.

27-30

NUORO, SARDEGNA
SAGRA DEL REDENTORE
FEAST OF THE REDEMPTION

This is another chance to see the incredibly rich
costumes of Sardinia, this time focusing on the
fabrics, colors, and jewelry of Nuoro.

THIRD WEEKEND

SAN VITO, SARDEGNA
SAGRA DELLE LAUNEDDAS
FESTIVAL OF ANCIENT WIND
INSTRUMENTS

Music historians consider the Sardinian *launeddas*
one of Europe's most ancient wind instruments,
and this festival is the perfect forum for experiencing its haunting melodies.

FOURTH SUNDAY

SAN DANIELE DEL FRIULI,
FRIULI-VENEZIA GIULIA
SAGRA DEL PROSCIUTTO DI SAN DANIELE
HAM FESTIVAL

This annual festival showcases the sweet and
nutty *prosciutto di San Daniele*. You can move
from one stand to the next, tasting ham and
sipping the wonderful Friuliano wines.

SEPTEMBER

ALL MONTH

CASTELLAMONTE, PIEMONTE
MOSTRA DELLA CERAMICA
CERAMICS EXHIBITION

This is Castellamonte's chance to show off
its characteristic ceramic wares, especially
the curious room-heating stoves or *stufe* so
popular in northern Italy.

1, 2, 3

ORTISEI, TRENTINO ALTO-ADIGE
FIERA UNIKA
WOODCARVING FESTIVAL

The town tennis center is transformed into an
exhibition of woodcrafts for three days, showcasing the rustic figural works and devotional
objects for which Ortisei craftspeople are
renowned.

FIRST SUNDAY

VENICE, VENETO
REGATTA
REGATTA

In this heated race between Italy's four former maritime republics (Amalfi, Genoa, Pisa, and Venice), the Grand Canal becomes a moving stage for historic gondolas and other boats carrying passengers with the fantastical costumes and masks of Venice.

SECOND SUNDAY

QUARTU SANT'ELENA, SARDEGNA
SANT'ELENA
SAINT ELENA

Honoring the patron saint of Quartu Sant'Elena, outside of the capital city of Cagliari, is reason for showcasing southern Sardinia's most typical costumes and jewelry.

SECOND WEEK

CASTEL SAN NICCOLÒ, TOSCANA
MOSTRA DELLA PIETRA LAVORATA
STONE WORKING EXHIBITION

Nearly 400 stone carvers from all over Italy converge on this small town near Arezzo, with live demonstrations and exhibitions of stone from every corner of the peninsula.

8

LANCIANO, ABRUZZO
MADONNA DEL PONTE
MADONNA DEL PONTE

This celebration of the Madonna del Ponte includes a parade in which peasants carry copper pots on their heads filled with typical specialties of the area.

13

LUCCA, TOSCANA
SANTA CROCE
FEAST OF THE HOLY CROSS

During this important local feast day, artisans around Lucca converge here to demonstrate old-fashioned trades and crafts.

LATE SEPTEMBER

FOGGIA, PUGLIA
MOSTRA DELL'ARTIGIANATO PUGLIESE
CRAFT FESTIVAL

This festival showcases the best crafts from this region that makes up the heel of Italy's boot.

OCTOBER

SECOND WEEK OF OCTOBER

CASTELFIDARDO, LE MARCHE
PREMIO INTERNAZAIONALE CITTÀ DI CASTELFIDARDO
CITY OF CASTELFIDARDO INTERNATIONAL ACCORDION PRIZE

Accordion musicians from all over the globe convene in this accordion capital to show off their talents and vie for one of several awards.

NOVEMBER

FIRST WEEKEND

CELLE LIGURE, CAMPANIA
BORGOINFESTA
TOWN CELEBRATION

Local artisans of all trades display their wares in this annual festival.

DECEMBER

THROUGHOUT THE MONTH

TRENTO, TRENTINO-ALTO ADIGE
MERCATO DI NATALE
CHRISTMAS MARKET

The streets stretching out from the Piazza Fiera spill over with fabulous handmade Christmas decorations, nativity scenes, candles, wooden toys, and knitted alpine clothing. Music, food, and holiday lights in a mountain setting make this one of Italy's most evocative holiday events.

THROUGHOUT THE MONTH

BOLZANO, TRENTINO-ALTO ADIGE
MERCATO DI NATALE
CHRISTMAS MARKET

On the piazza Walther, the central square of this mountain town near Austria's border, a month-long Christmas Market showcases wooden toys, nativity scenes, and the local specialty, cuckoo clocks.

FIRST WEEKEND

SAURIS, FRUILI-VENEZIA GIULIA

MERCATO DI NATALE

CHRISTMAS MARKET

In this mountain town of northeastern Italy, merchants offer gorgeously packaged gift baskets full of the local cured ham that is so delicious. Streets spill over with Christmas crafts, including hand-carved wooden toys and ornaments.

SECOND WEEK OF DECEMBER

FLORENCE, TOSCANA

MARTA

CRAFT EXHIBITION

This event is a smaller version of the International Craft Exhibition that takes place every April (see page 203), but focuses more on holiday crafts, such as nativity figures, Christmas ornaments, and toys. It is primarily geared toward the gift trade.

MID-DECEMBER

NAPLES, CAMPANIA

NATALE

CHRISTMAS CELEBRATIONS

Artisans create fabulous displays of angels, saints, and other nativity figures on the via San Gregorio Armeno, the street renowned for the city's best nativity artisans. People also trek to city churches to see the fabulous historical crèches that are the showpieces of these sanctuaries.

MID-DECEMBER

LECCE, PUGLIA

MERCATO DEI PUPI

DOLL MARKET

For two weeks in December, Lecce's Piazza Sant'Oronzo becomes the center of a thriving trade of nativity figures and dolls crafted of papier-mâché and terra-cotta. This is the town's premier gathering of local artisans.

LATE DECEMBER

GROTTAGLIE, PUGLIA

MOSTRA-CONCORSO DEL PRESEPE

HOLIDAY NATIVITY COMPETITION AND SHOW

The renowned ceramicists of Grottaglie open their doors at the end of the year to showcase the best of their Christmas works: ceramic vessels with Madonnas, saints, and other religious figures, as well as nativity figures crafted of terra-cotta.

About the Author

Laura Morelli is an art historian and writer with a passion for the world's artisanal traditions. She holds an undergraduate degree in languages, and earned a Ph.D. in art history from Yale University. She has taught at Trinity College, Tufts University, and Northeastern University, and has spoken to public audiences across the United States and Europe. Laura is a contributing editor to *National Geographic Traveler*, and created the guidebook series that includes *Made in France* and *Made in the Southwest*, also published by Universe. A native of coastal Georgia, Laura has lived in five countries, including four years in Italy.

www.lauramorelli.com